I Know
Who I Am

I Know
Who I Am

A CARIBBEAN WOMAN'S
IDENTITY IN CANADA

YVONNE BOBB-SMITH

Women's Press/Toronto

I Know Who I Am: A Caribbean Woman's Identity in Canada
By Yvonne Bobb-Smith

First published in 2003 by
Women's Press, an imprint of Canadian Scholars' Press Inc.
180 Bloor Street West, Suite 801
Toronto, Ontario
M5S 2V6

www.womenspress.ca

Canadian Scholars' Press/Women's Press gratefully acknowledges financial support for our publishing activities from the Ontario Arts Council, the Canada Council for the Arts, the Government of Canada through the Book Publishing Industry Development Program (BPIDP), and the Government of Ontario through the Ontario Book Publishers Tax Credit Program and through the Ontario Book Initiative.

National Library of Canada Cataloguing in Publication Data

Bobb-Smith, Yvonne, 1931-
        I know who I am : a Caribbean woman's identity in Canada

Includes bibliographical references.
ISBN 0-88961-414-8

        1. Women, Black—Canada. 2. Blacks—Canada—Race identity. 3. Caribbean Canadians. 4. Race discrimination—Canada. I. Title.

HQ1453.B62 2003   305.48'8969729071   C2003904414-9

Cover design by Drew Hawkins
Text design by Susan Thomas/Digital Zone
Text layout by Brad Horning

03   04   05   06   07   08   6   5   4   3   2

Printed and bound in Canada by AGMV Marquis Imprimeur Inc.

ONTARIO ARTS COUNCIL
CONSEIL DES ARTS DE L'ONTARIO

THE CANADA COUNCIL
FOR THE ARTS
SINCE 1957

LE CONSEIL DES ARTS
DU CANADA
DEPUIS 1957

Canadä

For

Youthdawtas and youthsons
All pickney an dem
Ovah de world
Fuh allyuh to
Neva fraid
Jus big up
A oo yuh is

For

All the young people everywhere in the world:
Never be afraid to claim your identities.

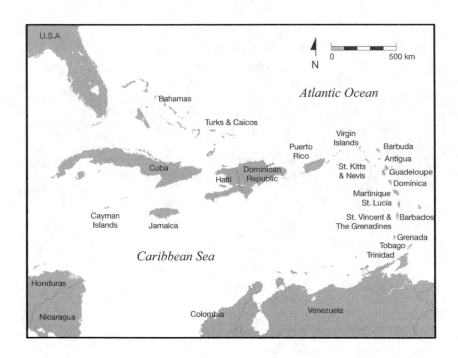

Table of Contents

Preface

Ramabai Espinet

This is a noisy text — replete with the sounds of Caribbean women's voices, migrant voices erupting out of an alien space, and giving voice to experiences hidden from plain sight, swallowed whole or camouflaged for the necessary purpose of survival. Yvonne's searching interviews move behind the easy construction of "Strong Black Caribbean Woman" to find the particularity of her subjects' individual struggles, their stubbornness, their humour, and the sheer grit and determination that enabled them to resist adversity and emerge into creative recognition of their own potentials.

The Caribbean in all its mesmerizing diversity appears on these pages. The plurality of experience is given substance by ethnic and racial differences, but there are also cases of overlapping racialized identities and complex discussions concerning the difficulties in individual negotiations surrounding this vexed issue of race, often without resolution. Racialized categories have different valencies depending on location, and what is important in the Caribbean becomes contextualized differently in diasporic space, yet in this text elision is not at all the preferred alternative.

The structure of the work is intriguing, as Yvonne's own experiences are integrated into the analytical framework of the text, refracting and problematizing concerns that are personal as well as deeply political. Considerable risk-taking occurs here as the process of becoming, of constructing one's unique subjectivity, is carefully anatomized in order to lay bare the arduous efforts by which these subjects realize that their recreation of "home" is often deeply inflected by desires springing from an earlier home.

For me, Yvonne's achievement in creating this work represents the fruit of her life of activism on behalf of women and her deep consciousness of oppression, especially that of racial inequity, which often demanded immediate attention and protest even if redress remained elusive. It also speaks to the degree of her commitment as an information specialist, driven by a grasp of what it meant to make knowledge accessible and available to everyone.

I am honoured to be writing this preface. Yvonne was one of the decisive exemplars of woman's autonomy and independence to me when I first encountered her, eons ago, as a daringly Afro-ed young hip librarian, expressing a discourse of black consciousness rarely heard at that time in the Caribbean. She was vital, exuberant, challenging, and brimming with ideas about how to create innovative ways of disseminating information in the immediate post-Independence period in Trinidad and Tobago. She is, years later, all of these things and more. Her activism and her enthusiastic commitment to providing information has not diminished over the years (her email list was a famous Caribbean link for many of us in Toronto and elsewhere) but she has moved now into more research oriented pursuits. I salute her amazing tenacity, her enduring belief in social and political transformation, and, always, her grace. The praisesong that follows is my congratulatory tribute to Yvonne in celebration of this wonderfully eclectic and original text, *I Know Who I Am*.

Praise Song for Miz Bobb

❧ I   A Borokit Dances By
In the middle of the masquerade
Swish, flash! Is Tan Tan in red flare skirt
Madras and foulard, a moko jumbie
Reaching for the sky
A full woman, cocoa-brown
Legs for days, tight waist
Meeting up with Saga Boy
His wicked, teasing smile
His pssst, dou-dou
Nutten sweeter than you dou-dou

Dancing, wining
I pass by
A chrysalis in brown bodyskin
Cocooned, exposed, showing
Motion for so, shaking up mih peffen
Is me!   From down below
From below the gravestone I come
A ghoul in crocus bag, a shroud
Rough ropeskin lashing
The road that make to walk on Carnival Day

And Tan Georgie, my own Tan Tan
Singing through my head
Through the jamjamjam of the iron man
All I'll ever need, this kaiso beat
Chipping over pitchroad, las lap
Coming down, all I need now, and
Now for now   I dance here
Island queen, Belmont diablesse
Dancing like a borokit
A sumari turning round and round

Winding through the midnight streets
Monday mas, J'ouvert morning
Macumere, Bonjay
No lagahoo in sight now
No lashing jab jab to catch me now
From j'ouvert to las lap
Tan Georgie I never stop
I never stop to eat or drink
Not to sleep self; I carray
I ramajay   Bonjay

I don't give a damn
Not at all at all
Is me, I know who I is
I and I win dis freedom
From tantana to danse macabre
From de glories of greece to de grandeur of rome
Tan Georgie, I play with all a dem
With Bailey, McWilliams, Morris and Minshall
Dancing through these streets
Narrow and mean

Concentric circles spiralling open
And snapping shut like jalousies again
Sometimes in my face
Courage fighting up with me
Sometimes, an unseen hand steadying me
Like you, Tan Georgie, improvising
Making it up over and over
Renting out the front room
Baking something, selling something
Give up? For what? Man leh me live mih life

~ II Belle Eau Road
That possession I knew early
Sure as the evenness of days
Yellow poui and flamboyant
The smell of wet grass on mornings
Darkness creeping through the hills
Down those twisting streets
Tinpan music following the dark
Picking up the tune and, like magic
Ping-ponging it back   Home is
The same as return

After tasting life and running
Frightened of sailor mas and powder
Neighb Jimbo doctor mas, his shoe-box
Hiding something, rude, forbidden
Listening to nancy story and Ma Mamba
Listening for tassa drums at twilight
Up the long gap to our house
The ruins of old Boissiere's estate
Behind the fence, peeping to observe
Courage starts at home

Heaps of rice dwindling as
Hindu gods collect their offerings
Listening for sacrificial goats bawling
In Piggott yard   Was Shango
Double ten, Divali, Hosay
Lord Executor up the hill
A Potogee man ketching his nen-nen
Near the streets narrow and twisting
Like coral or mapipire snake
Down to the Savannah stretching below

Crocheted doilies stiff starched
Guardians of centre tables, crepe paper flowers
Antimacassars, morris suites, wall pockets
Mama's blue enamel cups put away
Courage riding tall through Panka Estate
Up to Mount Moriah Road
Watching Tan Georgie walking through the town
Her strong legs, her good dress, the red brocade
Seeing about her own business at the Town Hall
And never, never going to church

Courage striking up a chord
In Panka Lane, Tan Georgie laughing
Child, what it is to be nervous?
Laughing because is only one time to dead
Holding me tight tight
Tan Georgie so sure, so in charge
Whispering in my ear, under the cherry tree
Make yuh own life
You is the brightest   Take courage
And run like hell with it

III   The Girl Who Speaks With Her Hands
Caught in the web of history
I, laughing, streaked across the map
Of that island world I knew
Reaching for a larger geography
Open, accepting, kind even
And finding only a horizon
More pitiless and unforgiving
More locked in stone white cold
That that narrow-bore world
That made me

Then, all I saw were the contours
Of a near sky pitching back
To hill and valley, bamboo
And dry river, black skin
Light skin, brown skin
Good hair, soft hair, bad hair
The coastline curling around the
City at the sea's edge, its hills
Smoky blue on evenings, the road
Dipping into Carenage

Where I knew and did not know
Everything — who I was, and when
And where and how   And later
Talking, talking, hands, fingers drawing lines
Through air and sea and sky
Trapped inside boxes shrinking in rain
Snow, hail, sleet, losing
Gaining, starting up again
And how, how does betrayal stop?
Where to find a resting-spot

Like the gap at Belle Eau Road
Like smoke and steel pan in the early dark
Like Tan Georgie, her strong arms
And always, those hands, mine somehow
Cutting, slicing, caressing the air
Forward moving in concentric circles
Across ocean and river-bed and silt
Moving away from home   a girl
Speaking with her hands opening and closing and
Landing on cool pitch, on Belle Eau Road.

Ramabai Espinet
Toronto, May 2003

Acknowledgments

Foremost, and always on my mind for their indomitable courage and strengths of resilience, is this group of women who have passed on: my Mother (Irie), Mama Carr, Ma Norah Dottin, Tan Georgie Elcock, Cousin Helen Manswell, Auntie Olive Robertson, Ma Muriel Sturge, Ma Blanche Talma, and Mother Myra Yawching. I am forever grateful to these beautiful elder Caribbean women, for having left me a legacy of resistance. No doubt, this legacy has extended to some of their female offspring, with whom I enjoy a magnificent network of sisterhood, resonating in the achievements of these mothers.

It is not a tradition for many Caribbean people to tell their stories to "strangers". Therefore, I owe a deep and special gratitude to the 45 Caribbean women in Canada who honoured me with such a privilege to expose their experiences in this body of Caribbean knowledge. I remain grateful to these women for the insights I drew from their stories. I drew inspiration for this book when I heard my colleague Dr Afua Cooper exclaim, "I know who I am", as she debated the idea, on a TV panel, that racism submerges a Caribbean identity. Hence the title!

One part of the journey of this book was the mixing of my maturity of practical experience with academia during the period 1991–1998, at the Ontario Institute for Studies in Education, University of Toronto. First, I owe, with thanks, my presence there to Dr. Alan Thomas and Dr. Kathleen Rockhill who envisioned, on my admission, that I would make a contribution. Also, thanks to Dr. George Dei and Dr. Edmund Sullivan for their insightful advice.

Most of all, I am much indebted to my friend and thesis supervisor, Dr Sherene Razack. I thank Sherene immensely for the tremendous benefits I derived from her sincere and profound teaching method. Without her vision, her earnest responses to my thesis ideas, as well as her tact, patience, and warmth in friendship, this book would not have been made possible. An Ontario Government Scholarship helped considerably in my carrying out the research, for which I am grateful.

I have had a number of friends who, directly or indirectly, contributed to the making of this book. First of all, I bear in my memory the encouraging words of my dearest and deceased friend, Daphne Harper, in her final days, who exclaimed about my thesis findings, "Bobby, take it to the schools!" Special to me, has been Selwyn McLean's dedication and interest to edit this work during the process of my writing. His detailed critique of the text, together with his compliments, was truly empowering. Thank you very much, Selo! Also, I am very grateful to Ramabai Espinet for her insights in the preface of this book. Her thoughts can be measured in terms of her knowing who I am — the Trini — in the library days at home. Her words have always helped me to retain the highest level of self-confidence. As well, I thank Dr Akua Benjamin, for her support and conviction that this work needed to be done.

Several other friends have given me encouragement in recent years. I thank Honor Ford-Smith for our conversations about "we" region, together with the warmth of our friendship. There is also the "cheering crowd", whose support, at whatever distance, meant much to me, and to whom I am grateful: Larry Brookwell, Norma Ferguson, Denise Herrera-Jackson, the Roaches, Itah Sadu, Phyllis Shepherd, Simboo Singh, Anne-Marie Stewart, Maggie Synnott, Peter Smith, and Gemma Trott (Canada). Also, Grace Talma and Geoff Frankson (Trinidad and Tobago), and Hermia Morton-Anthony (St. Kitts and Nevis — a Caribbean posse.

This book, as a venture, informing the nature of a Caribbean legacy of resistance, was also nurtured spiritually, through my contacts with cousins and siblings who reside far away from me: the Elcocks; the Robertson clan (Trinidad and Tobago); Marigold Robertson-Saul and her offspring (England); and Bettylou Deschamps, my sister, and her crew (Trinidad and Tobago/England). I thank you all for helping me to maintain a connection to a family identity I cherish: the one that has showed me how to "get troo".

ACKNOWLEDGMENTS

I will always remember my great surprise when Jack Wayne, President of Canadian Scholars' Press (CSPI) and Women's Press, enthusiastically made such positive comments to me upon his reading of my thesis. Thank you, Jack! I deeply appreciate your sincerity and confidence about this book's future. I also thank Althea Prince, Managing Editor, CSPI, for her gentle encouragement and confidence in the content of my work, and Rebecca Conolly for her patience and dedication. As well, I acknowledge gratefully the professional work provided by all members of the staff at Canadian Scholars' Press/Women's Press.
Give Praise!

Yvonne Bobb-Smith
Toronto, Canada

Introduction:
Tek de bull by de horn[1]

During my childhood, when I was gazing at the little social and economic advances older Caribbean women were making in their everyday lives, I had no idea I would address their actions in terms of "independence" and "resistance", let alone theorize them as concepts in this book. As I grew older, I was concerned that these measures of survival may never be recognized. I realize that Caribbean women, like other women marginalized by society, particularly in the diaspora of Canada, form a silent majority whose subjugated knowledge and histories of resistance seem never to go beyond their immediate environments. Added to that, this book aims at rectifying general assumptions that persist in diasporas, internationally, that a Caribbean woman's identity is essentially that of the "immigrant woman", that is, with all the negative connotations of blackness, passivity, and working in unskilled jobs. But how could I change this picture of identity intellectually? So far, much of my personal oppression arise from experiences that have given meaning to my skin colour only, which defines externally who I am as opposed to whom I know myself to be. Thus, I want to refute any argument that skin colour is enough to enable anyone's understanding of life experiences of women in different contexts of domination. Therefore, as my interest to explore identity, I target Caribbean women's experiences in Canada and their survival. This book, *I Know Who I Am*, investigates my own story and the stories of 45 Caribbean women of different backgrounds and heritages, in order to understand how they speak of the consequences of racism and sexism in their everyday lives as a means of their strategizing resistance. I am aware that discriminatory

1

practices can constitute and reconstitute identity as these women become varying targets in the public sphere. As a result, these Caribbean women's stories amount to stories of survival that inform us about their evasion of victimization and their measure of empowerment.

My own story is typical of many Caribbean women who migrate to Canada. Mainly touched by the effects of economic forces, we migrate with goals and ambitions for possibilities of education, of vocation, and of developing potential.[2] Despite the negative and repetitive aspects of the stories told, I observe that many Caribbean women focus on resolving problems of racial discrimination through mobilizing and organizing communities. This book deals with those issues. It focuses on these women's capability to deconstruct a stereotypical identity, "immigrant woman", in which they uniquely distinguish themselves through collective resistance. Yet, I want most of all that this work be understood as a treatise to reconceptualize identity, and to re-imagine "home" as an educative institution.

Introducing the subjects

I begin, in Chapter Two, Part 1, with the self-definitions of the 46 Caribbean women in this study. I then proceed, in Part 2, to connect some of their stories to my own. We represent diverse heritages, cultures, class positions, and sexual orientation, having in common migration from the Caribbean and subsequent residences in Canada between ten to 25 years. We are a group whose self-ascribed identities reveal our self-actualization. Our stories demonstrate how, as Caribbean women, we reinvent our identities to resist the victim identity of an "immigrant woman" pathologized through racism and sexism in the society of Canada. The stories illustrate how we Caribbean women can use agency to self-define through goals of education, networking coordination, and community organizing. We strategize these goals of resistance so that we are justified in broadly identifying ourselves as community activists. Added to that, our stories indicate how many of us Caribbean women ascribe to ourselves multiple heritages.

Tracing Caribbean history:
The road to subjectivity

Then, in Chapter Three, to justify this diversity, I historicize our experiences, tracing the journey, which socially constituted the Caribbean, from colonization of the Aboriginal peoples to twentieth-century nationalism. Consequently, this tracing exposes the interconnectedness of our histories which enables me to theorize a collective subjectivity that I term a *Caribbean woman's subjectivity*.

I use, as appropriate to my analysis, the term subjectivity, mindful of Kathryn Woodward's (1997: 39) assertion that, though identity and subjectivity are sometimes interchangeable, they are different, in that subjectivity is derived "in a social context where language and culture give meaning to our experience of ourselves". This social context represents the objectivity that produces subjectivity.[3] Subjectivity, as a concept, allows us to explore, psychologically, how we invest our identities in certain positions that establish forms of behaviour. As I hold this notion, I can isolate the subjective as my focus, placing less emphasis on race, notwithstanding the gendered nature that flags these Caribbean women's experiences in the diaspora.[4] Yet, I am thinking, like Amina Mama (1995: 129) that I am not projecting subjectivity as a universal approach to understanding experience in the way that class or gender does in social science analysis. I am using it to develop a methodology that can survive the analysis of both individual and collective experiences of this group which, although it shares a common geographic background, is, in itself, diverse. I believe subjectivity provides a grounded theoretical analysis which enables me to embrace notions of multiplicity and anti-essentialism as my critique. These notions, if generally overlooked, marginalize certain groups from the Caribbean and deny the interconnectedness of histories. I, however, would not ignore the potency of a racial identity that merges with gender for particular kinds of experiences, mindful of what Mama (1995) writes: "For Black women, the dominant order is both racially oppressive in gendered ways and sexually oppressive in racialised ways" (123). I seek, then, to go beyond generic and imprecise labeling to articulate a Caribbean woman's identity.

My anti-essentialist approach, I note, is supported in the texts of scholars like Sherene Razack's *Looking White People in the Eye* (1998), Paul Gilroy's *The Black Atlantic* (1993), and Cornel West's *Keeping Faith: Philosophy and Race in America* (1993), which show concerns about the prevalence to essentialize subordinated groups. For instance, in a chapter from *Keeping Faith*, entitled "The New Cultural Politics of Difference", West claims notions of the "real black community" and "positive images" are value-laden, socially loaded and ideologically charged (19), as he endorses Stuart Hall (1992: 19), who states that there has to be: "the end of innocence or the end of the innocent notion of the essential Black subject...the recognition that 'Black' is essentially a politically and culturally *constructed* category".

Furthermore in the same chapter, West (1992: 19) argues that Black women in the diaspora, through their inclusive critique of "class, empire, age, sexual orientation and nature", have decimated the "essential Black subject". I, therefore, confirm my stance not to repress heterogeneity and diversity as distinct features of a Caribbean identity. These features are increasingly evident in political, social, and cultural movements which affirm and celebrate the multifaceted nature of identities in the Caribbean region. I am less interested in the macro view of identity, and, for that reason, I specifically rely on the notion of subjectivity and historical formation. Thus, the concept of subjectivity enables me to explore these Caribbean women's experiences in the contexts of our political and social environments from childhood in the Caribbean to residence in the diaspora of Canada. In other words, subjectivity allows me to investigate how these women see themselves as subjects, and how notions of themselves are constructed on the basis of their initiatives for social change. As well, I can locate these subjects through their experiences from childhood socialization to adulthood in community activism.[5]

With regard to experience, I choose to rely on Joan Scott's (1992: 25-34) theory that deconstructs modernist ways in which historians use evidence of experience in history. She argues that stories are not to be accepted as self-evident truths, as they are in the modernist view of experience. She asserts that history often assigns experience as unique to individuals and so makes people the starting point of knowledge, thus naturalizing categories such as man, Black or White, which become "characteristics of individuals". Furthermore, she insists, "it is the historical process that, through discourse, positions subjects and produces experiences" (25). In other words, we are to understand how individual identities are constituted in relations of power as well as objects in discourse. Hence, I found the other reason for my Caribbean historical journey, that is, to understand how Caribbean women, as subjects, "are constituted discursively", and how their construction involved "agency". Their agency, as Scott puts it, was "created through situations and statuses conferred on them" as they inhabit multiple competing systems. I can theorize on this basis because, subjectivity, as a concept, is fluid and unstable, unlike identity, so that references to the multiple identities over time in which these Caribbean women experienced their lives, can be endorsed. That is, I can admit memories of childhood and young adulthood to their period of migration and residence in Canada.

In this historical journey of Chapter Three, we learn how Caribbean people's actions were shaped and constrained by the contexts in which they operated. Victimized by imperial systems, which were masterminded by the planter ruling class to produce wealth for themselves, these Caribbean peoples countered acts of domination with vehement resistance. Stretched from the fifteenth to the nineteenth century, these systems were inconsistent and variant. Dehumanization, harsh brutality, and devastation were experienced by several peoples in the region. To a very great extent we note that, through genocide, Amerindians became marginalized and erased, and that through slavery, Africans, over three centuries, were exploited, oppressed, and victimized in most inhuman ways. Then, to a lesser extent of severity, European poor and disenfranchised peoples experienced a system in servitude, while Asians, other Africans, and Europeans were contracted in indentureship to maintain capitalism up to early twentieth-century colonialism (Mangru 1996; Look Lai 1993; Hall 1989; Williams 1969; Goveia 1965). Tracing this process tells us that Caribbean peoples, in their diversity, have been remarkable and passionate in reconstructing their identities through collective resistance. In particular, the resistance of Caribbean women was reflected differently, yet similarly, in the consistent pattern of the struggles against sexism, that created a dominant notion of womanhood. This historical journey, then, explains the interconnectedness and interrelatedness of the histories of Caribbean women, which produce different discourses in colonialism, and provide an understanding that resistance distinguishes the collective identity of a Caribbean person.

Looking for that identity: Resistance

In order to define a Caribbean woman's identity, Chapter Four explores Canadian scholarly literature, as well as Caribbean fictional and non-fictional writings. First, I examine Canadian scholarly literature in these categories: general writings about Caribbean migration to Canada; Caribbean feminist work on immigration, race, and gender; and non-Caribbean feminist work on immigration and gender. Knowledge produced from these non-Caribbean scholarly pieces can be an attempt to deconstruct the immigrant woman identity which mostly puts the conditions of migrant Caribbean women into perspective (Boyd 1975, 1987; Calliste 1993; Macklin 1992; Brand 1984; Silvera 1989; W. Ng 1982; R. Ng 1988). Among the Caribbean scholars (Calliste 1993; Brand 1984; Silvera 1989), while arguments have characterized the struggle and the shifts in identity for a life of adaptation, yet they have been constrained to transform the stereotype, "immigrant woman". I discover that images of Caribbean women are neither a reflection of my own knowledge of a Caribbean identity nor my understanding of Caribbean history. Where there were suggestions of resistance in a Caribbean woman's identity, an essentialist idea of Black, associated with victimhood, is, by and large, retained. I am left asking questions: *Who are these women? Do I know them currently as Caribbean women? How will they identify themselves? How are they surviving?*

To recover my sense of what history taught me, I explored a Caribbean woman's identity through, first, regional Caribbean feminist research studies and, then, imaginative writings by Caribbean women in the diaspora. Within these sites, the picture greatly improves. I note that Caribbean scholarship materializes Caribbean women as full subjects, with stories that go beyond discrimination and victimization. These works demonstrate a thematic structure that includes how some Caribbean women survived, economically, how they were empowered to do so, and how they maintained emotional support to earn their survival (Barrow 1986; Brodber 1986; Massiah 1986; Odie-Ali 1986; D. Powell 1986). It is among these writings that the notion of "independence" emerges to fulfill my vision of a Caribbean woman's identity. For instance, Brodber asserts that independence exists as a value in a Caribbean female ideology (1986: 28). Reflecting on my childhood observation, I can specify independence as the feature in a Caribbean woman's subjectivity that enables me to understand responses to resistance.

Independence

I next choose to explore this identity of a Caribbean woman in some imaginative writings contextualized both in the Caribbean and in Canada, because I believe that these works are crucial to my analysis as they amount to narrations by the only voices able to deconstruct imperialist representations of identities of Caribbean women (Said 1993: xii). Caribbean women writers create from their memory women characters who are representative of a past in which they continued a legacy of assertiveness for resistance and survival. I select ten Caribbean women authors of fiction, short stories, and poetry, whose writings are located in the diaspora of Canada, England, and the United States of America, but whose origins are Caribbean. They are: Jean Rhys (1992) from Dominica; Joan Riley (1987) and Afua Cooper (1992) from Jamaica; Mahadai Das (1988) from Guyana; Jamaica Kincaid (1991) from Antigua; and Ramabai Espinet (1991), Dionne Brand (1988), and Claire Harris (1992) from Trinidad and Tobago. In general, these writers help me to feminize "independence", neither as a trait nor characteristic, but as an ethic. I call it an ethic, in postmodern terms, so as neither to identify the notion as a quality a Caribbean woman has, nor to locate it in the liberal sense of freedom to pursue one's own interest. The latter, of course, is a modernist view with no clear defining links to community. In my terms, this concept, *independence*, contains a value which drives an individual Caribbean woman to be conscious of the dominance and control that threaten knowledge of herself. Having recognized that consciousness, she can make appropriate responses. The opposite to the use of that ethic is to accept controlling images of womanhood. As an ethic, independence is not a permanent feature, but is derived from levels of self-empowerment and informed through experience. This book illustrates, through voices of Caribbean women, that their use of strategies to resist and to engage in efforts of survival were driven by learning to employ an ethic of independence. Thus, using subjectivity to analyze experiences, I can confirm that independence is not a trait but a direct means of responding to domination. The knowledge of who a Caribbean woman is likely to be is transformed because, collectively, a group of Caribbean women has used strategies of resistance to exercise that independence. Therefore, I will proceed to situate their actions in the Canadian social contexts in which many have resided for up to 25 years.

Caribbean women in Canada: A new home

A specific flow of labour from the Caribbean to Canada occurred in the sixties to meet a demand for domestics, which seemed insatiable. The increasing growth of a middle class in Canada, combined with White women's struggle for liberation, caused consistent pressure on the Canadian government to bring Caribbean women to Canada. As Wolseley W. Anderson (1993: 35) notes, there has always been the "push-pull" factor that operates in colonialism, whereby individuals are pushed out of Third World countries to meet the extensive needs of labour in industrialized countries like Canada. The result was a Caribbean/Canada agreement that promulgated two Domestic Schemes and increased the number of women who immigrated to Canada independently. Agnes Calliste (1989) studies the experiences in the fifties of some Caribbean women who were brought from Guyana, Jamaica, and Trinidad and Tobago to serve as domestic workers here. The landed immigrant status granted to these women on entry was by no means a sign of Canada's largess but, as Calliste argues, was highly indicative of racist factors that suggested that Caribbean women would most likely remain permanently as domestics.[6] She also notes that, although on the surface the Domestic Schemes appeared to be a satisfactory means of dealing with problems of unemployment in the Caribbean versus high employment in Canada, race played a large role in constructing these women's identities. In some of her other works, Calliste (1989, 1993) documents some contradictions of the period, when trained nurses and nursing assistants from the Caribbean were brought here, although immigration policies and admission requirements of health care institutions were discriminatory, resulting in a de-skilling of the migrant nurses. These Caribbean women initiated their own strategies of resistance with Black and Caribbean community support. However, in my study of Caribbean women, the migratory pattern indicated that many of these women were also of the independent category, while some belonged to the extended family, and very few were dependent on a spouse. Their stories tell of how critically conscious they were about the social issues of their time in Canada, as well as how their potentials were minimized through the experience of racism, even while Canadian feminism was engaging in mainstream organizing.

❧ What is the meaning of "home"?

Chapter Five defines and develops the notion of a Caribbean woman's subjectivity through the repetitive parts of their stories in which *home* is central to a personal identity formation. Generally, *home* is understood in a dichotomy, that is, it is seen, first, as a birthplace and, second, as a place of migration or exile. For some scholars neither of these positions is an easy fit because they suggest a sense of belonging and giving opportunities for women to develop, yet, at the same time, do not represent liberation for women. For instance, Inderpal Grewal (1996) argues that, in India, at the turn of the nineteenth century, while home might be construed as a fixed place, it served as a site of nationalist resistance and feminism, which Indian women had to leave to seek freedom. Another notion of home, which Jasbir K. Puar (1996) uses, is that Indian women's experience in the diaspora cannot be oversimplified within a dual position — home/a birthplace, away from home/ displacement — because, in either site, women do not become liberated. I recognize these feminist positions as encouragement to define home as some measure of self, but, from a Caribbean perspective, the difference lies in an attempt to define home not in physical and immobile terms.

❧ Home is a learning site

Many of the Caribbean women's narratives, in which "home" is central, deconstruct a standard notion of fixed place—one with many physical locations and a variety of structures—because their homes have become learning sites for resistance. Home is full of complexities and contradictions, not only encompassing the geography of familiar spaces and groupings within communities, but linking the private to the public, where tangible or intangible struggles are experienced against domination. Yet, as Chapter Six explores, for these Caribbean women, home is highly regarded as a site which taught them resistance, as well as the value of community. In the home they saw older women struggle both privately and publicly against domination as, one, they assumed major responsibility for family, and, two, they often activated community effort, in a variety of forms, against social injustices. At each location, through their activism, they resisted many of the issues arising out of capitalism and colonialism so as to enable themselves and others to cope with economic and social domination. While home is nostalgic, contradictory, and full of contestations, according to Carol Boyce Davies (1994) "it is a critical link in the articulation of identity. It is a play of resistance to domination", that is, it can certify our origins (115). For the women in this study, their memories of home embrace this range of experiences, from negative to positive, through which strengths of resistance percolate. Thus, home remains in their consciousness. It is inextricably tied with a notion of survival, a notion of community, and a fully intangible site where they can employ resistance to all forms of domination. Therefore, because their stories are replete with representations of home as a learning site, I strongly argue that this is the place that taught them to transform a traditional identity through the use of independence as an ethic.

Having established that home is an educational institution, I draw attention to how these Caribbean women sought to appropriate a power passed on to them from older Caribbean women of the region, a legacy which enables them to use the *ethic of independence*. As I suggest in Chapter Four, this is neither a trait nor a characteristic in a Caribbean women's self-definition, but a response to domination and oppression. Quotations from their stories fully articulate the meaning of this concept. Caribbean women's entire history is fraught with encounters of racism and sexism, because many Caribbean women are subjected to degrading images of who they are supposed to be and to immense discrimination (Morton 1991). Despite the resulting alienation from, and degradation of, their identities in mainstream society, these women rely on education, networking, and community activism as survival strategies. These ways of negotiating their identities are linked to the ethic of independence, which they learned to employ in the home.

⮞ Resisting Canadian feminism in a striving for "home"

Chapter Seven traces a picture of the Canadian context as a space for negotiating the identity Caribbean women brought with them to Canada.

Generally speaking, in the seventies, White feminism, in spite of the momentum gained in the women's movement, still did not grapple with the issues of differences among women (Adamson, Briskin, and McPhail 1988; Stasiulis 1987). They continued to emphasize the issues of gender, equality, sexuality, reproduction, and abortion. Migrant women, however, including "Asian, African and Caribbean women" were organizing to work on racism in several areas significant to preserving an identity "across lines of race and class" (Stasiulis 1987: 66). Caribbean women, along with other migrant women, experienced obstacles to adjustment and settlement in basic areas of housing, employment, education, social services, and so on. These negative experiences can be translated into oppressions of marginalization and powerlessness. The White women's movement received funding from many provincial and federal agencies and, with its purpose to homogenize and essentialize woman as a category, expanded into numbers of women's organizations. Yet, because race was not a part of the primary politics of the movement (because it was not a White woman's issue), organizers failed to capture totally the number of vibrant Caribbean women who were experiencing the effects of alienation but who refused to be ignored and revictimized.

This book shows how many Caribbean women sought to develop their own feminist space, while not lessening their commitment to strategies of resistance with their "brothers" in the wider struggle. It traces Caribbean women's activism in several sites, including immigration/refugee issues, social service agencies, and cultural production.

Strategies of resistance to live in Canada

In Chapter Eight, I discuss how the use of the ethic of independence enabled these Caribbean women to transform their identities. It demonstrates what these women undertook as initiatives to overcome their oppression, and how these activities had a cumulative effect that distinguished them as women. It tells us that Caribbean women can negotiate their identities consistently to survive through the use of various forms of resistance. I argue that these women are re-imagining themselves as able survivors. Their statements, which bear themes of assertiveness, resilience, and creativity, illustrate how the magic of learning resistance works to counter oppressions. It was among older Caribbean women, and sometimes men, as these stories by Caribbean women in Canada recall, that they saw tremendous strengths of independence displayed in a variety of ways in the Caribbean region. They saw these as strategies of resistance, which were manifested in a range of activities. For instance, some of these Caribbean women, consistent with their historical backgrounds, remember times in which resistance to oppressions was portrayed in humour, spirituality, and cultural renewal. However, their more profound attempts at surviving were to refigure the lessons taught to them. One of these lessons is the value of education as a goal that fully strengthens any of their efforts in opposition. However, I argue that education may likely be a contradiction, since it forges an adoption of White cultural and social customs, while the struggle anticipates resistance to such domination. However, Caribbean women in Canada claimed that many of these older women, regretting their own lack of educational accomplishments, affirmed that education was essential for self-empowerment and liberation. Therefore, in the diaspora, these Caribbean women tell us how they used education primarily as a tool for self-development. More pertinently, education was a means to sustain institutional transformative work through anti-racism efforts, as well as to mobilize their communities. Yet, it was not only formal education that was important, but the development of critical consciousness that enabled many of these women in Canada in the eighties to progress into an activism of revolutionary politics. Both these assets, education and critical consciousness, directed the process of recognizing and questioning the cumulative experience of oppression. The variety of experiences of immigrants from diverse regions and backgrounds most likely had disarming effects, against which many Caribbean women needed strength to cogitate acts of resistance. In order to manifest this strength, these Caribbean women precipitated, for a collective purpose, networking as a strategy of resistance.

Networking, as a component of learning at home, is not to be simplified. In general, it evolved historically as a subversive strategy of resistance against all forms of oppression. I refer here to the many stories related to escapes different people made from all the imperial systems, particularly slavery, where networking enabled the building of maroon communities.[7] It was used as a strategy to replace the loss and erasure of identities of origin, as well as to defeat imperialist systems aimed to *civilize* the Caribbean region in social structures such as the family.[8] A fundamental definition of networking is that it serves to create social and cultural bonds, as well as to protect and preserve cultural beliefs and practices, and it can be used to precipitate levels of political consciousness. The networks which emerged in the Canadian environment were developed to either resist marginalization or to avoid the possible encroachment of individualism that marks life in a metropolitan society. However, networking is institutionalized in a variety of forms throughout the Caribbean region.[9] These Caribbean women offer much anecdotal evidence of their search for connection and interaction with persons whose cultural identities appear to be mutual. In the collective data, with few exceptions, these Caribbean women claim that to find others like themselves was highly significant as a means of safeguarding those values that help to define *home:* food, language, laughter, music (Ho 1991; 1989). Networking, as some of them would describe, was important to recreating home, that is, a place which may not always have oppressions, but where there can be positive connotations. This strategy of resistance, for some of these women, led to community activism.

Reaction to racism in Canada produced initiatives carried out by Caribbean women and men who frequently established, through contacts made in networking, both community organizations and projects. Racism, as institutionalized in Canada, presents challenges to Black and Caribbean peoples mainly in employment, accommodation, and education. Some of the Caribbean women in this study, therefore, began community activism in the *Black Education Project* (BEP), in Toronto, and the *Negro Community Centre* in Montreal, which were spaces carved by and for Caribbean people to challenge racism in the society.

For instance, in brief, let us look at how BEP was formed. During the early eighties there was serious concern among Caribbean parents about the possible fate of their children as victims of the formal curriculum and the hidden curriculum systematized and processed in Toronto schools. First, the formal curricula of schools throughout Canada ignore perspectives in the humanities and social sciences that reflect the thoughts of persons from societies that have been historically and currently exploited and marginalized. Second, Caribbean students, who comprise a distinct group, are racialized through a hidden curricular, and thus are isolated from mainstream society. That is, the systemic social and cultural environment of schools, coupled with educators' value systems, are racially tainted and operate in such a way that Caribbean children are easily made to feel excluded (Henry 2000). Therefore, educational projects (for example, BEP), conducted voluntarily by Caribbean men, and women, amounted to one of the ways that enabled the community to solidify, while it challenged the climate of racial bigotry and prejudice in the education system.

In Chapter Eight, the voices of the Caribbean women themselves demonstrate radicalism in the approaches some of them took to assert their rights as Caribbean women to formalize community organizing in Toronto. For this reason, I argue that these Caribbean women, through their own ideas of feminist activism outside the mainstream women's movement, have created an *alternative women's movement* in Canada. I claim that the emergence of this movement must be recognized as a departure from the usual positioning of many Caribbean women in community organizing, that is, to serve almost always in a marginal capacity. In addition, this opening of a movement led by Caribbean women demonstrates, in terms of identity, liberation from the pathologized view of these women as "immigrant women". It is evident that these Caribbean women have formulated a "culture of resistance" in Canada (Collins 1990: 18). According to Collins, this non-monolithic culture defines a collective power of the oppressed. This power is created to enable them to see the world differently from the dominant group. It also forms a legacy of resistance in the continuous struggle. Thus, my findings, which are extracted from a continuum — Caribbean history, fiction and research, and the lived experiences of Caribbean women in the diaspora of Canada — are congruent with a prevailing significance of resistance as a means of survival in different communities that encounter multiple oppressions because of domination and capitalism.[10] All stories by Caribbean women in this study speak of a consciousness of the struggle, often within individual communities but sometimes with reference to the broader picture, such as a residual consciousness of Black Power, evident in the support of the African Liberation Movement both in Toronto and Montreal.

However, many of these Caribbean women, who engaged in the "Black" movement, express their perception about a conflict between presumed gender equality and their subordinated positions in those activities. Many of them, through struggles in everyday life, mostly with racism and sexism, identified with Afrocentrism and brought a national Black women's movement into resurgence in 1981. This movement was later institutionalized as the National Congress of Black Women of Canada, with the mushrooming of provincial and municipal chapters. Working in the communities as activists, and understanding the oppressions and needs of other migrant women, they formed The Coalition of Visible Minority Women in Ontario. While other individual activities of Caribbean women's organizing, that manifested as resistance in Canada, would differentiate the Black women's movement, there is some validity in assessing the overall impact of the activities of this group in the study as culminating in an alternative women's movement.

A future concept of identity

In conclusion, Chapter Nine theorizes a future concept of identity by summarizing how teaching, studying, and analyzing human experience in a wide range of contexts can reconceptualize our thinking about identity. First, Caribbean women's identities, viewed in the binary of Black and White or African and Indian, can become problematized. We avoid this dual notion when we tap into history and find there are multiple identities and multiple differences to be associated with the overall idea of *identity*. The historic journey described in Chapter Three, together with the lived experiences of the subjects in this book, helps us to discover that some Caribbean women construct their own subjectivities. That is, many Caribbean women have arguably different ways of surviving that reflect their own historic creativity and intellectualism, which have emerged from multiple realities. Many of these women are *agents*, rather than victims under societal and capitalist pressures, because their knowledge of how to use independence as a response to domination moves them beyond boundaries established for women in the patriarchal sense. This we see in the stories each of them has used to demonstrate the struggle that displaced dominant ideologies about womanhood. Thus, we may conclude that this ethic of independence could become a humanitarian one for women in the twenty-first century.

Next, this book makes us reflect on how survival and resistance are learnt entities which centralize the educational setting of home. This work convinces us that learning to survive is connected to histories of oppressions and to the ways in which communities, subordinated and exploited by hegemonic powers, are sustained. My aim is to enable the reader to rethink how we use experience to bring us from the objectivity of oppression to a subjectivity charged with responsibility for resistance and survival. The purpose in my work is to demonstrate how a politicized identity may or may not be used by the oppressed. The voices of Caribbean women, who have lived in Canada for over 25 years, bring a reality to this book. Their words comprise one collective story of Caribbean women in Canada, who, in continuing the journey of resistance, can say, *I Know Who I Am.*

Notes

1 Standard English translation: *Discussing the challenges in this work.*

2 Many Caribbean countries have attained national independence, yet the vestiges of the colonial system remain — capitalist class structure, pigment hierarchy, and cultural hegemony—to stifle initiatives and limit opportunities.

3 I am grateful to Selwyn McLean for bringing this insight into our conversation.

4 I interpret Sherene Razack's (1998) argument on anti-essentialism as my having to come to recognize that there is a tension between stressing multiplicity and a need to retain a focus on race, and that to talk about differences brings into account my own subject position.

5 According to Amina Mama (1995), subjectivity can "be studied at any point in the life cycle" of an adult, because it does not presuppose the individual is in a fixed or unitary form (129).

6 My own experience of a future beyond the Domestic Scheme illustrates how resistance to racism can change perceptions of identity.

7 Maroon communities, historically, were derived from the determination of enslaved Africans to escape total domination. Therefore, during the centuries of slavery, many of these men and women, to survive the holocaust of slavery, removed themselves from the stranglehold of plantation life. Their flight took them to distant parts of the islands where they established their own groupings to carry out African cultural traditions.

8 In all migrations to the Caribbean during the days of servitude, slavery, and indentureship, capitalists paid no regard to difference in culture, language, and religion (Goveia 1965; Gonzalez 1969; E. Williams 1970; Higman 1984; Look Lai 1993; Mangru 1996). As well, throughout history, the ruling class engineered structures of community that could reflect their own identities, one of which was the nuclear family. Caribbean peoples standardized networking, as a tool of resistance, when they crossed borders of race, culture, and ethnicity to survive.

9   Many people in the Caribbean regard, as important for survival, a pastime of informal gatherings over refreshments. These sometimes result in serious debate and banter, becoming a pedagogy for dissemination of information and knowledge. This, in Trinidad and Tobago, is called a "lime", which is regarded by some as a learning environment in the broadest possible sense.

10 Patricia Hill Collins (1990) also defines the term "culture of resistance" in *Black Feminist Thought* as one which ought not "to imply that a monolithic culture of resistance exists". In examining African American women in acts of resistance, she notes that the meaning included the contradictions either through "compliance with or resistance to oppression" (18, note 4). However, in my study, I found that stories relay the fact that these Caribbean women, in varying ways, were more committed to acts of resistance through community organizing.

TWO

Caribbean-Canadian
Women Self-Define:
Me see meself as...[1]

Part 1: Caribbean-Canadian women
identify themselves

The Caribbean-Canadian women in this study identified with their current and ancestral linkages, and issued statements about their subjectivities. Their names are anonymous. Some of their quotations helped me to write this book. The reader may refer to this list, as necessary, for further clarification of the subjects' voices.

Abena (African): I have always identified myself as a Black feminist activist because, given my experience, I can be nothing but feminist. I have worked alongside women and the struggle of women for so long. I have worked with five generations of people. You are looking at someone who has worked with five generations of men. I would have worked with five generations of people in the struggle, and I am only xx years old! You say to yourself, what else can you do! As I identified more and more with the gay community, I could feel them [Black community] turning away and treating me with more and more disdain. I don't know, they who had relied on me for such a long time for support.

Abike (European; Chinese; African): Having migrated to Canada and lived in residence, I kind of acculturated to Canada in many aspects of my life, but, in many other aspects of my life, I have found my own way. For instance, building on my Caribbean roots, and having identified myself as Black, irrespective of the White father in the background, I took specific steps to know more about what I consider to be my culture. I made my pilgrimage. I went all over West and East Africa. When I look in the mirror, my dominant physical characteristics are African in origin — the textures, my physical and facial characteristics, my build, and my whole orientation is African. When I study my own modus operandi, it is in keeping with some of the original traditions of sharing, of looking after the collectivity, of looking after the community, of being part of a group. I am married to a Black man, who is from Nigeria, but born of Guyanese parents...his father was a Black nationalist and so am I, a Black nationalist and PanAfricanist.

Aita (African): I define myself first and foremost as a Black woman, not narrowly bound in terms of nationalist ideology, and I don't see myself so much as a PanAfricanist because PanAfricanism has its place. Just as I say that I grow up and I see all that goes on, is just so we have a sense of our power. It wait until it comes to North America for it to come to fruition, but we are powerful, and can be powerful, and nothing en go stop us if we put our mind to doing something.

Alice (African; Amerindian-Carib): I think I became Caribbean when I came to Canada. I left thinking I was Canadian, and then I came to Canada thinking I was Caribbean. And that was interesting, meeting women from Jamaica or Trinidad or Barbados or, not Trinidad since my family earlier lived in Grenada and Trinidad, but from Barbados, and those places and having a sense that, you know, we came from the same cultural basis. Yah that, once I became a Caribbean woman, and so I think I have to acknowledge that there are very many women from all over the Caribbean, and men who played a part in who I am now.

Amanda (European; Mixed race): I am a Trinidadian. I still consider myself a Trinidadian, but the changes taking place in Trinidad — the crime — I don't think I would want to live there.

Anne (African): I see myself as a Black female, still Caribbean even though I have spent more time here than I have spent in the Caribbean. I still identify very strongly with my Caribbean roots, you know. I see myself as very much really conscious of what's going here in Canada, and I am living it on a daily basis, working in a mainstream organization. I see myself not as arrived, I haven't arrived anywhere. I see myself in a position to make a contribution, and I can make a contribution to those people in my community, either by seeking them out, because of the position I am in, hiring them, or making sure that they are hired. I see myself as a spokesperson for them especially when we are talking about policies. I see myself, being able to help others, and also as a voice really, because we have very few Blacks who really get promoted to directors or managers, where they have impact on policies and decisions.

Annzinga (European; Portuguese; African): I found that I didn't have difficulty mobilizing people...and it is something people talk about, they talk about in the sense that they think I have the skill or ability. But I am not conscious about it. I guess it is part of my reluctance in talking because I don't put labels on myself. I don't see what people see in me. This definition of my self — what does that mean?...there is a finality to that...I hear people introduce themselves as an activist, I don't know. Definitely I would say I am a Black woman, I am a Caribbean woman. I am very much a Black woman from Trinidad, that's who I am — that's where my roots, my culture, and my outlook, whatever.... I have not found anything in Canadian culture that would make me give up Trinidadian culture. Because of so much what I talked to you before had to do with work that I did, when people ask the question you usually think about a political activity.

Aretha (Mixed race; African): I have a bit of a struggle with that [identity], because when I became a Canadian citizen, it was very, very emotional for me, as I had difficulty letting go of Trinidad/Tobagonian. I did not realize how nationalistic I was, so I always think Trinidad and Tobago first, then Canada afterwards. Black woman is important for political reasons in this country. I announce that in a loud voice, there is no need to doubt it. I walk in, you should see that I am Black. I am Canadian of Trinidad and Tobago origin, I say on the job, but deep down inside I am a very Caribbean woman. I am here enjoying what Canada has to offer, but I have given very much to Canada so there is reciprocity. And Canada should accept what this Caribbean woman is giving of herself to it. I am a Caribbean woman living in Canada!

Ariel (Mixed race; African): Woman — African origins, with some European blood-ties, or whatever you want to call it. In terms of identity I see myself as a Black African.

Bianca (Mixed race): Primarily, I am a grandmother, a mother, and a Black woman. I talk about myself as a Caribbean woman, but I am also a Jamaican woman. As well, I am a citizen of Canada. Funny for the length of time I live here, with all my family, and others who are important to me, but deep down I can't say here is home. I still talk about home as Jamaica. I am a Human Rights activist, a Trade Unionist, and a human being, who, with all these different parts, make me who I am.

Cheryl (East Indian): I know that sometimes people behind the politicians have more power than the people upfront. Maybe it is not my personality to be a upfront politician. I am do more behind the scenes, okay, and that's why I didn't want to be upfront, and I wasn't ready for it. I am a private person, too, in so many ways. And then my writing was always in the back of my mind. I work as a community worker for my bread, and I enjoy doing it, but my passion in life, what I would like to do one of these days, is to sit and just write, you know. But it is really hard for us, for reasons I don't have to tell you, so I rather work in the background. I had opportunities to do that, but I was disillusioned because [of] what I saw: the racism, the sexism, you know, the ignorance, and the games. I wanted to seem to be a Canadian — a citizen of this country, not just a little, something by the wayside. You know I felt one of the ways in which you can seem to belong more is if you act, you know, and let the public see that you are not just interested in race relations and equity issues, which a lot of minorities do, and especially the Caribbean people, because they started the whole issue for fighting for equity. You don't want to seem to belong to this and to seem to be doing a limited type of activity. I wanted to embrace everything.

Clarita (African): I'm a mother and a social worker and this and that. I'm a daughter, I'm a sister, etc., etc. I'm a friend to one or two people. I don't think that I can define myself as any of these things without putting Trinidad in front of it. ... I'm saying that when even as I hear of some of the unfortunate things that happen in Trinidad, I think they're unfortunate, but, it doesn't terminate a desire to go home.

Daisy (European; African): I think I could say that I see myself as a strong Black woman. I did not always see myself as strong, but then, because I was always thrown into situations, as I mentioned before, where I had to speak up, then people see me as strong, and people tell me I'm strong, so I think that is strength for myself. And I think you have to be yourself. I think I have a deep faith and a deep trust in God, and I think that is what helps see me through a lot of things, because things weren't always easy and smooth flowing even when we came here to a Black congregation.

Doreen (African): I was a part of, and still [am] part of, the "Assembly of Spiritual Awareness", that is: we deal with the spiritual...the authentic part of our ancestors' spiritual tradition where we believe there is a God; you believe in your ancestors and in the method of their spiritual worship, not the distorted way that Europeans projected us. I know, with me, the more, the greater the challenge ... I do not know where I get the energy, I do not know where I get the strength, but the fighting spirit is within me. We are the key to the survival of the African race in the Caribbean — the women, the strength that we have. When the men will get a little downhearted, the women will fight relentlessly. We have that determination, that inner strength!

Evelynne (East Indian): I have not grown with restriction, and yet I know who I am. I am not African, I am not Chinese, I am not English, but I know where my roots are. And I know I would not like to go to India and marry an Indian man. I am a Caribbean woman! What is a Caribbean woman? She is a pepper-pot, and I think I got quite a lot of pepper in me too!

Fern (Chinese): "I am me. I think I am unique with my background and with my life. I treasure my background in Trinidad and Tobago. I think I have got the best of both worlds.

Haniffa (East Indian): I am a Black woman. My roots are Caribbean, Guyanese. I hold both Guyanese and Canadian citizenship. My sense of religion is Islam. I grew up in an environment where all religions were equally celebrated, and I have a high degree of respect for people's preference and choice of religion. This experience developed a strong sense of community and family responsibility in addition to my home family. I consider myself to be a Black woman. I do not think that one can be outside the Black and White definition. You are either Black or White; you cannot be blackish, brown, or yellow. Your racial group is not the colour — it is your political, economic, and social bias that identifies if you are Black or White.

Kamla (East Indian): I think I am a person who came from a humble beginning; I continue to feel that way. I am a humble person, no matter where I go, what I do, or where I am. I am very ambitious. My goal would be to do my own business. I really like people; I am a people-person. I have things going for myself. I think the reason that I am successful is that I like people, helping, talking to them. I help personally or professionally. I would like to be looked upon as one of those kinds of individuals: a people-person. I want to say that the Black community does not include people like me, and I consider myself a Caribbean woman. I consider myself a Black person. I may not be Black in the sense as one refers to it in this continent, but I am not White. When you reflect on who you are and what you are and where you fit into this society, people like us are not identified in any form or fashion, because you have the Whites, and you have the Caribbeans who will talk about "Black". Well, what's the Blacks? I feel people like us are left out.

Kim (Chinese): [No statement made.]

Lauretta (European; East Indian; African; Amerindian; Jew): I see myself as a child of God, and I get my strength from being a child of God, and my direction — a daughter out of the Caribbean, who works towards the harmonious co-existence of people.

Lena (African): I look at myself as a person who made good use of my background, because I discovered that there was richness in my Caribbean upbringing. I am a woman who is not bitter from the experiences that I considered negative in my life. They were not negative, now that I reflect; they were part of my process, part of my life processes that you must go through if you are going to survive. Some of the things I found difficult have brought character and strength, and we know that we have made a contribution. I know that I made a contribution from

25

what people tell me. There is nobody, wherever I go in Toronto, who does not know me for that name. And the only reason is because of the work that I did, and the contribution I made. My name is connected to Black Theatre Canada, and that, to me, is a great compliment. I know the work which was created was very meaningful. But I really loved to be a teacher. I never became one, but in a sense I am one. Now, I know that, looking back. Teachers are not only those who go to the school and teach. You become a teacher also by sharing.

Lucinda (European; Mixed race; African): "I am an individual, and I am proud of who I am as a woman; and I don't make the colour — black or white, light or brown, English or African — take away anything from me as an individual. My identity is: I am a Black, mixed-race individual who come out of many cultural and good people; and when I look at who I am, most of all, I am a human being and next thing, I am a woman. That is something nobody can take away from me.

Mabel (African): I am conscious of my blackness and my identity. I don't take life seriously. My experiences are shaped by my travel in Tanzania for three years, and through Nigeria for four years, and then coming from the Caribbean. I feel I have a very wide worldview that I could put my experiences in. Community, that is, family and friends and others, is very important to me because it gives me a sense of belonging and helps to keep me going.

Marilyn (Chinese): I am proud to be Trinidadian. I do not see myself as Caribbean because I have never seen the Caribbean except going to Barbados. I have to tell everybody because they look at me and they say, "You have an accent". They expect me to sound like a Hong Kong Chinese, or somebody else. I am from Trinidad! I know my feelings because when I go home, I love the mountains, I feel I am at home, I love the water! When I hear the steel band, my heart goes...if I hear the bass, I cry! I am a daughter; that is very important to me. I am a daughter, a mother, and a "me" after. I was brought [up] to be last. This is the way with Orientals. We are taught to be quiet, submissive, and passive. I always put myself last. I am trying to overcome that feeling, but it is difficult.

Marise (Mixed race; Portuguese; African): I think that, for me, there is no cultural community on the planet I feel comfortable with, because I think that all cultural definitions have come out of the colonialist heritage which is patriarchal, heterosexual, you-name-it. And for women like myself, and possibly men, it is very difficult to identify by any existing definition, which have come from the organization of nation states and the European colonialist background. That is a problem for me, and it is a problem for me in joining culturally defined groups from the Caribbean. And there is the difficulty of accessing groups which exist because I am a lesbian, and many are male-dominated. You only have two choices: go in and accept domination, or stay out!

Maya (African): I want people to see me as a Black feminist. What does that mean? For me it is a case of seeing me more as a person, to describe me in words, in terms of my character, things that I stand for, and what I actually do, will be more valuable to me than giving myself a label, as a character. I can say I am a person of integrity; I believe I have a sense of commitment to my blackness and to being a woman; and to strive for freedom not only for myself as a Black woman, but for other women, and, in fact, for everybody who is oppressed; to value people and to work for the better humankind; and to get rid of the oppressions we experience. This is where my commitment lies.

Naomi (African; European): I am a Caribbean Black woman. I don't want to be called an African Canadian because it was made clear to me that it is wrong for us from the Caribbean to call ourselves African. Although I have lived in Canada all these years,

I still hold on to Barbados because it is my cultural background from which I drew the strength to live here. I don't want to ever give up the cultural things which made me who I am: a Barbadian with Canadian citizenship, a piece of the mosaic. This way I get a sense of comparison which I pass on to my children to define their way of living. Comparison helps them to make choices. They know what Barbados stands for, and can understand and respect people who belong there, and put Canada and Barbados together. Call me a Black woman from the West Indies!

Nikki (European; African): I want others to see me as a very fair person, as a person who can listen to both sides of a story and come to a conclusion with a balance. I want people to see me as a warm person; and I know I sometimes don't give the impression of warmth. I see myself as a Black woman, yet I still see myself, in a number of ways, as a woman from the Caribbean. As I was saying there must be some European because the grandfather that I knew was very fair — if you look at my hair! When I look at his side of his family, there is a range of light-skinned to white.

Nisa (European; Mixed race; African): I am all-Jamaican!

Olive (European; African): One of the things I know that I do, that I am very interesting — I am a connector, and I am connected. It seems to me I am that all the time. Everything I do I want to bring other people into it, or every time I hear about something I think to myself: I wonder if I can help make an opportunity for somebody there. So that means being connected and being a connector. There is no doubt in my mind about being a Caribbean woman: I think the high school girl thing, the being my father's daughter thing, all of that makes me be a certain kind of person. As well, I am a dreamer, I dream all the time. I love to tell stories. I love to sing calypso.

Radika (Mixed race; East Indian; African; Amerindian): So, our first three weeks in Canada, we are in the hotel alone, and my Mom looking for jobs, and our Indo-Trinidadian friends mostly inviting us to their homes just to show off. So today when I identify mostly with the Black people of my community, the African side of my community, it is because I find that the people in the African side, for me, have been more caring, supportive, and not having pretension of hypocrisy about them. So that it was why I say that I am Black. I don't want to be called anything but a Black woman because to me that's the identity I require.

Rebeka (European; Mixed race; Amerindian): As a Black Caribbean woman, I like to think of myself as somebody who is open to learning things, who can gain clarity about what my strengths are, and what my contributions might be in the world. The direction I would like to go in, and continue, is one where I am working on issues of change and challenging the status quo. It doesn't always happen, but this is something I feel that, as a Caribbean person, and knowing the experience of colonialism, imperialism, as a woman knowing the experience of sexism, and as a Black person knowing the experience of racism, these are not about life, but about death, suppression, and downpressing; that what I would want my life to be is something to open that up, to remove it, so that you have a life, you are flourishing, you have joy and ability to contribute to whatever you want to. So that is what I want to be thought of as.

Rosetta (Mixed race; Black; Chinese; East Indian; White): I can't remember how I identified myself, so I think I'll identify myself more clearly for you. My name is really in transition also. I'm thinking in terms of my identity. I was named by some African friends, I think ten or more years, more then ten years ago. I was named M__, and I had a naming ceremony, and recently I thought about it off and on, I recently thought to officially or legally change my name. And M__ means "I have found the one I love". And I would like to use my African name as part of my identity, in terms of my writing. I would like to write and do independent research, and I would like to be known by my African name. Because, for me, it embodies my roots that I started, I think, seriously searching when I was quite young.

Rowena (European; Mixed race; East Indian; African; Syrian-Lebanese; Amerindian): I never identified myself first by my sexual orientation, that just happened by the wayside; no, that sounds trivial, because the experience of it is a political one. That is not my focal identity, I mean; I identify myself as a Caribbean woman. I would say in the eighties I identified and called myself a Black woman. As I say, more and more that women were claiming a racial identity. For example, I was called "Black and Women of Colour". That was a sort of umbrella term used, which encompassed all women. Now me is a woman of mixed race, so I feel it would be stupid of me to dredge up any one of those and claim it for myself. Because, if I refer to myself as an Afro-Caribbean woman, people would laugh me out, and *I* would laugh myself out! I have come across some little stiff times in dealing with some of my Black sisters, who kind of want to treat me scrabby² because I is light-skinned and middle class. Then they would proceed to identify me for myself. But I had decided a long time ago that nobody was going to create an identity for me, and that I would be who I am — I am a mixed-race, middle-class woman.

Simone (European; Portuguese; Africa): Yes, I'm a Canadian, very much a Canadian, I feel. I love this city. I love it. I've never been one of those who moan and groan about Canada. I even like winter. I love where I came from. I feel it has made me a strong person to survive in North America. I wonder what it would have been like if I had grown up here. I have had such a strong sense of myself that I never feel that anyone is better than me. In fact, I usually feel that I am so much further ahead than many born here. I don't even presume to think that I am a victim. I've never walked around feeling like a victim. I've never been stopped anywhere I want to go. I believe a Canadian is anybody who so identifies him/herself.

Saida (Jamaican): I'm just a plain, ordinary, down-to-earth person. Me, I'm Black anyway! Me, I'm Black, and I'm a Jamaican. If they want to call me African, go ahead! I was born in Jamaica, and that's the only thing I know. And I still say I'm a Jamaican. And if I have to say anything, I would say I'm of Cuban descent because my father's from Cuba. But my mother's a Jamaican also, so I just stick to Jamaican. I was born Jamaican.

Sastra (East Indian): I have a struggle with the immigrant women group I now support, that is, calling ourselves "visible and immigrant minority women". I struggle out of the question: How long will we have this title? Will we ever feel we are Canadian of Caribbean ancestry — wherever we are from? I am told by my friends just by having that title it gives people a sense of power, sense of purpose. I respect what they say, but argue that if I call myself "an immigrant woman" the word itself does not connote power. I was resisting that — "Don't call me that", I'd say, "I come from Guyana, and I want an opportunity to organize and contribute to my community". So I have always had this internal struggle: Who am I in Canada? I had to take the agency for everything I got involved in — the first move or the last move, nobody came looking for me, and I had to take that initiative. So I felt I have used both the experience I have internalized, as I was socialized by my mother as well as my aunt, and the belonging to community groups.

Sumanta (East Indian/South Asian): Well! Now I definitely describe myself as Indo-Caribbean, Trinidadian, or woman of colour, depending on the context I am in. My organizing is happening in different areas too. In the past two years I have been conscious of being an Indo-Caribbean, and I have been trying to organize in that area, and trying to assert that identity in a specific way, as I am on the Board of xxx, and I try to push that identity of Indo-Caribbean.

Toni (African; Amerindian; Jew): I define a little different here — I define I am a woman, and my mother's daughter (I don't even think of being my father's daughter), because she is a blend and a mixture of so many things. I think I identify with being very Jamaican, being Caribbean, but I identify with being a woman. I think of myself as being Canadian, because I have a Canadian child. But I think of it as something transient because I really think of myself as an international woman. If I don't enjoy Canada any more, I see no reason why I can't pack my bags and go off to somewhere else, as I think I have no limited boundaries. *This* isn't it. I could go where I am needed. Jamaica is my nucleus. But being this kind of bastardized mixture, because now that I am here, I never valued the native part of me as it was devalued in the Caribbean. I value it very much now. I value my Jewish grandmother, my Black grandmother, my Arab ... and I don't care if nobody else sees it ... I value the fact that I am a woman. Jamaican yes! Woman first. But to hell! If I contribute something to Canada, and Canada does not want me, I will give it to somebody else!

Vanessa (European; Mixed race; African; Amerindian): I consider myself to be Canadian of Caribbean heritage. I am proud of my sensitivity to age. I believe that heritage has contributed to my sensitivity of other cultures and my understanding of diversity. I also believe that my family influences have contributed to my confidence and sense of security. These early influences have played a part in whatever achievements that I have gained over the years.

Yaa (African): For me, I see myself as an African-Caribbean woman. I see myself as coming from a strong line of Black women. It has given me pretty powerful tools to cope with a very rough life. I never had any idea that Canada would turn out to be a hell hole that it is. Well, there were good times too, but! I see myself as not an individual. I don't see myself as the "I"-

"Me"- "Yaa". I see myself as very much connected to a community — often times what I feel and what I do isn't in a vacuum, it is from a Caribbean or Black community. Even so I made a conscious decision that any work that I do is within a Caribbean community, and that is why I am at xxx. I see myself as taking on struggles, I try to balance my work with women's issues and youth and children's. I feel if I were to stop doing that work, I would wither up and die. It is integral to my survival and to my peace of mind.

Yelena (European; Mixed race; East Indian; Chinese; Portuguese; Carib): I claim a Caribbean identity. I claim Trini, I don't say Caribbean. I say Trini, because that is a separate piece of the Caribbean. Being Jamaican, or being Bajan, or Trini is being different things, although we all come from the Caribbean. But, I also acknowledge the privilege of access that I have of being mixed race at this time. I have to acknowledge what I have. I can quite easily let myself be exoticized, which happens a lot, but I try not to let it happen. Now I have access into the Vietnamese community, Korean, Japanese — any community of colour — which other workers do not have.

Yvonne (African; Carib; Indian; Coco-Panyol): I am an independent woman striving to live my life like a prayer. I yearn to experience more and more understanding and respect among people. I am a sister, a friend, an auntie, and a godmother. I am woman-centred coming from a Caribbean social-cultural framework of "women-looking-out-for-women" and often men. My Caribbeanness springs from the connection which I make to a history of struggle and recreation of a diversity of cultures. I call it participation in a tapestry. I have a sense of diversity which stems from Belmont, a location of Trinidad and Tobago, which I specifically call *home*, where Pan [steelband] was born.

Zindzi (African): Whatever name they call me — consultant, educator, activist, and now professor — I am really a teacher at heart, rooted in African soil, nurtured by the sun of small Caribbean islands, and coming to full personhood in cities all over the world.

Zora (African): So I see myself as, what we used to say, a Black woman in Canada, but now an African-Canadian woman. So I don't, necessarily, I mean, I do not want to find out about Guyana alone, that is I can't get myself caught up in that area only. I'm a Guyanese, so I'm not a Jamaican, and I'm not a Trinidadian, and whatever, you know. I feel that we sort of all belong together.

Part 2: Who are Caribbean women in Canada?: *Mout' open 'tory jump out*[3]

I had no idea of the extent to which my identity, the sense of self I cherished, would be challenged until my encounter with Canadian racism. I recall when I thought I was fully in control of my life: there I was making some notes in my organizer, and sipping a cup of coffee. Then, a White woman placed her used tray in front of me, and proceeded out of the coffee shop. When I glared at her she offered no apology; I felt enveloped in a destabilizing silence that made me question who I knew I was. Was I who she imagined I was? I began to reflect that instances of racism have the potential to lessen the positive levels of my self-perception, particularly when they occur unexpectedly. I am amazed, for example, when I have felt my self-worth reduced as White Canadians are puzzled at my knowledge of Eurocentric literature or art. Equally, I was horrified when, as ostensibly a new migrant, Third World people in Canada, presumably culturally assimilated, distrusted my competence to undertake responsibilities which I have repeatedly accomplished in the Caribbean.

Nevertheless, I knew in Trinidad and Tobago that the pain of prejudice existed, because of my "black" skin, as well as my own personal status — an orphan — that produced degrees of emotional alienation.

Yet I survived because of "home", where I could feel connected and where I could position myself to believe I belonged to a community, even if there was the presence of cultural or racial boundaries.[4] I could imagine I knew people and they knew who I was, because

the street of Belle Eau Road, Belmont, where I spent much of my young life, was the place to which I belonged. I felt heady about dipping in and out of cultures. For me, exciting things used to happen at different times in this district of my upbringing. I can recall the Da Silvas (Portuguese) who would be celebrating "something", asking us to join them for Madeira wine and garlic pork. Then George Lee (Chinese), our shopkeeper, would invite us to his restaurant for a feast on Double-Ten (10 October). That was very special as it was Mama's birthday. How fascinating an experience it was to see the oldest daughter of the Barradas' family (Spanish) flaunting her hips through her tight-fitting skirt, and holding a proud head bedecked with colourful headties in the guise of Carmen Miranda.[5] I wanted to emulate this woman. The romance story of the Swedish nun and the African priest would titillate my fancy — they had done the forbidden — left their respective religious orders for their marriage. I could only watch with yearning their beautiful garden at the front of their home that I presume might have been evidence of their relationship. Sometimes I felt the anxiety of waiting for the approach of the Hosay (Muslim) festival on Belle Eau Road because of the continuous sound of the tassa drums resonating from the not-too-distant hills. Of course, I was intrigued with the idea that the gods would come to collect food offerings left by Indian men in the driveway leading to our house. I kept looking every day in amazement at the large heap of rice gradually disappearing. No sooner had my interest lessened in that festival, then I would hear the loud, repeated rhythms of Pan (a musical band whose instruments were steel drums). It was fun to override the cacophony and decipher the tunes attempted: this artform was so new! Then it was the ringing of the bells, when religious rituals began at dusk in the Piggotts' (African-Yoruba) yard, together with bawling goats used as sacrifices to their gods. Older people used to identify this family as authentic Africans who were practicing the Shango religion. For me, that was Belle Eau Road, Belmont; that was where I belonged for many of my impressionable years.

This part of my story illustrates how I imagined myself as belonging, and indicates how I might have constructed my subjectivity, without truly feeling restricted by race. That is, I kept seeing myself occupying a space among these diverse heritages, notwithstanding the prevailing negative stereotype towards people with dark skin colour, which has been developed through social stratification in the colonial Caribbean society. When such identification is accorded inferiority, I, and perhaps many others, find that the identity within me is disrupted.[6] I recall an activist in the Toronto Caribbean community saying,

> Identity is to be understood as within, waiting to be expressed in ideas, behaviour, visions, and desires seen in our politics, literature, drama, creativity, and so on, and to be shared.[7]

This definition of identity is appropriate for my ideas of exploring Caribbean women's experiences in this book. I believe that when the stereotype — as in "Black" — objectifies me, I recognize my identity yielding to lack of privilege and inequality. Thus, I hastily generate strategies of resistance in an attempt to undermine any structures that could subjugate me. But I do not intend to make my story progress so as to essentialize a Caribbean woman's identity. I am going to introduce related personal quotes from the stories of other Caribbean women to interlace the experiences of women born in the Caribbean and living in Canada. Our histories are interconnected through imperialist systems that established the Caribbean region. Therefore, in this chapter, these voices will punctuate my story to distinguish this identity connection.

As I tell this story, I think of the process of constructing my subjectivity. My socialization into Caribbean womanhood was partly the result of observing the behaviours of many older women, and their attitudes towards responsibilities in their homes. These older Caribbean women were consistently self-reliant, in spite of limited formal education, restricted autonomy, and little or no dependence on spousal unions. For instance, I remember my great-aunt, Tan Georgie.[8] In the forties and fifties, a gender ideology in the Caribbean, designated a woman's role to be contained as a housewife, the dominantly nurturing role in the home.[9] The male, in the role of income provider, did not see the home as the main site of his activities. Yet Tan Georgie, as I fondly recognize this older married woman, developed and expedited a baking business from her home. A continuous learner, with a penchant for discussion, she seemed never to be victimized by the delinquency of employment of her spouse. While undertaking her other domestic responsibilities, she produced, for sale, the most delicious breads through the use of a large traditional oven in her backyard.[10] In other words, she greatly reduced those effects of poverty, which could have become a menace to her subjectivity. It was apparent that she earned both an emotional and economic independence that enabled her to maintain a progressive lifestyle for herself and family. The outcome of these material and spiritual roots can be seen today, the twenty-first century, in the security and comfort of a lifestyle experienced by three of her children during their senior years.[11]

Zora: I saw my mother struggling to retain a comfortable position, after we lost our commercial bakery because of my father's gambling habits. When it collapsed, Mother took it over. She turned the ovens over for use of our community, so that people in the town paid to do their own baking of quantity stuff. Later she began, herself, baking in the home, and gradually she recovered our level of comfort. (Interview 31, 10 August 1995)

Aita: I am from a humble background — [my] mother was a domestic worker and my father a teacher. Yet, she taught herself to read. You would see her religiously in the evening going through a pile of old *Reader's Digest*. We used to say she was a trooper when she comes to take up our school work ... if you stumble at all she made you go back and read it. (Interview 20, 14 June 1995)

I was born into an extended family which knew how best to stretch the boundary between middle- and low-income classes to emerge in some often nebulous position between the haves and the have-nots. I imagined much of the hard work of those adults in acquiring material wealth was done in order to maintain their pride and integrity, and to deflect the stigma they felt as descendants of the historic enslaved and indentured peoples. Other Caribbean women in Canada tell their stories about home in different, yet similar, ways:

Sastra: My mother's Mowsi aunt (so she was my great aunt) was a woman who expressed her independence in a number of ways — she was widowed, she had a love affair, she had a child, she was the only Indian woman among many Afro-Guyanese people in the village. She was a first woman in many cases: to go to high school, to refuse an arranged marriage, to matriculate, to get into the Civil Service. (Interview 36, 29 August 1995)

Lena: Back home ..., me? An ordinary, middle-class person? We were poor! Therefore, we did not have such things like an identity. I, as a young person, did not consider myself to be anything special. (Interview 27, 28 June 1995)

Yaa: My construction as a woman, as a female child, is my memory of the number of women in my household, who played a role in raising me. I retain vivid images of very strong women back home. My grandmother played an important role in my life. I see her as somebody who worked very hard...she was a maid in a hotel. Her little money provided for the family. I had an aunt who made clothes for me with ends of fabric. I am always able to reflect on how these older women made it in the Caribbean. (Interview 10, 15 June 1995)

Simone: I was born into what I would call a middle-class family, yet we were a struggling family. In my early years my parents were quite poor but we were more upwardly mobile than others in their generation. My grandfather, whom I never met, was White — and that makes for a lot of feelings of where one should fit in a family in the Caribbean, colour being a very distinctive denominator. My mother was black-skinned, and my grandmother, at one point, I remember her telling me, "I hate everything black, except your mother." (Interview 23, 22 June 1995)

Lucinda: My mom, back home, who is much fairer than I am, went through so much discrimination, because she was poor. I remember her telling us a story that she went for a job once as a housekeeper, and the woman looked at her and said, "We can't hire you because they wouldn't know who is the servant, who is the master." (Interview 24, 21 June 1995)

Nikki: My mother, undoubtedly she was a strong woman. She was involved in community work as a member of the Anglican Church, and was involved in the Mother's Union. (Interview 22, 17 June 1995)

Roberta: Momma worked in the house. Occasionally she would do things like cleaning fish all night and returning in the morning during the fishing season. She was doing men's things. (Interview 18, 7 June 1995)

These stories tell us that the socialization process differs only in degree among Caribbean people who are materially distinct in class (Senior 1991: 25–43), yet, theoretically, they are similarly grounded, particularly by exceptional older women, in a resistance to economic and patriarchal domination. The construct of a Caribbean woman's subjectivity emerges from a legacy of historic capitalist exploitation inherent in the imperialist systems — genocide, servitude, slavery, and indentureship — which, for many people, had to be resisted continuously through generations.

I grew up among many adults whose occupations were diverse and which appeared to position them in a middle class. For example, an exemplary work pattern included that of my biological mother, a nurse, who redefined herself through her co-founding of the Trinidad and Tobago Nursing Council.[12] Next, there are those relatives, mainly men, who were propelled to energize their identities, through their involvement in the trade union movement, as blue-collar workers in the sugar estates and the oil fields of Trinidad and Tobago.[13] Added to that were the few men who were public servants, and a few women who did clerical work in department stores, as well, there were some who owned small businesses. Yet, all were experiencing the limitations of economic progress through the White colonial system. Lastly, was the rare case of my adoptive father who was a writer, and whose publications in the fifties and sixties, articulated, through story and critique, the effects of colonialism on the identities of Caribbean people.[14] This was how I was socialized to understand, on the one hand, that the dynamics of working life was consistent with a struggle against domination/oppression in a "race/colour" system, and, on the other, the utter importance of strategies to provide a livelihood for acquiring the essentials — house, food, and schooling — so as to retain a human dignity.

Mabel: My grandfather, like so many Caribbean people, worked in the Panama Canal. He sent money home to my grandmother who didn't work outside the home, and they built a comfortable home. They were the only ones in the village with running water and so on. I would say I was middle class. (Interview 33, 23 August 1995)

Marilyn: My Dad was very proud, so he would not allow us to work in his snackette.[15] He did not want us to be abused. He did not want customers — anybody — to say what a lovely daughter he had. So he was very protective. My Mom, now, proclaimed that she will not let her daughter marry any man who runs a snackette, and work as hard as she did. (Interview 39, 6 September 1995)

Yelena: My grandmother was strong and independent. She ended up having to raise four sons on her own, because her husband gambled the family's fortunes away. She used to buy coffee beans and grind them and send her sons out on the street to sell. (Interview 28, 29 June 1995)

Aretha: I did not know what class I was in; I just knew I was okay, and I had to get this education which was extremely important, more than even to earn money (Interview 34, 29 August 1995).

Yaa: We were dirt poor! This whole emphasis on education, they (grandmother, mother and aunts) felt that I could use that as a means to break out of the poverty trap. It was really interesting; I won a scholarship through sitting the 11-plus exam. (Interview 10, 15 June 1995)

I also remember how important education was to my elders whose wisdom I respected. These Caribbean women of strengths, and just as many supportive Caribbean men, encouraged me to be, intellectually, all I could be. None of them dreamed that, when I became a young adult, I would take up an immigration option, one of the few affordable means, to fill a quota of domestic service workers from the Caribbean to Canada. Amazed at the daring I had used to continue to shape my life, my extended family remained silently supportive. My decision, of course, articulated the measure of poverty in our lives as a family. Yet my determination to improve my position emphasized that I had been socialized to regard myself capable of progress through achieving a strong education. I can now state, in reflection, that education, as a strategy of resistance, was a part of a Caribbean ideology. My challenge, therefore, was to make a difference beyond the stereotype that enunciated misadventure and failure with blackness.

In the Caribbean, degrees of material deprivation that can produce inequality are effects of economic domination and control. People, however, of cross heritages and cultures with these experiences can build solidarity. Even though racism appears to be subliminal, I repeat, I was conscious that to be a Black person, perhaps without distinguishing myself, might result in my experiencing the obstacles that are inherent with prejudice. Therefore, the only means through which I could access opportunities to deflect any form of misfortune to pursue my educational goal, was to use Canada's Domestic Scheme which began in the fifties. Thus, fortified with my educational background and a subjective rationale for my assertiveness and motivation, I became a domestic service worker in Canada. I was a graduate of Bishop Anstey High School, the first secondary school for girls in Trinidad and Tobago, and I had begun my career as librarian in a junior position in the Central Library service of my country. Consequently, I was studying for a British diploma in librarianship through the British overseas program as the next best thing to university education. Arriving in Toronto, I was placed with a family in an upper-class district. There, my White employers quickly recognized my skills went beyond household routine tasks to the level of teaching and counselling their sons. I overheard their boasting of their good fortune to have got someone like me who was capable of being more than a routine domestic worker in their household. Yet this might have been a compliment in the reverse, because of how racist ideologies are formed and exist, that is, to have "Black" individuals represented as tokens of equality. I heard stories from other Caribbean women, which were opposite to my own, and which accounted for privilege in whiteness being used to subjugate blackness.

> **Saida**: I came here as a domestic worker, and my first experience was with a White woman who had a toilet brush in her house, yet she let me use my hands to wash the bowl. (Interview 17, 8 June 1995)

> **Ariel**: When you come up under the Domestic Scheme you have to be cautious. But I did not like housework back home! In my first job I did not mind taking care of children — I love children — but then I was told to cook as well. I went to Manpower and Immigration, and actually demanded that I get a job with my qualifications and skills. (Interview 15, 13 June 1995)

These experiences tell of the kind of social legacy of resistance that many of these women often internalized. They bring with them an awareness of systems of power, in the history of domination, from the Caribbean region. These systems have exploited, devastated, and deprived a large majority of racially different people. Therefore, any form of experience of race oppression in the early days in Canada, did not deter any of us — Saida, Ariel, or myself — from achieving our personal goals. We displayed the agency to abandon domestic service for more rewarding occupations before the end of our contracts. For Delta, after three months, she took a suggestion from a friend to apply for her first training job as a nursing assistant.[16] For Ariel, as her quote states, it yook guts to insist on a job position that would be more appropriate to how she defined herself. For me, it was through similar assertiveness that I initiated a job search during the last three months of my contract. I responded to a *Globe and Mail* newspaper advertisement, and subsequently became employed at the Faculty of Law Library of the University of Toronto as a library assistant, a job similar to the one I held in Trinidad and Tobago prior to migrating. This prompt and positive result marked the continuation of my journey, and made me feel that Canada was respecting of an individual's skills, and was a place where there was great potential to provide the opportunities in the world to people. However, my thinking about this was altered because of Mrs. R.'s retort of disbelief that it was possible for me to be employed outside of the domestic service. I experienced vividly the falsehood of racial supremacy and the denigration of my Caribbean identity. But these utterances, made in the privacy of the employer's home, were not effective at the level of government, so I left this employment one month before the end of the contract. My story, so far, tells how I found my way in Canada. I now link it to other Caribbean women's stories, as they briefly provide reasons for migrating, and their early immigrant experiences.

Naomi: When I came to Canada, my qualifications were discredited. I had proof of the certificates in every subject that qualified me for teaching, and even signed by Canadian professors who were sent from Canada to the Barbados College. (Interview 42, 23 October 1996)

Zindzi: I came to Canada to go to university because I wanted to have a separate identity from my sister. I was trying to see how far I could remove myself from the familial props. I wanted to see how good I would be on my own. So, in a way, this was a move to independence that got me to Canada. (Interview 9, 13 May 1995)

Nikki: When I came here I worked in a factory for two years — it was very heavy work — I was in a basement hanging raw leather on the ceiling. I came from the Caribbean as a high school graduate and had secretarial skills. (Interview 22, 17 June 1995)

Kamla: With the difficulties I had at home [Caribbean], the only recourse, I thought, was to leave. I first came as a visitor and applied for permanent residence. That was the procedure they used then. I got a job in a factory, even though I showed proof of the "O" levels at home. [High school diploma equivalent] (Interview 38, 5 September 1995)

Haniffa: I am of Indian ancestry; I lived in a Caribbean city where there was a large mixture of people. Yet, everybody liked each other, fought for each other – it was very much like on an equal basis, that is, you know it is your neighbour. When I began high school here it was very traumatic to understand the ramifications, that is, of racism. With 12 Black people in the school, we had to fend for each other. (Interview 4, 2 August 1994)

Olive: I came to Canada to get away from a life that was becoming very kind of nightmarish. I signed in at the YWCA on Woodlawn. Next day I was walking along College Street and saw this big building. I thought it might have a library, so I asked and the receptionist told me it was on the seventh floor, where I saw this lady. I said, "I am a librarian. I am looking for a job." And she said start on Monday. That's how I got my first job. (Interview 6, 1 September 1994)

These stories show that migration and adjustment for Caribbean women can be differentiated as variants of class and individual identities.

The next two years found me in a new capacity, fully independent, during which time I left the Law Library and moved on to a similar position in the Toronto Public Library Service. Neither of these jobs challenged me intellectually, nor helped me to gain a true comfort level. Therefore, I applied, and was admitted, to a Bachelor of Arts degree program at the University of Toronto, major in Philosophy. I had progressed from domestic service worker to university student over a period of two years of migrating, motivated by the sheer desire to construct my own identity. To ensure some security, both physical and financial, I took up an au pair position with a Toronto family, during the first year of university. This live-in arrangement curtailed much of my freedom to avail myself of extra curricula opportunities. However, during my second year of the program, like many of my Caribbean peers, I took up the challenge to split my time between course work and paid work in industry; the rewards of both, along with obtaining bursaries, enabled me to live in the comfort of a university residence for women.

Seven years after migration, my success was in achieving two Bachelor degrees — Arts, and Library Science. Thus, the experience of being "forced" to assume a domestic service worker identity (very often despised and socially degraded) had been subsumed. In addition, it was deeply inspiring that my work in the philosophy major had impressed my professor to the point of his recommending me, in writing, for admission to the Masters program in the department of Philosophy. I did not, however, complete an application because of my concern about a program in a White and male academic environment. I also knew I had neither financial resources nor the kinds of emotional strengths to cope with that apparent degree of adversity.[17] However, my journey in tertiary education continued on my return to Canada in the eighties, which I discuss later in this chapter.

My findings in this study showed that education as a strategy of resistance was a part of a Caribbean ideology. We observe how much education is primarily used to challenge gender stereotyping and to support strategies for self-defining. Some Caribbean women now recollect how this was conceived in the family setting at home.

> **Aretha**: Education was key, extremely valuable, and more important than to earn money. (Interview 34, 29 August 1995)

> **Sastra**: Education for me was a word for my age group of Guyanese, especially East Indian women. Education was not on my agenda; it was for my brother. (Interview 36, 29 August 1995)

> **Sumanta**: My mother always pushed me to school ... she valued education a lot (Interview 40, 19 September 1995).

Later in this book, I discuss, in depth, how education, as a primary strategy of resistance, was deployed by a majority of Caribbean women, like me, to define our identities in the contexts of racism and sexism. Yet, definitions of who we are go beyond the construct of education to that of community activism which was used to create spaces for Caribbean women in Canada, and to capture the intellect and imagination of many of us.

In the sixties, however, national independence was a political priority for the Caribbean region. As a result, several Caribbean students in Toronto, during my undergraduate years, kept close contact with political developments in this region as a means of self-assurance about their eventual return home.

Conscious of the diminishing identity, Caribbean people, as a group in Canada, had at the time, with so few of us around, we worked to uncover a Caribbean identity through cultural activities on the campus within the West Indian Students' Association of the University of Toronto — an organization which still exists in the twenty-first century. We were a racially conscious, eager group of students with political agendas, who neither ignored challenges to confront university authorities on racism issues, nor missed opportunities to exhibit Caribbean culture. Serving in this organization reduced some of the alienation inherent in the campus culture of a majority White population. Yet, this was a contesting space for me as a Caribbean woman, since Caribbean men slightly outnumbered Caribbean women in these voluntary leadership positions. For instance, I was never nominated for executive positions — President, Vice President — even though members openly recognized my organizing skills and my dedication to our goals. Somehow it stands to reason since issues of sexism prevail. Caribbean female students, almost equal in numbers to the Caribbean males on campus, were fairly well represented in this Association, yet, at that time, no Caribbean woman ever became President.[18] I, however, ignored any attitude that might have been deemed to create my discomfort, and enjoyed my pursuits in the routines of organizing meetings from the positions of Public Relations Officer or Secretary that I held during my four years on the campus. Oddly enough, these activities, during my undergraduate years, might have prepared me for the next step in my journey of community organizing. During the year of study for a degree at the Faculty of Library Science, I was elected Vice President of the class of 1963. There was only one other Caribbean (Black) woman in the school. The White dominated milieu of middle-class women and men was frequently very alienating. However, there were a few people, including the President, who was a White Australian male, with whom I could share concerns about a curriculum that was less than progressive at that time. As a result, we teamed up to encourage the Students' Council Executive to negotiate with the Faculty for a systematic transformation of the Library Science pedagogy that would include approaches to nurture community-based and diversity-focused curricula. I graduated with a Bachelor of Library Science degree in 1963.

I was fully aware that "Black woman", as a constructed identity, would not cease to haunt me, since the Faculty of the Library Science perceived me as a suitable candidate for public library service, preferably outside of Toronto. With deference to their judgment, I attended a few interviews at public libraries in Southwestern Ontario, and received offers which I graciously refused while relying on my own initiatives. Once more I put to work my knowledge of a legacy of resistance, as I deconstructed a controlling image — passivity and dependence — to initiate my own Caribbean/Black woman's identity (Boyce Davies 1994). The result was that I was very impressive at an interview at The Canadian Hospital Association (CHA), where I was hired for its special library — a site that could have been easily construed as a reserve for a White, middle class person. My tenure there was full of challenges as, with the help of one clerk, I converted the holding of books and documents into an organized library research facility to provide Canada-wide service. Notwithstanding the *everyday racism* at the workplace, my enthusiasm and success in the job brought recognition along with a degree of professional acceptance from colleagues.[19] Much to my amazement, I was recommended by one of the accountants who used the CHA library to do some consulting with the Library of the Institute of Chartered Accountants, following which I got a similar contract with the firm, Woods, Gordon Management Consultants. This was during the years of 1964–1966 when "moonlighting" was not considered respectable for women, particularly since I had to conduct these duties between 5:00 and 11:00 pm. Yet, I never lost consciousness of the prevailing racism, as my otherwise normal work experiences always had a flavour of condescension from the White side. However, I also remained in a supportive network with friends and acquaintances in the Caribbean and Black community in Canada. As a result, I chose to become engaged with advocacy work around my love for Caribbean literature. I joined other friends in founding an arts society for the purpose of promoting art and literature by Caribbean and Black peoples throughout Canada.

> **Abike**: When I decided that Canada was my home, I was extremely involved in the Black community. I was co-founder of the National Black Coalition. I worked with the Negro Citizenship Association in the late fifties, when we tried to integrate the Diamond and LaSalle taxi industries. I went with Black groups to Quebec City to advocate for human rights in this province. The list is legendary. (Interview 13, 16 June 1995)

However, by 1966, I felt overcome through experiences that minimized or marginalized my identity. I had not felt connected to Canada in a wholesome way even with my attachment to Black and Caribbean issues. Having gained ten productive years in Canada, I returned to Trinidad and Tobago for a 20 year sojourn. At home, I claimed the space and gained the privilege, by taking up the challenges in a society under reconstruction after colonialism. The then Prime Minister of Trinidad and Tobago, Dr. Eric Williams, had proclaimed his government's mission of reconstruction. I held a position as Medical Librarian, which gave me the main responsibility to implement this country's Medical Library service. I recall how my desire to make success of this challenging responsibility made me experience a sense of difference. Some health and administrative professionals, who were unaccustomed to working with a woman as expert and decision maker, were negative about my reconstruction of the mission of the "Medical Library". I organized the library to embrace the information needs of nursing, paramedical and health administration personnel, conscious of the barriers of elitism which always seems to surround doctors as professionals. Added to that, my national television program, designed to inform the country about the role of a medical library in people's lives, was often regarded as unacceptable. I, however, pursued many other challenges, confident that my work must depict social change. I realized, then, that most of my behaviour fell outside the construction of a Caribbean female identity. But, undoubtedly, my high motivation stemmed from examples of resistance, which I had internalized from observing assertive Caribbean women. I had developed some concerns about exclusion from certain social circles, but that was not a deterrent. Experiencing the loss of some friendships did not stop me, because I realized the reason was my confident and professional attitude. This was not an asset that was totally admired by many Caribbean men and some women alike. Assertiveness would appear as confrontational and contradictory to the gendered perception of Caribbean womanhood. For instance, in 1974, I was the chair of a Library Sub-Committee whose members were all women. We presented the government of Trinidad and Tobago with a Library Statement on Intellectual Freedom.[20] This expressed our opposition to censorship legislation enacted by a government which was enjoying enormous popularity from a majority of the population. My colleagues and I felt largely triumphant when our statement received some recognition from a few overseas Trinidadian nationals, yet we were generally ignored locally.

Community activism, the experiences of which I address in Chapters Seven and Eight, was the challenge that continued to fuel my energies and to enable me to develop and enhance my public relations skills. Therefore, I readily accepted the challenge to switch from being a librarian, and to take up a role that would intensify my public involvement. In 1975, I was successful in my application for the job of Secretary to the Trinidad and

Tobago Bureau of Standards, which entailed administrative and public relations responsibilities. Foremost, with a team of Director and staff, I worked to establish and develop a meaningful role for this state agency. Again, I found myself working towards encouraging links between the public and the state. The challenge was greater than previously at the library, and more politically oriented. I was aware of my shifting into a place where a Caribbean male would feel more comfortable, and where Caribbean women were not expected to be seen. This was the sort of dichotomy that heightened the prevailing attitude of a patriarchal system, and energized the developing role of resistance among Caribbean women.

Also, having been recently married only compounded the matter of juggling the dual responsibility of "wife" and "manager". I believe, on looking back, that my motivational level peaks when the situation is ripe with opportunities to plant initiatives and expect valuable outcomes. Therefore, in spite of the new challenges in my private life, I continued my mission to perpetuate ideas or alternatives that would deconstruct colonialist methods. Among these was the system, agreed upon with my peers in the Bureau, which I directed and supervised to ensure integrity in an ongoing public education program, as well as in the Bureau's national, regional, and international responses in the discourses of consumerism and standardization. The relevant activities inspired my confidence as a public speaker, and encouraged the depth of my political commitment towards nationalism. However, this nagging desire for new challenges caused me to look elsewhere once the Bureau was fully operational. In 1980, I joined the Iron & Steel Company of Trinidad and Tobago as Administrative Manager, and two years later I was appointed Corporate Secretary. I again found myself the outsider in the "boys' club". This new workplace would be marked by its semblance of being a jungle: tough and male dominated. I was competing, as a Black woman, in a very senior authoritative position, with the ramifications of the social structure: gender and colour. But I never allowed negative attitudes to control me. I remained self-reliant and conscious of a political vision as an ingredient for power in my self-definition.

Throughout my career at home, my interest in social justice and women's issues was retained as I was outspoken in corporate and university classrooms and through the media. I believe, on the one hand, that I gained notability at the national level for my outspokenness; while, on the other hand, my position on issues such as exploitation of domestic service workers, caused me to be branded as "communist". Such gossip did not confuse me as I mixed with people of like mind, some of them women, who also worked with visions of equality and social justice. I had become a voice for women of Trinidad and Tobago, as well as, for the large percentage of my country's citizens who were experiencing difficulties with consumerism.[21] I felt a strong sense of patriotism and pride for my national consciousness building in my country. This developed consciousness formed part of a Caribbean identity which helped us to emerge from the degradation of colonialism. I felt I was able to negotiate my identity as a Caribbean woman and national, among people with whom I belonged, sometimes balancing on an uneven terrain of gender and power. I had academic qualifications that were respected. I had overcome the uncertainties that came with being Black during my youth. I had affirmed my management and leadership capability. Altogether, I had been able to integrate my career, my voluntarism, and my personal life in a remarkable way to make a statement of who I then was.

My subsequent return to Canada in 1986 was based on my need to continue the process of self-definition. I felt I might benefit greatly in a metropolitan society from the kind of opportunities I had imagined that would enable me to fulfill some personal goals. While I had overcome many uncertainties presented by racism in my country, there were still some oppressive situations of race and gender that seemed difficult to counter, in Trinidad and Tobago, at that time. Consequently I relinquished the privileged position I held there, and took recourse in my return to Canada where, again, I used education to strategize a definition of my own liberation. I began that journey to equalize my chances of fitting into a growing market of the library and information profession, when, through part-time studies,[22] I acquired a Master's degree in Library and Information Science (MLS) from the University of Toronto in 1990. In 1991, I entered the doctoral program in Adult Education at the Ontario Institute for Studies in Education/University of Toronto, inspired by an elective, which I took during the MLS program, and which explored issues of women's organizing in Latin America and the Caribbean.[23] In 1998, I obtained a doctorate from the same university. My thesis was the foundation which provided the opportunity to create this book.

Therefore, at the beginning of the twenty-first century, having seen the results of deploying some strategies to sustain my identity, I can better understand the conflicts between the price of alienation and the value of self-actualization. I am empowered to build a bridge between my "home" and my "residence" in Canada. This new empowerment has been energized by my role in teaching Caribbean cultural traditions and the significance of Caribbean literature on society, at universities in Canada, using an interdisciplinary approach. Somehow, my dealing with issues of identity is now more tangible and safe. For one thing, my academic work has done much to satisfy my intellectual curiosity about how we see ourselves and how others see us — a notion that has been analyzed in many social science disciplines. Yet, I am focusing on how the experiences of some Caribbean-Canadian women can collectively furnish ideas about how marginalized people can distinguish their identities outside of the binary: Black/White.

My story finds its link with other Caribbean women's experiences in Canada, particularly women who helped to make this study complete, and who ascribe their identities in Part 1 of this chapter. I identify this group, which includes me, as Caribbean-Canadian women. My next step is to discuss the historic experiences to which we all, though different, are connected, and are justified, collectively, to hold a Caribbean identity. To my mind, my story is one of resistance and survival.

It is a story of someone who becomes an "immigrant woman", and, like others, reduces considerably the constraints which weaken that identity through resistance, and moves beyond to affirm: *I know who I am*.

Notes

1   Standard English translation: *This is how I identify myself.*

2   "Scrabby" treatment is to have one's ideas or responses, when given in conversations, dismissed or inferiorized.

3   Standard English translation: *Once a person begins to say a little about herself or himself, much of the secret will be revealed.*

4   This idea of specifying community in association with identity has been well advanced in Benedict Anderson's *Imagined Communities* (1991), where he argues that the project of imperialism encouraged people, who occupy a common geographical space and who do not know each other, to have in their minds a communal sense of belonging.

5   In the fifties Hollywood contributed to the exoticism of the Spanish by producing a female actor, partially English-speaking, who became a legend because of her dancing and singing and who offered a mystique of womanhood through exhibiting her sensuous and titillating behaviour.

6   In the Caribbean, habitual acceptance of white and light skin colour as the mark of superiority and purity is the result of the plantation society and the brutal subjugation of Africans by Europeans, with its resulting miscegenation and consequent social stratification. As Rex Nettleford discusses in *Mirror, Mirror* (1970), through racial consciousness, a black-skinned person, competing with others marked as brown, white, or Asian, has to double her/his efforts to achieve. Added to that, many people who are distinctly of African heritage experience a construction of their identities as hopeless and problematic and with less chance for social mobility in the society.

7   In conversation with Selwyn McLean, Chairperson of the Toronto Caribbean People's Assembly, November 1994.

8   My maternal grandmother's sister, Mrs. Georgiana Elcock, fondly called "Tan", a vernacular term for "aunt". She lived the longest of her generation, at a location in San Fernando, which was once a colonial estate named "Panka".

9   For an analysis of gender ideologies, see Barrow (1998).

10   I recall when Tan Georgie used to serve us, the visiting children of the extended family, hot buns, sweetbread, and pone. These delicious refreshments awaited us after we had exhausted ourselves with play: picking cherries, pitching marbles, bat and ball, and so on. In 1977, David Moore, Trinbagonian artist, captured the traditional oven in one of his oil paintings.

11   I refer to Dorothy, Joslyn, and Hugh Elcock.

12   I learnt about my mother's activities when I was a medical librarian in Trinidad and Tobago and was collecting medical, nursing, and health archives for the Medical Library.

13   I refer to the trade union movement in the 1930s and 1940s led by Uriah Buzz Butler to improve working conditions.

14   Among other published articles and essays in the Caribbean, Canada, and England, see Carr 1966; Carr and Clarke [n.d.].

15   A convenience store.

16   The conditions of the Domestic Scheme included, contractual labour for 12 months, plus a provision of the immigration requirement to hold a landed immigrant status.

17   Of secondary significance to my decision not to try to pursue a Masters in Philosophy was the discomfort I had about not being able to access Third World scholarship of thought, and I was concerned that, with a perspective only on White philosophy, I might have to remain permanently in Canada.

18   Several of my colleagues of those undergraduate years have often indulged with me in memories of the WISA days and the male era.

19   The actions of prejudice in everyday and informal contexts, which Blacks (and others who are oppressed through race) experience as theorized by Essed (1991).

20   Some of the women, I recall, were Yvonne (Sarjeant) Bobb, Daphne Harper (deceased), Vere Achong, Ursula Raymond, Lois Barrow, and Barbara Farquhar.

21   Activities in public were due to my serving as a member of a Cabinet Committee, the Prices Commission, during the early 1980s, as well as, my duties in education in my job as Secretary, the Trinidad and Tobago Bureau of Standards. Hence, I was told that my name, Yvonne Bobb, became a household word.

22   One year after my return, in 1987, and during the beginning of my 18-month career at the Bank of Montreal as a Legal Information Analyst, I began courses towards a Master of Library Science degree.

23   During the doctoral program, I organized an OISE/UT Caribbean Women's group to meet at my apartment, in Toronto, as regularly as we could, so as to provide a space for networking: sharing issues of nostalgia, discussing challenges, warding off isolation. These meetings consisted of a small number of Caribbean women who were on the sojourn with me during 1991–96.

THREE

Interconnected Histories
in the Caribbean: Caribbean Women
as Rebels and Spitfires[1]:
Back in a time a hole lot o' we[2]

> If I have to define myself as coming from a particular part of the world I like to think of myself as a Caribbean person; because the Caribbean embraces so much, it's like saying you're a poet. For psychically, you're at once connected to Europe, Asia, Africa and the Americas. (Grace Nichols, Caribbean woman writer, 1989)

Introduction

How can we claim, as Grace Nichols has done above, a Caribbean identity? What brings this imagined community to this claim?[3] How could the Caribbean-Canadian women in this book make these claims? Joan Scott (1992) and Hermani Bannerji (1991) have individually reminded us that stories of survival have precedents in history that produced and positioned women as subjects. Therefore, in this chapter, I trace the manner in which colonizers populated this geographic region, which encompasses an area containing an archipelago of islands and two mainland portions of the continents of Central and South America. The people of this region named Caribbean have a common history of domination and resistance in spite of their complex diversity. I provide a synopsis of the historic pattern that underpins the stories of Caribbean women during 500 years of imperialism in the Anglophone Caribbean. I abridge the experiences of imperial systems — genocide, servitude, slavery, indentureship, and colonialism — mainly to point out how diversity was constructed and how resistance enormously distinguishes a Caribbean identity. In addition,

I discuss how we theorize the process of "creolization", which is peculiar to this region and which provides reasons for the notion of collective resistance as a distinguishing mark for all Caribbeans, upon which these Caribbean-Canadian women can also claim an identity. I conclude by drawing a picture of the legacy of Caribbean women's historic resistance to stress its significance in the formation of their identities.

The historical journey

✷ White "West Indian" fortune

In all modern imperial colonies during colonization, the elite White population consisted of large-scale planters or estate owners, who were distinctive in their political and economic power through their absenteeism and their ability to control the movement of enforced labour, as well as to direct class mobility throughout (Cox 1984). Those of the highest level in the social structure — English, French, Dutch, Spanish — were government authorities and planters, while some held other "respectable" positions in a variety of skilled professions and occupations essential for a livable society (Brathwaite 1971). Historically famous for its subjugation of others mainly by race, but also by class, the White elite was divided. Foreign and visiting Europeans resented the creolized version of their peers and the degrading conditions of poor Whites through time (Beckles 1989b). The Caribbean being an "integrationist" society, there was modification of European ideologies, though Whites dominated the upper echelons of this region well into the twentieth century (Lowenthal 1972). Nevertheless, the planter and authoritative class were fully responsible for the dominance of imperialist systems to achieve capitalist gains through dehumanizing conditions.

✷ Imperial systems: Genocide—Caribs, Arawaks, and others

Human presence in the Caribbean dates back to 3100 BC, yet the colonizing "pirates" claimed the region as their own. The bitter encounter of Amerindian peoples with European imperialists resulted in loss of sovereignty, sexual exploitation, and gradual extinction over 300 years. Added to that was loss of identity. Colonizers re-named the natives of the Caribbean "Indians"[4] to dehumanize them, reducing their multiple identities by recognizing only two tribes, Caribs and Arawaks, designating them as hostile and passive respectively. Typical of imperialist strategy, social relations were established by this staged divisiveness among the oppressed and through miscegenation which created a group who were forced to show "mixed loyalties" (Craton 1986: 97). Yet the masses of Amerindians refused to assent to the "encomienda",[5] enslavement, and loss of religion because of their ethical values, and thus the colonizers rendered them to be "inadequate and unsuitable" as slaves (Badillo 1995: 65).[6] Amerindians, with relatively limited technology, confronted European oppression through protracted wars to remove a colonial presence that meant the appropriation of their lands.[7] For instance, the refusal of the Kalinagos (Caribs) throughout the first 300 years of European settlement to bow down to oppression was a thorough example of the "anti-colonial and anti-slavery tradition" that speaks to collective resistance (Beckles 1992: 13). As well, their solidarity with enslaved and freed Africans became another major strategy of resistance to imperialism, as alliances redefined them as Black Caribs in the struggle for the islands of the Lesser Antilles (Beckles 1992; Craton 1986).[8] Thus, from the late 1500s and thereafter, the Amerindians displayed patterns of resistance which were to be repeated by many oppressed peoples in the Caribbean over the centuries (Craton 1986). The system of genocide of the Aboriginal people meant there was a tremendous loss of human potential and identity. This loss created an inevitable need for the system to find new sources of labour. As a result, Europeans, the English and French in particular, turned to their own metropolitan cities for White "not free but involuntary labour", as well as "convicts and malefactors" to become indentured servants in the seventeenth century (E. Williams 1970: 96, 99).

❧ Imperial systems: White "West Indian" Servitude

The system of servitude indicated that White people were not only symbols of "wealth, power, and status", they also belonged to oppressed groups engaged in labour development of the region (Beckles 1989: 175). These marginalized and poor European people mostly were kidnapped from the streets or taken out of prisons, and were granted contracts that gave them freedom after serving a three- to five-year term, as well as three to five acres of land (E. Williams 1970: 96). There was a "systematic application of legally sanctioned force and violence" on these indentured workers whom the planters racialized, stereotyped, and auctioned without respect for law (Beckles 1989b: 5). The ruthlessness of the elite often resulted in confrontation, and hence riots and strikes that erupted on estates when "servants" found their rights undermined (Beckles 1989b: 101). White servants often escaped from the plantation and, as a result, British planters retaliated with a legal pass system for control. Yet, this system and other restrictive laws did not stop the struggles against continuing abominable treatment. There were often conspiracies by Whites in servitude to take control of the island. However, planter absenteeism caused a "leveling up" of some oppressed Whites, and when the population of enslaved Blacks in the Caribbean increased in the early 1700s, their resistance objectives changed, as "radical servants became more reformist" (Beckles 1989b: 99).

❧ Imperial systems: Slavery — "I am a slave from a land so far"[9]

In the sixteenth century, Africans first came to the Caribbean in few numbers as menial workers on colonial ships. However, in the seventeenth century, European opinion determined that the "laborious toil" of Africans was needed to cultivate Caribbean soil so as to produce the sugar industry. Thus, the slave trade began, and a sugar economy was created (E. Williams 1970: 136). Unlike the incentives in servitude, the colonizers offered no promises of tenure or of lands. West Africans mainly were forced or kidnapped and brought to the region as property. But the forced African presence transformed the social and demographic picture of the Caribbean region because they brought a range of complexities of religion, language, and culture to produce an "internal diversity" (Higman 1984: 4). Yet, the colonizers structured social relations to dehumanize them and to homogenize the identities of these highly diverse peoples, while dismantling the structures of societies to which Africans were accustomed in their civilization.[10]

Slavery, a holocaust system, was totally brutal and devastating to Africans who remained in subjugation for three centuries as the largest majority of the oppressed. Nevertheless, over the years, strategies of resistance reflected a consistent pattern to cripple and crush the plantation economy and to produce terms of survival. First, there were rebellions, or "slave plots" conducted with the courageous leadership of Africans to bring about political and economic instability in the plantation society.[11] Next, Africans' determination to escape resulted in the institution of Maroon — fugitive slave — communities, which validated their attempts to control their own lives through resistance. Being able to remove themselves from the plantation was a noteworthy strategy, first to encourage African solidarity, and then to expedite open rebellions, which often resulted in demands for treaties. Moreover, the fact that some Africans were manumitted indicated there was a slave economy that facilitated some purchases out of slavery.[12] In addition, as frequently as they could, enslaved Africans showed their independence from cultural domination by re-creating and cultivating an African cultural identity that increased the Whites' fear of the power of the oppressed. For example, African retention of cultural and religious practices, notwithstanding the attitude of the European planters to diminish or control them, was a mark of maintaining an identity. Resistance, therefore, both physical and psychological, was frequently used as a strategy to achieve some gains in everyday life and to maintain a sense of self. Thus, it can be interpreted that, in the long run, any rebellious activity by the enslaved to initiate and establish any semblance of freedom was a use of their intelligence to undermine authorities, and this contributed to the abolition of slavery. When slavery ended, planters, disregarding the grave conditions in the sugar market and the retaliation of independence from emancipated Africans, turned mainly to Asia to establish another system of servility: indentureship.

∾ Imperial systems: Indentureship — Jahaji Bhaji[13]

In the mid-nineteenth century, indentureship was used as the cure for poor industrial relations with freed Africans and the planters' commitment to continue an almost failed sugar economy. People were brought into the system from China, Africa, and Europe. This nineteenth-century "encomienda'" marked another shift in identity, fostering a stratification of race/colour/class in the plantation society. The new structure differentiated inequity and oppression of different people, in a superficial way, but, through the colonizers' propensity to create injustices, indentureship fostered racial ambiguity and animosity up to the twenty-first century. To begin with, unlike slavery and similar to servitude, this system offered some incentives to immigrants, such as return passages at the end of their contracts, yet labour conditions were still atrocious. However, in spite of many contract failures and the extent to which they experienced a variety of oppressions, a majority of Asians made the Caribbean their "home".

Among the Asian population, diversity of culture, language, and religion was significant, yet the planters assumed no difference. Their labour was fully exploited and their cultures demonized based on a construction of a stereotype: "docile, cheerful, willing, tractable and industrious" (Mangru 1996: 43). However, the planters' discriminatory practices and labour injustices met with retaliation mainly by Indian and Chinese workers. Large numbers of these indentured workers resisted physically and in a fashion similar to people in the past, that is, through desertion, suicide, malingering, and other disruptive behaviours (Mangru 1996; Look Lai 1993). Indians, in particular, vigourously reconstructed religious practices to adapt to the social environment, as evidenced in the repressed celebrations of the Muharram festival in Trinidad and Tobago and the Tadjah festival in Guyana (Mangru 1996; Singh 1988). This was a strategy to resist being Christianized.

Other identities within the indentureship system included a small number of Africans, Madeiran Portuguese, and Syrian-Lebanese, for whom the system was arbitrary. African workers, in the main, ignored rules of indentureship and solidified with African peasant communities to protest colonial domination and economic disparity (Schuler 1980: 31). The Portuguese, who were secured as cheap labour in the interest of White racial supremacy, buffered the tensions in the social structure between the accomplishment of Whites and the meagre economic standing of Blacks. Some of them, however, experienced racial tensions and subjugation from the planter class; yet, because of rules of pigmentocracy[14] they readily commanded the retail trade and depressed the struggling Black merchant class (Moore 1993: 156). A similar experience of racialization, together with class mobility, could be attributed to the Syrian-Lebanese group as they became "clearly upwardly mobile" in the early twentieth century (Brereton 1993: 39). Therefore, under the indentureship system, capitalist gains continued to be sought through inhumanity towards a diverse group of people. Nevertheless, patterns of resistance were indicated differently as each group of migrants to the Caribbean, voluntary or involuntary, displayed their courage and resilience to total domination either through economic success for some and/or through achieving cultural integration within a growing African/European Creole society. Accompanying these varying labour systems directed at increasing profits was a structure that fostered miscegenation.

❧ European forced miscegenation

The colonizers' ambivalence towards practices of miscegenation might be depicted as encouragement towards sexual exploitation of African females to reproduce "'slaves", or to a rejection of the experience based on the ideology of respectability and White pride. In whatever way society manifested its accommodation or outrage, the role of miscegenation was clear in influencing the structure of a Caribbean identity because "color was a significant factor in occupational allocation" (Higman 1984: 84). For example, the children of European men and enslaved African and perhaps Amerindian women, being of mixed ancestry, were often sheltered from the rigours of plantation life (Higman 1984: 194). Though largely unemployed in urban areas, they could engage in labour requiring domestic and mechanical skills (Knight 1990). Yet, coloured people in the Caribbean, who were educated and professional, experienced many "civil disabilities" which undermined their confidence. They were subjected to disenfranchisement, limitations on property, and ineligibility for government positions (Campbell 1992). These "disabilities", along with employment discrimination in the Roman Catholic church, formed the basis for collective resistance among the coloured people throughout the Caribbean. By the mid-eighteenth century, colonial authorities investigated their protest and created laws of reform. Thus, in the colonial system, permanent privilege was a myth for those outside the working class. "Coloured" middle-class people were very often in the struggle for "real equality", because racism was intended to provide the elite White, and no other group, with power and privilege.

❧ Voluntary migration: Jews

The inclusion of Jews from Europe and Palestine in the Caribbean region began as early as the seventeenth century, when Jewish communities were established as a group having "common language, culture and heritage" (Loker 1991: 19–20).[15] Jews were allowed to occupy territory in which the British, French, and Dutch had settled. For reasons of race, however, the colonizers encouraged their migration over 300 years because their presence "facilitated the settlement of white power" (Loker 1991: 24) and racist practices. Yet, because of the prevalence of anti-Semitism in Europe, the legal status of Jews differed among the colonies as the size of their communities was controlled by the White elite similar to what was happening in Europe at the time. Their class position was rectified through their commercial ventures, but they were not permitted to engage in the slave trade, though, like Christians, they were slave owners. The maintenance of their religious practices, while they engaged in merchandising activities, served as a cultural marker and positioned them to display resistance to total domination.

ᕱ Voluntary miscegenation

In Trinidad and Tobago during the late twentieth century, there has been an unmasking of ethnic identification of people rarely recognized as belonging to distinct and small groups. These ethnicities have created a phenomenon in racial mixing because they exist outside the boundaries of the African/European dichotomy of the Caribbean plantation society. That is, these are groups that comprise two or more distinct heritages, creating a combination which reduces Black or White as a strong distinction. These forms of racial mixing, no doubt, are native to many parts of the region and form an impressive part of the tapestry of a Caribbean identity, yet, because formal knowledge about them is limited, they remain under-recognized. The intense cosmopolitan nature of Trinidad and Tobago, however, and the existence of some degree of relevant scholarly research, enable a brief description of three groups as examples: Dougla, Spanish, and Coco-Panyol.

First, Dougla — defined as "the mixed offspring of 'black' [African] and 'East Indian' parents" born in the Caribbean" — is not yet quantifiable. This category lacks formal inscription in the colonial hierarchy, even though there has been acknowledgment of it (Segal 1993: 96–97). People in this group have experienced ambivalence and discrimination by other heritages to the extent that they have been considered as outcasts. Examples of their persecution have been analyzed in Rhoda E. Reddock's 1999 article, "Jahaji Bhai: The Emergence of Dougla Poetics in Trinidad and Tobago".

Next, the Spanish are a multivalent category, in which "economic and social boundaries" correlate with race, ethnicity, and religion (Khan 1993: 287). This group might have origins in the late eighteenth century at the end of Spanish rule in Trinidad, when British concepts of racial types and equivalent inequalities were used to perpetuate a social stratification. Sometimes ethnicities like these get constructed along familial, or popular, lines.[16] Again, indications of their constructed identity are subsumed under the embracing of ethnic difference in a general way.

The final construct, Coco-Panyol, is a subculture of religious, linguistic, and social systems found in a community with peasant-class origins dating as far back as 1498 to 1797, the period of Spanish rule in Trinidad and Tobago.[17] This group consists of people considered to be "racially mixed African/ Amerindian/Spanish descent" (Moodie-Kublalsingh 1994: 2). Their identity is distinguished through their work on cocoa estates, which were owned by descendants of Spanish settlers or Venezuelan planters in the late nineteenth century. They are also known for their perpetuation of parang culture, which is evident in Christmas celebrations in Trinidad and which employs a syncretism of Trinidad English, Spanish, and French patois in its lyrics.

While these ethnicities have not been fully legitimized, they are often idealized in the colour hierarchy. In the Caribbean, lighter degrees of colour, created by racial mixing, are preferred as a sign of enhanced status and overall recognition in the social and economic spheres of society. Resistance within these ethnicities is noted through their attempts to develop communities outside the hegemonic standards and to validate their existence through naming and through idiosyncrasies that may distinguish them as people of Caribbean origins.

This concise historical tracing reflects how Caribbean women are able to identify themselves biologically and psychologically within a vast spectrum of "racial" differences, as well as in practices of resistance. We can view historic experiences as a means of understanding how the self-ascriptions seen in Chapter Two, Part 1 can defy a methodology which applies the binary: Black/White. A Caribbean historic and linear journey brings to us an awareness of the interconnectedness and the interrelatedness of individual histories constructed under imperialism. When we visit this historical construct of connecting identities and related experiences, with due respect to individual differences, we find its significance is embedded in a theory of creolization.

Creolization: A cultural marker of Caribbean identity

The Caribbean region is "a reminder of the disruption and eventual subversions" of people whose origins are diverse (Balutansky and Sourieau 1998: 2). Through these adversities there has been a process that *creolizes* the variant forms of a Caribbean identity, coordinating the shifting and fragmentation of unitary origins. My theory about creolization as a defining component of a Caribbean women's identity intends to move beyond some perspectives that I discuss. Therefore, creolization theoretically leads us to the process of understanding a collective cultural identity, which is not monolithic, but one to which fragments adhere. It legitimizes the identities of Caribbean-Canadian women in this study who have constructed subjectivities through the effects of the plantation society where the persuasion of the dominant culture was often in contestation with the borrowings and origins of other cultures.

Creolization was argued and explained earliest in the seminal work of Edward Kamau Brathwaite, which was continued by other Caribbean scholars, such as Rex Nettleford, who use perspectives of pluralism, interculturation, and assimilation to define its meaning. The African/European dichotomy has been used as the pivot around which cultural diversity and identity need to revolve. Others have built on this argument by equating creolization with "Black culture", thus seeing the African/European model of Caribbean culture as a dominant entity. These scholars also see the power of Creole in the process of creolization in a role to modernize other heritages, particularly those claiming an Indian identity (Allahar 1993; Mohammed 1988). Their arguments seem to correlate creolization with social mobility as well as economic and social status.

The pluralist thought, which emphasizes the African/European cultures as major components in contestation, develops the idea of a monolithic culture, erases the Aboriginal experience during the first century of colonial establishment, and diminishes the Asian and other experiences in post-emancipation days. However, any African/Eurocentric argument about multiplicity in Caribbean identity disrupts the stereotype of a segregated and stable system of Black and White. But one has to emphasize that all the groups delineated in earlier paragraphs, whose experiences of socialization and identification were different, hold some responsibility for the innovation of what we can call a Caribbean experience. People in groups accomplish this from their respective positions as they move between acceptance and resistance of colonial culture. Their actions to indigenize ways of life, distinct from western culture, have continued to establish creolization as a process, rather than a fixed entity. For instance, Brathwaite (1971) sensitizes us to the struggle to formulate a Jamaican Creole hegemony out of the derivatives of African/European social organization, referring to the mixing, matching, and recreation of both cultures which took place during 1790–1820. However, the construct of any indigenous culture was marred by the self-seeking non-European Creoles who, to improve their status, mimicked British culture in the Anglophone Caribbean. He writes, "it was one of the tragedies of slavery and the conditions under which creolization had to take place that it should have produced this kind of mimicry; should have produced such 'mimic-men'..." (Brathwaite 1971: 300).

Rex Nettleford, who also engages in the discourse, reminds us that identity operates at different levels of "power, domination, resistance and violence" by generations of Africans and Europeans. Moreover, one of his concerns is that there is a continuous struggle to expose the prominence of African culture as opposed to British culture and to harmonize what he terms a "Caribbean experience" (Nettleford 1993: 185). His other concern is about how this historical creolizing process has produced a continuum to embrace newly arrived immigrants, "East Indians, Chinese, Arabs and even the more recent transitory North American visitor" (Nettleford 1993: 185). In other words, his assertion is that "others" need to conform to the creolization process that contains major creative contributions of the African and European presence, and indeed to the African Creole. This uniqueness of the Caribbean identity which he applauds and therefore suggests, needs to be continued.

❧ The challenge of constructing a Caribbean identity

My notion of collective resistance through examining history locates the role of creolization as a rationale for collectivity and cohesiveness, as present both in ideologies and activities. In other words, people are responsible for the social and cultural changes and exchanges under colonial domination, which have produced a heterogeneous identity in the Caribbean region, given the quantum of the African-European contribution. Hence, I proceed to consider how groups within the indentureship experience can become an integral part of the creolization process that adheres to mainstream culture. This discussion is with specific reference to Guyana, Jamaica, and Trinidad and Tobago where numbers of indentured workers are greater than in other Caribbean islands.

The Chinese, in their experience of indentureship, combated the horrors of domination, and assimilated Creole culture during the early to mid-twentieth century. In Guyana, Trinidad, and Jamaica, though Chinese groups were different, with both Hakka and Cantonese origins, they adopted the same two strategies of adjustment to enable them to cope with marginalization. These strategies were intermarriage or concubinage with African and coloured women and conversion to Christianity. Thus, miscegenation was a leading force (Brathwaite 1971) in staging cultural identity, while religious conversion proved to be a tactic for accommodating dominance. While successful mobility caused the Chinese-Caribbeans to become targets of violence, Ho further argues that, in Guyana, Jamaica, and Trinidad and Tobago, there was a definite and rapid process by them to accommodate to local culture in food and social relations. Yet, they established ethnic social organizations, some of which consisted of "multi-generational membership" and most of which were centres for sports, recreation, and celebrations (Ho 1989: 11). Activities in these spaces both in Guyana and Trinidad and Tobago, she goes on to state, could hardly be called "Chinese" as, she emphasizes, *Creole* orchestras played *Creole* music to which people responded.[18] However, in Jamaica, where assimilation was the most difficult of the three countries, Chinese people remained mostly isolated and maintained separate, effective social centres, educational, health, and welfare institutions. Such establishments enabled them to maintain "cultural distinctiveness from Creoles and perpetuated their social isolation" (Ho 1989: 15). Ho's analysis concludes that "the process of creolization had eroded most Chinese institutions and culture", though there is a differentiation in the ways that ethnic communities avail themselves of Creole culture (1989: 12). She defines creolization as "the process whereby populations that are neither European nor African become enculturated in Caribbean (African-European) culture" (Ho 1989:3).

This analysis, for me, omits the cultural exchanges that take place between the Chinese and African/European Creole groups. Among some of the well-known cultural traditions in the Caribbean are two: Chinese food, which has developed a flavour that suits Caribbean tastes in separate locales, and recreation, such as gambling, or "whe whe",[19] which was integrated into African beliefs around survival and which was at one time criminalized, although currently it has been nationalized.[20] Thus, there are contributing elements of culture from groups outside the African/European dichotomy that are engaged in the process of creolization.

The Indians, in their experience of indentureship, also tackled the issue of a Caribbean identity distinctly by assimilating and adding to the experience of creolization. But some Caribbean-born scholars see creolization as not making sense in the socially and politically diverse environments contained in the region. According to Anton Allahar (1993), one cannot unify or establish a culturally homogenizing process as totalizing as definitions of creolization appear to be. We have too much at stake, like the contrasting economic conditions of Guyana and Trinidad and Tobago, where the latter is industrialized and can provide conditions for the modernization of Indian culture. Thus, the creolizing process is dissimilar in each country of the region.

Patricia Mohammed (1988) asserts that creolization did occur in general for Indians when industrial transformation and depression in the sugar industry forced Indian communities to restructure and to gradually increase intercultural relations within the larger society. However, she reminds us that creolization emerged from the term "Creole", which was used to distinguish ethnicities, that is, descendants of enslaved Africans from indentured Indian immigrants. Thus, "creolization was viewed as synonymous with absorption of black culture at the expense of one's own—a process referred to as acculturation" (Mohammed 1988: 381). And that is partly correct. The settlers' order of divisiveness was often controlled by labels. Thus, Mohammed observes contradictions among Indian indentured immigrants to participation in the process. On the one hand, the willingness of Indo-Trinidadian women to participate in acculturation was manifested in the calypsos of the day.[21] Interestingly enough, while these women changed their names to English, or were alleged to have consorted with men of other races, they encouraged African-Trinidadian men, in spite of covert animosity within their communities, to participate in their culture, that is, to partake of Indian food.[22] However, on the other hand, assimilation was not the option, for, unlike the Chinese, Indo-Trinidadian men did not use intimate relations to absorb into the ongoing culture, "despite the scarcity of Indian women" (Mohammed 1988: 384).

The mutual contempt, sparked by colonial divisiveness, among Africans and Indians inhibited a rapid progress of creolization, even though history depicted the cultural cohesion that took place when Africans witnessed Indian drumming and dancing (Mangru 1996; Laxmi and Ajai Mansingh 1999).[23] Yet, this picture is not totally accurate, as separatism continued to occur in certain places in order to maintain traditions that could force Indian women into domesticity.[24] The picture is also not generalizable, as Indian women's acculturation was dependent on their religious affiliation and the democratization of education that a large percentage of the Indian population embraced. These were issues arising from political movements or the effectiveness of modernization that influenced the ethnic practices in the Indian-Caribbean community for Indian women. There was free education for boys and girls. Indian households were nuclearized. Indian diets included Creole dishes. The change in traditional dress to western-style outfits was apparent. Many of these changes were observed in the attitudes of the young who pursued inter-ethnic relationships. Findings of this nature caused Mohammed (1988) to suggest that there needs to be a differentiation made "between creolization and modernization" so as to recognize the significance of a political and social commitment to a new society (392).

Exploring these views helps me to argue, as I try to define a *Caribbean identity*, that any theory of creolization that can embrace the experiences of domination and resistance must concede that it is not a homogenizing process at all, but that it brings together differences and interchanges between ethnic groups with collective contributions that resist social or cultural hegemony. The history of resistance, as traced earlier in this chapter, has a principal role in the formation of a Caribbean identity. Resistance is thus linked to Creolization. That is, the activities in which, for instance, all Anglophone Caribbean peoples were engaged, often distinctly in order to reject becoming totally British, marks the process of establishing political change.

Creolization, therefore, is *that* change. It provides a cultural space or breeding ground for counter-hegemonic values and standards. These are perpetuated by the oppressed; therefore, cultural patterns are less regulated from the top (ruling class), and more negotiated and controlled from the bottom (working class).[25] The process of creolization assists in creating and recreating identities as they have emerged from a political process that structured and organized many diverse peoples and cultures under capitalism. The imperialist paradigm produced genocide, servitude, slavery, indentureship, and colonialism from which a construction of Caribbean (Creole) society emerges and is perpetuated. It is impossible to categorize this society in terms of the dichotomy Black/White or, as Nigel Bolland (1992: 64) argues, against merely seeing it as different groups responding to each other and to their environments. I am supporting his argument in that I see Caribbean creolization as filtered through the overarching system of domination/subordination; people's use of agency in resistance; the interconnectedness of (women's) histories; and the interrelatedness of (women's) experiences to produce different, yet similar, subjectivities. It is through these lenses that we can locate this thinking in a "dialectical analysis of society [which] draws attention to the interrelated and mutually constitutive nature of 'individual', 'society', and 'culture' and of human agency and social structure" (Bolland 1992: 65).

There is a flaw in analyzing the creolization process as though people are engaged in "dropping in", or that it is a blending and mixing exercise, or a structure determined or regulated by some past historical precedents. One notes that two major groups, African and Indian, voluntarily and continuously fuse parts of their culture in music, particularly to develop new constructions in resistance to social and political divisiveness.[26] Similarly, Christianity of European origins has been Africanized. I deeply consider Caribbean peoples' everyday practices in resistance to dominance as subversive elements that form a "culture of the opposition". These practices are not innocuous; they are acts of manipulation and aggression, whether they are religious or secular; they are acts, behaviours, and activities that people are forced to perform in relations of power within domination. They provide the material for a dialectical analysis for our understanding of creolization as a process (Burton 1997; Bolland 1992).

Thinking of the intricate dimensions around which culture evolves is a way of seeing how to build a theory of the creolization process. Caribbean history informs that this process has to be inclusive from the first encounter Aboriginal peoples had with Europeans, and, as such, has produced several insights because creolization is not a regulatory process, it is a continuous, perpetuating one. We begin by seeing:

- the repetitive dynamics of plantation society to produce language, culture and identity;
- the ambivalence of some people to prioritize an indigenous culture;
- the contribution of culture from each group serving as an instrument of survival;
- the continuous recreating, meeting, and overlapping of cultures, so that individuals and groups, more or less, contain fragments of each;

- the movements of syncretism and hybridity that recognize differences yet retain individuality;
- the symptomatic belonging to fragments of race, class, and culture.

These are the culminating insights that enable us to draw the conclusion that creolization theoretically is neither complete nor at a final stage in creating a Caribbean identity, as the people's propensity to change is its only law.

Having said that, I recognize the centrality of African culture in relation to other cultures. Its centrality is valid, because of the thousands of Africans of heterogeneous identities who, over 300 years and more, have made the largest contribution to that Caribbean cultural identity, and because the African-Caribbean persistence in retaining their cultural practices, often covertly, and in spite of control, was a form of empowerment to their communities. Their agency to resist total domination and to indigenize their ancestral cultural traditions resonates in the history and psychology of the Caribbean ethos (Smart and Nehusi 2000; W. Carty 1991). Yet, this tenacity resonates in other cultures, for example, the Indian-Caribbean, whose contributions are no longer in the margins, but have become more and more centralized.

Thus, the composite picture of indigenizing cultures can be theorized as creolization. But it is important for me to correlate that process with individual and collective resistance activities that distinguish a Caribbean identity. Thus, I conclude that a Caribbean woman's identity is represented not only through diverse cultures, languages, and heritages, it is also to be found through the ways in which Caribbean consciousness is structured and has emerged from experiences of genocide, servitude, slavery, indentureship, and colonialism. These systems engineered and regulated the construction of Caribbean women's subjectivities. Yet, their lived experiences have displayed agency not only to reformulate their identities in multiple ways, but to empower them for the struggle to bring about social change.

Caribbean women in resistance activities

Women in the Anglophone Caribbean — European, African, and Asian, with the exception of Amerindian women — were forced to migrate from male-biased but different imperial systems to the region. Each group of Caribbean women experienced the double jeopardy — imperialism and patriarchy — differently as gender struggles arose beyond conflicts of race and class. Each group differently employed strategies of resistance to denigration and extremely harsh conditions of labour, punishment, and sexual exploitation, including freedom, denial and other inequities. Because of the prolonged existence of slavery, with its dehumanizing racial prejudices, African women, the largest majority in the systems, experienced gross indignities (Shepherd 1995; Reddock 1994; Bush 1990; Dadzie 1990; Beckles 1989a, 1989b; Higman 1984; Mathurin 1975).[27] Many Caribbean feminist studies have pointed out that those Caribbean women's acts of resistance to domination/subordination historically created an ideology to refute gender hegemony (Barrow 1998).

❧ Amerindian women

The enslavement of Amerindians, though short-lived and arbitrary, indicates that Amerindian women were subjected to sexual exploitation. These women displayed strengths of courage and resilience to cultural dispossession through abandonment of marriages with White men (mostly arranged), which subjected them to an ambiguous status. Also, even obscured, ignored, or demonized for their cultural/religious beliefs, which were interpreted as magically potent, Amerindian women responded in ways that disrupted the colonizers' gender ideologies and stereotypes (Warner 1998; Melville 1997). Thus, Amerindian women's actions began the continuum of linking Caribbean women's experience of gendered resistance to colonial domination.

❧ White women

White women's resistance is indicated in their independent action towards migration, made possible through the system of servitude. Their labour potential totally disregarded within Great Britain during the seventeenth century, they traveled long distances and in defiance of social norms in order to be selected for service in the indentureship system to the Caribbean. Their status was ranked as "voluntary servants" or "labouring white women" who were "considered unfit for marriage" (Beckles 1989b: 46) In spite of their experiences of gender subordination on the plantations, they could have found several means of redefining themselves in the slave society because of their race.[28] White women, as studies show, predicated their politics on the "subjection and brutalisation of non-white women" (Beckles 1999: 60). Motivated through the system of patriarchy that suppressed them as females, they sought their own means of economic survival, which was linked to the reproduction of slavery and indentureship. That is, they became slave owners, or managers of plantation houses or other forms of entrepreneurship that could control enslaved men and women. Yet, many of them often led lives of interculturation as, from a class position, they adopted customs of African women; that is, some of them entered into market trade or copied everyday routines, while others parented "a number of free born mulattos" with "black" and "coloured" men (Beckles 1999: 132). Collectively these amount to actions that shattered the patriarchal myth of femininity and domesticity. From this gender and historical perspective, these White women's actions can be acknowledged as a contribution to resistance of patriarchy and imperialism.

෴ African women

The "anti-slavery" consciousness of African women, fostered through their initial resistance "to capture and sale", forged distinct patterns of resistance in race and gender at the point of embarkation and which continued during the plantation years (Beckles 1988: 34). Many African women in the Caribbean "did not succumb to apathy and resignation" because of the repressive nature of slavery, or the hard monotony of work, or the disrespect of sexual exploitation on plantations (Bush 1990: 56). Their vengeful attitude both in domestic and field labour against the brutality of slavery can be counted in a legendary list of behaviours and activities, from personal to political, that occurred and which were unexpected from women (Bush 1990; Beckles 1989a; Mathurin 1975). Resistance activities were often initiated, supported, and expedited by African women. Of these, two main political activities were repeated: the inciting of rebellions and the establishment of Maroon communities (Dadzie 1990; Bush 1990; Beckles 1989a, 1989b; Mathurin 1975).[29] Thus, acts of homicide on White men by African enslaved women, which politicized them, were not uncommon in "self-defense and preservation of dignity" (Beckles 1988: 164). The other political act, "a commonly reported anti-slavery action", was their escape into Maroon communities to build a space for African solidarity where language and religion could be supreme and from which opposition to White power could attempt to flourish (Beckles 1988: 165).

Equally significant to counter gender stereotypes was these African women's skill in developing economic independence when they were restricted to either field or domestic work. African enslaved women in seventeenth-century Jamaica, for instance, were primarily responsible for the system, well known in the twenty-first century, as higglering:[30] an internal marketing strategy, which provided the enslaved with an independent economic culture, and which the planters had great difficulty in controlling legally (Beckles 1989a). Similarly, in the emancipation period, some African and coloured women who found themselves victimized by gendered approaches to labour staged their own idea of developing economic independence. They became lodging-housekeepers and "strategized" appropriately to gendered constructs of a Caribbean woman's spirituality, nurturing, and sexuality (Kerr 1995: 197–212).

In plantation economies, labour exploitation and savage punishment were considered norms in the planters' treatment of both sexes. Sexual exploitation, however, increased the vulnerability of subordinated African women. For economic reasons, planters and other White men in authority claimed their right to African women's bodies.[31] While there was much bitter defiance, generally speaking passive resistance was apparent when some African and coloured women strategized "social-sexual relations with free men, particularly whites" to reduce their chances for both labour and sexual exploitation (Beckles 1989a: 67). This non-violent strategy by Caribbean women entering relations of concubinage, while countering the inhumanity of sexual abuse, reduced the sordid conditions of slavery, not only for themselves, but for the "master's" children who, often categorized as free, were materially provided for in the long term.[32] (Beckles 1989a). Other African women, however, resorted to violent strategies of resistance, such as abortion and infanticide (Bush 1990), to overcome a system that established forced procreation of the young for continued enslavement.

➷ Indian women

The indentureship experience of Indian women was predicated upon British imperialism and Indian patriarchy. First of all, the system recruited large numbers of men, alleged to have more value in the sugar industry. Again, in another male-biased system, many Indian women emigrated independently, much as White women did, and thus ruptured the Indian ideologies about female dependence and Indian marriage (Reddock 1994). These indentured women were targets of oppression by both the colonizers and men of their own ethnicity. Many struggled to gain and maintain self-autonomy through economic independence, and some rejected arranged or forced marriages. For example, Indian women in Jamaica initiated "income-gathering activities" when they were forced out of the plantations after the end of the indentureship system that precipitated social and industrial changes in the 1850s. Relocating in urban areas, they made market-gardening and house-to-house retailing viable income-generating sources. As well, they resisted early betrothal, opting for a choice of mate that could improve their lives financially (Shepherd 1993: 248). Some other acts of resistance resulted.

Added to that, Indian women's early experience of indentureship was politicized in that they openly supported male resistance to arrests of Indians. In 1872, their protests against industrial exploitation, which took place in Essequibo, Guyana, were significant and highly visible as they were, in confrontation, "armed with hackia sticks" (Mangru 1996: 74). In other situations they replenished the artillery of "infuriated strikers" who hurled volleys of missiles through windows of managers' houses (Mangru 1996: 122). Indian women's participation in the politics of oppression, at that time, disrupted the myth of their passivity and docility and contributed to the Caribbean legacy of resistance. Sometimes, for instance, their agency to resist arranged marriages would cost them their lives (Espinet 1993).

➷ Coloured and middle-class Caribbean women

The well-known ambivalence of the Methodist church towards the abolition movement was central to the revolutionary role of some coloured and middle-class Caribbean women against White and Christian religious practices in pro-emancipation days (Ferguson 1993a). The activism of the two Hart sisters of Antigua serve as an example. These Caribbean women, in defiance of their middle-class position and their religious faith, which failed to see the humanity of their action, established the first Caribbean Sunday School in their home, accommodating both African enslaved children and economically deprived White children.[33] In response to the hypocrisy of the church to which she belonged, one of the sisters proclaimed her belief in human equality through her book, *History of Methodism, A Spiritual Autobiography.* This work severely criticized White supremacy, which had produced racial and social apartheid in the island (Ferguson 1993a: 17). This sample of resistance activities among those who could acquire some measure of privilege in the system of pigmentocracy appears to be the forerunner of the era that sparked a colonial women's movement in the Caribbean.

Thus, the histories of Caribbean women depict acts of resistance that emerged from an inner desire to redefine their identities and to remain in concert with the needs of the wider community. This suggests the manner in which some Caribbean women prescribed roles for themselves in resistance, which could be expressed, as I will show, in the community activism that occurred in the twentieth century.

Caribbean women's twentieth-century resistance: Colonialism

☐

The Caribbean women's movement was precipitated in the early twentieth century by the oppressions that stripped Caribbean populations of their social and economic rights. Influenced by, but not a total copy of, feminism in North America and the United Kingdom, this movement was instituted with both liberal and conservative agendas towards social change (Reddock 1994; French 1985; French and Ford-Smith 1986). That is, it reflected Jamaica's need, and indeed that of the Caribbean, to find solutions to unemployment, low wages, and other inequities while emphasizing the "housewifisation process" as suitable for women (French and Ford-Smith 1986: 324).[34] Organizations became a terrain for training local women in domestic work, while providing social services (Ford-Smith 1989:16). Yet, in Jamaica and Trinidad and Tobago, parallel organizations publicly emphasized their roles both to agitate for women's right to be represented at all levels of government and to notify the public of their ability to prove women's equality to men. These participants proclaimed that they possess "some qualities [that are] eminently desirable, [and] are vastly superior" (Ford-Smith 1989: 11, 12). In 1936, female representatives from Guyana, St. Lucia, and Barbados delivered profound speeches about women's political rights at the first Conference of the Coterie of Social Workers, held in Trinidad and Tobago. This conference, a site both of resistance to women's conformity to patriarchy and of liberation and achievement, formulated resolutions that included the regionalization of the movement, increased participation in social work activities, and a demand for their representation formally in Caribbean politics. Thus, at that time, the Caribbean women's movement, while using middle-class notions to seek social reform of others (Reddock 1994), acted in resistance with a high degree of radicalism towards the patriarchal assignment of domestic roles for Caribbean women.

Race and class, however, determined how this resistance can be categorized. For example, both in Jamaica and in Trinidad and Tobago, the "liberal maternalism" (Ford-Smith 1999) of the upper and middle classes produced tensions between the use of privilege in order to further self-interest along the lines of gender and the struggle to colonize the underclass woman to achieve respectability. Studies show that White Jamaican women[35] who were socialist-oriented became founding members of women's organizations to "civilize" Caribbean working-class women, yet they were active in struggles for political rights for Caribbean women (Ford-Smith 1999; Reddock 1994; Vassell 1995). Indeed, these early efforts to engage in racial and social upliftment activities became the means for a number of middle-class women with free time to achieve economic independence. Thus, activities designed to help the "underprivileged" raised the status of middle-class women during the second quarter of the twentieth century and also facilitated their skill development (Reddock 1994). Thus, resistance was not only about "doing good" and social achievement, it was also about seeking to transform gender practices that denied Caribbean women their "rights" and those activities that customize their identities as women.

Nevertheless, working-class Caribbean women initiated their own strategies of resistance, mainly specific to their class oppressions. These women, during the thirties, along with men in their class, experienced more bitterly the cumulated oppressions from post-emancipation to indentureship to postwar injustices resulting from colonial domination. A very active labour movement, therefore, embraced the enthusiasm of some Caribbean women, who were often represented in both leadership positions and the rank and file (Reddock 1994; French and Ford-Smith 1986).[36] Added to that, African and Indian women in Trinidad and Tobago, as labourers and domestic workers on the sugar estates, were fully involved during the riots and strikes that often disrupted the sugar economy in the Caribbean region. Yet, when working-class women of Trinidad and Tobago displayed any political potential, their actions were classified as prostitution: loose and unlawful (Reddock 1994). In Jamaica, at that time as well, when a similar group of women participated in several industrial strikes, or in marketing anywhere in the country, it was considered to be insubordination and obstinacy (French and Ford-Smith 1986: 265). Thus, Caribbean women's attempts to articulate their political views were mainly in conflict with the hegemonic standards that installed the category "woman" as totally dependent.

Women in Trinidad and Tobago formed their own unions when British-styled hierarchical structures, implemented in local unions, denied workers' rights to speak for themselves in their struggles. For instance, in the 1950s the Caribbean Women's National Assembly, a small organization of Trinidadian women with a strong socialist agenda, founded a domestic workers' trade union in the struggle for peace and equality (Reddock 1994).

These experiences of Caribbean women in labour organizations serve to demonstrate their agency in strategizing activities of resistance to counter colonial and patriarchal domination. Yet the 1953 lecture tour of Amy Ashwood Garvey, which fuelled a Black nationalist movement among many Caribbean middle-class women, did not appear to have included working-class women.[37] This sensitivity to nationalism came at a time when Caribbean countries had begun to create their routes to political independence. It was the beginning of Dr. Eric Williams's[38] era and education on social change, so that a few women's organizations in Trinidad and Tobago heavily supported political reforms to national independence there (Reddock 1994). Some of the organizations that were inspired by the Garvey tour of 1953 continued with momentum into the seventies and eighties and so stand to indicate the gains Caribbean women made in the efforts for gender, as well as political, liberation.

A number of Caribbean women's social welfare organizations with similar intent mushroomed throughout the Caribbean. For example, in the Anglophone Caribbean, there were the Federation of Women's

Institutes, the Montserrat Women's League, the Barbados Women's Self-Help Association, and the Belize Organization for Women and Development, to name but a few (French and Ford-Smith 1986). Yet, in community organizing in Jamaica and Trinidad and Tobago the dominance of race was displayed in that Caribbean women of African heritage and its mixtures were clearly in leading roles. Indo-Caribbean women participated in community organizing as an ethnic group during the period up to the sixties and onwards through religious organizations, but studies have stated that their activism was "less aggressive than their African counterparts" (Henderson 1973).[39] However, in the nineties, an organization, Women in Rice (WINRE), was formed largely by female rice growers, especially Indo-Caribbean women, to counter labour oppression. This organization is known to have made a remarkable contribution to agricultural development in Trinidad and Tobago. In addition, a Caribbean women's presence was increasingly felt in farmers' organizations in places like St. Vincent and Dominica to heighten awareness of these women's contributions in agriculture (CAFRA News, 1991).

Caribbean women's resistance in community activism epitomizes the presence of agency through radical attempts to transform the historical construction of their subjectivities. Here are two examples of Caribbean women's different ways of organizing around social justice issues. Following the surge of national independence in the sixties, each of these women's organizations worked in different ways to address community social injustices in the Caribbean.[40] First, the Housewives Association of Trinidad and Tobago (HATT), founded in 1971 by middle-class women, when political advances in that country had created widespread economic hardships, was a "social action" organization. This association was open to all women irrespective of political convictions, nationality, religious opinions, race, or colour. It organized around consumerism and, during the five years of its existence, disrupted the ways male strongholds in government and business carried out consumer practices. HATT's activities caused these women to develop a strong consciousness about Caribbean women's identity, power, and gender relations. As Faith Wiltshire (1990), an ardent community educator/worker and executive member, writes, "HATT was not just a consumer movement. It was really a women's movement which used consumerism as its drawing card. During its years of operation it helped many women to achieve high feelings of self-esteem".[41] While the resistance activities were educational and feminist for

HATT members, they were confrontational for the state and economic leadership.[42]

Sistren was founded in Jamaica in 1977 as a feminist organization in the particular context of political transformation. As Honor Ford-Smith (1989) relates, it was "the organized movement in a general sense [that] created the context out of which Sistren grew because it legitimized women's examination of their own struggles" (21). A mix of middle-class and working-class women formed this group and established practices through which they both made the personal political and examined their lives in the contexts of race, class, and gender politics. Their theory and practices differentiated this organization from all others in the Caribbean throughout the century. Unlike HATT's consumer research strategy, Sistren used theatre to analyze collective experiences and to seek to resolve pressing issues (Ford-Smith 1989).

Caribbean women's activism of the twentieth century was a mark of responsiveness to challenges found in the politics of patriarchy and imperialism. On the whole, the process of women's organizing was continuously infected with class-biased and White colonial influences.[43] These influences, however, were greatly reduced during the 1980s and 1990s by a change in focus on the theoretical question of Caribbean women in the nation. The Caribbean Association for Feminist Research and Action (CAFRA), an independent organization headquartered in Trinidad and Tobago, is an example of an organization of diverse women activists' groups that shows relative independence in pursuing "women's issues" mainly throughout the region. It is structured to embody issues of social justice as they affect Caribbean women, nationally and regionally, and to maintain viable links with communities of women.[44] In addition, there are also university-based women's studies departments as well as government agencies with a focus on Caribbean women's affairs throughout the Caribbean region. Nevertheless, Caribbean women's political activism historically works "between a rock and a hard place". That is, there is the struggle to challenge patriarchy, yet to remain supportive of Caribbean males in joint opposition against capitalist oppressions. There is also a struggle to realize that modern "isms" have not changed oppressive perceptions of Caribbean women's identities, which makes it most difficult to question the nation's production of power and social organization as these affect Caribbean women's positions (Mohammed 1985: 2).

Conclusion

My tracing of the history of the migratory process of Caribbean peoples, women in particular, facilitates my discussion by giving voice to the subjective experiences of Caribbean women in Canada, while not essentializing a Caribbean identity. This process is inclusive of the devastation of indigenous groups and the subsequent, mostly forced, and brutal migration of other peoples from a variety of geographical sources to supply the slave and cheap labour that created the riches of capitalism. The histories produced in this process are interconnected. While I cannot ignore the extent of the "Black" experience in which racial victimization and ethnic disparagement were fully inflicted, my point is that experiences of social relations, within the hierarchical structure of capitalism, are connected, though different groups, who in a chronological sense, were distanced from each other. Added to that, the variant groupings produced multiple identities which are interrelated because they form, through their activism, a "culture of resistance", as defined by Patricia Hill Collins (1990).[45] In other words, resistance for me has several meanings. It is a signifier mainly of the frequent oppositional intelligent activities by a critical mass of Caribbean people, indeed our women, to liberate themselves from various forms of domination. It is an action to reject victimization of self or community. It has an intention to counter total domination. My idea resonates in C.L.R. James's (1980) optimistic notion that the Caribbean people always have been responding and are responsive to fundamental and serious challenges.

Western history and popular opinion have too frequently identified Caribbeans through labels such as cannibalism, aggression, savagery, stupidity, docility, simplicity, and so on — labels that stigmatize, inferiorize, and homogenize Caribbean peoples, in particular Africans who have experienced the long tenure of slavery. These identifications have been replaced by the oppressed with certain other identifiable creolized formations, but activities that mark the eradication or limiting of western domination in a popular way are infrequently replete with conscious acclaim.[46] Yet my findings in the historical tracing are that resistance has consistently overridden barriers to humanity; thus, it has become a distinguishing mark of a Caribbean identity (Mangru 1996; Patterson 1993; Campbell 1992; Beckles 1987, 1988, 1989a, 1989b, 1992; Craton

1986). Needless to say, I have found that the Caribbean women's role has been clearly defined in strategies of resistance, both historically and currently, against gender ideologies that suppress their potential as human beings, particularly when their activism can disrupt patriarchal discourses. Having understood how these identities are constructed through the histories of Caribbean peoples, I move on, in my next chapter, to discuss current western and Caribbean thought separately that provides us with versions of what is a Caribbean woman's identity.

Notes

1   A description offered by Hilary McD. Beckles (1989a, 1987) to depict how Whites identified the actions of enslaved African women.

2   Standard English translation: *A history of diverse peoples.*

3   Colonialism indoctrinated colonized people to claim they belonged to the space into which colonizers, with their profit motive, placed them to produce a territory in which they, in turn, felt a oneness with others (B. Anderson 1991).

4   "The name 'Indian' and the image of India therefore were like fruit from the same tree of ignorance, racial arrogance and their attendant bigotry" (Carew 1989: 5).

5   According to Look Lai (1993: 51), the historian Eric Williams "described the indenture system as the nineteenth-century West Indian plantation counterpart of the *encomienda,*" which is a Spanish-style form of liberal slavery.

6   Badillo (1995: 97) suggests that no proper assessment has taken place exploring the magnitude of Amerindian slavery.

7   Poisoned arrows were the weapons Amerindians used most, as opposed to the military arsenal of the Europeans: soldiers, fire-arms, and cannons.

8   Some Caribs maintained "anti-colonial communities" on the outskirts of plantations to foster and encourage African anti-slavery (Beckles 1992: 7). A remarkable joint confrontation against the British took place in the 1700s with the takeover of St. Vincent by the Black Caribs in two bitterly contested wars, which ended with the deportation of Aboriginal peoples to Central America in 1797 (Craton 1986).

9   This is the title of a calypso, which was sung by the Mighty Sparrow (Dr Francisco Slinger), Trinbagonian Calypsonian in the 1970s. Taken from the CD: *Guidance* of the Millennium Series, 2002.

10   The origins of Africans were the Bight of Benin, Sierra Leone, Senegambia, and many more places from which emerged several ethnic identifications (Higman 1984). The diverse religious origins of the enslaved included Muslims from five nations — Mandinka, Fula, Susu, Ashanti, and Hausa. The followers were educated and wrote Arabic. Many did not succumb to the slaveowners' systemic brutal suppression of their language, and their dietary and family life. Thousands became Christian converts only as a subversion of punishment (Afroz 1995).

11   See Richard Hart's *Slaves Who Abolished Slavery: Blacks in Rebellion* (1985), the focus

of which — on resistance in Jamaica — names some of the leadership to which I refer. Also, C.L.R. James's *Black Jacobins* is a critical analysis of the Haitian rebellion led by Toussaint L'Ouverture that tells us about the power of an enslaved African.

12 Many of the enslaved Africans obtained their freedom through manumission by deed, purchase, will, or a gift for some favour. They even had themselves bought by people who could grant them manumission (Higman 1984: 380).

13 This term means in Hindu or Urdu "ship brother", which defined the new relationships Indian indentured workers made to fill the void of families and friends left behind in India (Birbalsingh 2000: xi).

14 Pigmentocracy is a colonial system based on skin colour to embrace the many shades between "black" and "white" and to assign class status to individuals.

15 This text consist of copies of original official documents, letters, summaries of commercial activities, lists of Jewish militia men, etc., which the author claims will substantiate Jewish history in the Caribbean.

16 See the novel *Ti Marie*, by Valerie Belgrave; it depicts the story of liberalism by the planter class to encourage loyalty, bonding, and racial mixing with the working class

17 Sylvia Moodie-Kublasingh's (1994) study during 1967 to 1986 of an existing group who claim to be descendants of peasants who established their homes in the cocoa estates of Trinidad and Tobago.

18 Christine Ho uses her autobiography to assess how her standard of living was "Creole". She spent her childhood in a suburban neighbourhood of the city, where hers was the only Chinese household in the vicinity. She also went to an Anglican school, and her friends were a mixture of "colored, creolized Chinese, Black and East Indian". She learnt "quintessentially creole" ways of "liming", that is, spending time in groups drinking and chatting leisurely, and she feted at public dances with Creole music played by a multi-racial mix (1989: 21, 22).

19 See, *The Chinese Game of Whe Whe in Trinidad: From Criminalization to Criminalization*, by Roy Dereck McCree, who discusses the origins and operations of this "illegal" game, introduced by Chinese indentured workers and frequently played among working-class, grassroots people of Trinidad and Tobago. Outlawed for alleged evil influences on the poor, it was adapted through an amendment of the law to establish computer-operated lotteries at the national level.

20 African beliefs in animism, that is, natural phenomena are endowed with forces and spirits, might have been linked to the methods of playing this game, Whe Whe, which includes the use of dreams and names of animals.

21 African male calypsonians have sung about Indian women and the sharing of their Indian culture since the thirties (Rohlehr 1990:251–57).

22 Calypsos with their usual double entendre (double meaning) tell us that baiting Africans into Indian culture was a form of ridicule of the perception of stereotypical needs of the Africans. Yet the act suggests interculturation.

23 In the early twentieth century, Basdeo Mangru (1993: 53) writes of the "Creoles" who "even held their own Tadjah, 'Black T' and incorporated African rites which the law did not permit". Laxmi and Ajai Mansingh (1999: 94) also write that "Hosay gained

some Afro-Jamaican converts who made their own tazias for the same religious reasons".

24   Mohammed (1988) reflects on Morton Klass's (1961) study of an Indian village which found that Indian culture was rigidly enforced. She explains some instances of Indian women's subordination by stating that they were not given the opportunity to receive basic education and that even when they were educated by Canadian missionaries, they were prepared to become good wives for "the converted Indian men who had become teachers in the Presbyterian schools" (Mohammed 1988: 389).

25   Grassroots or working-class people are responsible for the social movement of reggae and dancehall to the national and international levels (Stolzoff 2000). Similarly this same group of people are responsible for the success in maintaining the development of Pan, that is, the steelband movement, as well as the organization of Trinidad Carnival (Liverpool 2001).

26   The fusion of the rhythms of Tassa (Indo-Caribbean), Pan, and Calypso (Afro-Caribbean) is a case in point. Headlines appear fairly often in the Trinidad and Tobago press like this: "…Christians, Hindus and Baptists celebrate together"; each of these religions are recreations of dominant religions (Internet Express 2002).

27   Much more work has been done with respect to the African women's experience of enslavement than any other group of Caribbean women.

28   Historians often discuss White women's experiences of the horrible conditions on the plantation, but, as well, they have emphasized that race privilege exempted some of them who were granted status mobility as "pioneer wives" and others who became freewomen and worked as nurses.

29   The legend of Nanny is that in the Maroon community she held tremendous power during the First Maroon Wars of the seventeenth century. She displayed no fear of British soldiers, and it was alleged that the leader of the Windward Maroons refused to accept the British treaty on her advice. So strong was her prominence and power that she has become a mythologized character in Jamaican folk tale as having bullets bounce off her bottom (Hart 2002).

30   Higglering: an occupation done mainly by Caribbean women, individually, in which they retail goods: clothes, household accessories, and so on, like a present-day flea market.

31   Nothing or little is known to date of sexual exploitation of men.

32   The 32-year-long romantic relationship of estate owner, Thomas Thistlewood, with Phibbah, an enslaved woman who bore him a son, during his life in Jamaica until his death (1750–86) provides a glimpse of the social history of slavery as recorded in his diaries and transforms a perception of slave woman, is neither woman nor feminine. See Hall 1989.

33   Anne and Elizabeth Hart were daughters of an African-Caribbean plantation and slave owner, a poet and "*troubleshooter*" for the abolitionist movement, and a coloured mother (Ferguson 1992: 7).

34   French and Ford-Smith (1986: 324) write in their extensive unpublished work about public policy legalized during 1891–1911 that made women invisible in the workforce, by extending "domestic duties" to field labour and any other work women did

in agriculture. They wrote of these acts by the Jamaican government as intensifying a "housewifization policy", which means redefining women as housewives and relegating their labour to "invisibility and wagelessness". A similar argument was made by Reddock (1994: 183) for Trinidad and Tobago, where the Social Welfare Department established women's work in the site of the home as domestic and unpaid during the same period. Reddock defines the "housewifization process" as the "opposite of 'proletarianization' — whereby women are increasingly defined as non-workers, outside the active labour force, as non-earning housewives".

35 Particular references have been made in the studies mentioned above to Nellie Latrielle (Kilburn), Jamaica, and Beatrice Grieg, Trinidad and Tobago, to qualify Caribbean White women in the progress of the movement.

36 Major labour disturbances occurred throughout the Caribbean during the period 1900 to 1938, which marked twentieth-century colonialism. The provision of resources, such as land to peasants, food supplies, maintenance of hygiene, and adequate education by the British, had failed miserably to satisfy the needs of growing populations throughout the entire region. Hence people rioted in frequent successions (Reddock 1994; Williams 1970; French and Ford-Smith 1986).

37 Amy Ashwood Garvey was the first wife of Marcus Garvey, a PanAfricanist, and she was a co-founder of the United Negro Improvement Association (UNIA). She continued her work in PanAfricanism and feminism after the end of her marriage.

38 At the end of British colonial rule, Dr Eric Eustace Williams, Oxford scholar and historian, was elected Prime Minister from 1956 until his death in 1981. He made radical attempts to eradicate colonialism and to democratize the society, particularly in the area of education. His intellect and charisma were appealing qualities which endeared the hearts of many citizens, and which also motivated people beyond the call of duty.

39 In Trinidad and Tobago a 1992 list of non-governmental women's organizations itemizes nine as of Indian Trinidadian origin and two as Syrian/Lebanese.

40 A critical look at the development of women's organizations in Trinidad and Tobago after the sixties can be found in a two-part article by Patricia Mohammed (1985), "The women's movement in Trinidad and Tobago since the 1960s".

41 Wiltshire (1990: 34).

42 Less than one year after HATT was formed, its membership had grown to 800 women in a network of 17 branches, according to the Secretary's report for the period 1 September 1971 to 30 April 1972. As a member of the Education Committee, I facilitated consciousness-raising workshops at several venues where branches were formed. I infrequently chaired meetings.

43 For instance, while Amy Ashwood Garvey inspired middle-class women throughout her Caribbean tour in 1953 with her speeches about Black nationalism, her closest ally and friend was Sylvia Pankhurst, leading British feminist and member of the British communist party. Organizations such as the YWCA, the Business and Professional Women's Club, and the Soroptimists' Club were copies of those which were US- and British-based.

44 The advocacy work of the Caribbean Association for Feminist Research for Action

(CAFRA) influences policy at all levels of governments in the region to bring about gender equity. It publishes a biannual and bilingual (English and Spanish) journal, and hosts a series of seminars, workshops, and conferences that involve women from urban to remote areas of the Caribbean region.

45 I refer to *Black Feminist Thought*, where Hill Collins defines culture of resistance as the collective power of the oppressed, used to create ways of seeing the world and to form legacies.

46 I refer to the ways in which resistance against domination have been manifested in popular culture and language and in the aesthetics of the Caribbean. For instance, the use of creativity informally, whether in art or in economic ventures, to resist total domination is not often regarded as a triumph.

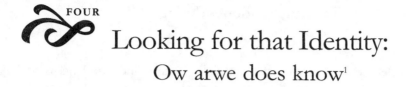

FOUR

Looking for that Identity:
Ow arwe does know[1]

As my tracing of Caribbean history in Chapter Three shows, Caribbean peoples, in general, maintained an identity because of resistance to oppression. Investigating history also proves that Caribbean women emerged as subjects with interconnected histories, and their subversive responses to domination were acts of resistance. The concept of resistance often points to a focused and masculine definition of collective confrontation and power to overthrow ideologies — for example, the rebellions in slavery (Aptheker 1989). But my idea here is that resistance, while it addresses the issues of daily life, goes beyond that level of struggle and moves in a transformative direction to redefine an imagined identity that was devastated by colonialism and patriarchy. Caribbean women, I observe, are motivated by defiance to carry out acts, either civil or cultural. My intention in this chapter, therefore, is to define *independence* as emerging from a Caribbean woman's agency to make a political statement effective. I recognize independence as a feminist ethic. I theorize that *subjectivity* is a dynamic process in which I can locate independence as part of a Caribbean woman's identity in Canada. I use the voices of some Caribbean women in my study to elucidate my meaning. These women speak for themselves because the discourse of "immigrant woman", which feminist analyses have not fully deconstructed, prevails to make a stereotype of identities of migrant women in Canada. Canadian scholarly literature has minimally exposed a potential for a Caribbean women's identity to contribute meaningfully to society. This feature of identification, however, is prevalent in Caribbean research studies within the region, as well as in fictional accounts of Caribbean women's lives in the diaspora. These Caribbean writings explore themes of resilience and courage as providing the independence perspective of a Caribbean women's identity.

Defining independence

In the gender ideology of almost any society, the term independence is commonly used to describe a masculine attribute or trait. As a result, when any action by a woman is recognized as such, she experiences, in the eyes of others, a loss of femininity, as well as an accusation of appropriating masculine values. My meaning of independence does not include that liberal sense of freedom, mainly attached to males, to pursue one's own interests. Neither is it to be taken up in the liberal sense of autonomy as though one is defining oneself as an individual without an unequivocal link with community (Razack 1998: 24, 25). My notion of independence is that there has to be a situation which, in the traditional notions of gender, is oppositional or contradictory to a Caribbean woman's vision of herself. She, therefore, finds a need to take a risk to exempt herself, altogether or periodically, from roles that are expected of her. The risk involves her use of agency to negotiate with and legitimize to her community the contrasts that will appear in her identity. I speak of independence as an ethic and not a quality or trait, because I associate its presence with the use of agency by Caribbean women to free themselves from victimization, when necessary, in the private or public sphere. In using independence as a tool for both self-definition and liberation, a Caribbean woman may know that her power can remain invisible and be associated mainly with nurturing. This meaning of independence is in keeping with a postmodernist notion of multiple selves in which one can have the responsibility for self-defining. I do not mean to endorse an identity of a Caribbean woman, mainly Black, as physically strong, aggressive, resilient, and so on, as was the perception of slave owners in plantation societies. My notion of independence recognizes Erna Brodber's (1986) definition: there is "a predilection for making…one's [her] decisions and depending on self while assessing how others may be pressed into assisting her" (23). Brodber's investigation of the lives of African Jamaican women prompted her to define how they survived the complexities of race and gender during the post-emancipation era.[2]

Next, independence is also a component of feminist ethics,[3] entailing a moral and social responsibility and providing an option to a Caribbean woman for its use, often for her own survival, but also for that of her community. The use of this ethic is dependent on sanctions, yet she may experience a penalty from her community for this choice. The community, a link to her identity, either consists of a family or of a wider network. It is a site where she interacts with people who have ample experiences of adversity through issues of colonialism and patriarchy. As a result, their sanctions are a contradictory mixture of encouragement and dissuasion. That is, often Caribbean peoples, understanding the injustices of the colonial system, may fear the negative consequences of a Caribbean woman's changed role when any diversion takes place from the tradition of being a "woman", that is, submissive and victimized. To elucidate this point, I refer to Makeda Silvera's (1991) short story which addresses the ambiguity in the community. The mother character has a female identity in the traditional sense, but she exhibits masculine traits. Mama, as she is named in the story, fulfils her many roles, which confused the minds of some: "Mama didn't look like half-woman half-man to me and I hated when the women on the street whispered so....It didn't puzzle me that Mama talked politics, drank white rum like a man, knitted and crocheted, tended her flowerbed and baked the best cakes and sweets" (28). Afua Cooper (1992), like Silvera, draws attention to the conflation of the feminine (procreating) and masculine (self-actualizing) in the experiences of the female characters in her work, when she writes: "My mother planted fields/ married a man/ bore ten children/ and still found time/ to run her own business" (26). Added to that was the subjugated knowledge of Cooper's characters about negotiating values around class standards that censure Caribbean women's behaviour: "we heard the missionary's car/ coming down the road/ she jumped over a culvert to hide/ because she had on a pair/ of my father's pants/ the church disapproved of women/ wearing men's clothing" (26). Yet, independence is an oppositional consciousness that enables Caribbean women, like those in my study, to survive the effects of colonialism, class exploitation, patriarchy, and heterosexism. To engage in a radical position, according to bell hooks (1990), is to search for "ways to construct self and identity that are oppositional and liberatory" (29). As I discuss later in this book, some of these Caribbean women in Canada, in memorializing the learning of resistance, develop strategies that were revolutionary for migrant women who are targets of victimization. For, as Simone says, "I have never been a victim. I don't feel like one. I never acted like one" (Interview 23, 22 June 1995) to bring forward a historic consciousness based on how some Caribbean women challenged imperialist and patriarchal regulations and control (Barrow 1998; Reddock 1994; Senior 1991; Beckles 1989a).[4]

๛ Exploring subjectivity to locate independence

The terms identity and subjectivity, as Kathryn Woodward (1997) reminds us, are used interchangeably, but overall they are different. On the one hand, we conceive identity as a way to understand how systems exist to categorize and classify individuals. These categories or classes bear symbols in our religion, our style of dress, our food, our skin colour, so that we gain some sense of how social relations are organized and how social practices are maintained. On the other hand, we understand subjectivity as an historical formation that is continuously being constituted and reconstituted over periods of time, in which we conceive and produce stories about ourselves. These stories can be contextualized, for, according to Amina Mama (1995), subjectivity can "be studied at any point in the life cycle" of an adult as it does not presuppose the individual is in a fixed or unitary form (129). This process further helps us to produce a deeper and truer identity formation.

Subjectivity, which provides us with a knowledge of who we are, "involves our most personal feelings and thoughts" (Woodward 1997: 39). This is not to suggest a focus on individualism. I adopt its usage as a concept that defines what we know of ourselves within, as opposed to what is out there to objectify us (Kuhn 2000). Thus, the Caribbean women in this study tell stories of their experiences when, either in the Caribbean or Canada, they have confronted precarious situations in their everyday lives, stories of how they coped with racism and sexism in both the private and public spheres. Each story, because of race and class, can be different, yet their responses collectively, drawn on the ethic of independence, constitute a "culture of resistance" (Collins 1990: 18). A culture of resistance enables an oppressed group to gain power to create better ways of seeing the world and of forming legacies. In examining identity as it is produced from the experiences of these Caribbean women, we find such a legacy of resistance.

๛ Illustrating the use of the ethic, independence

Each of the following Caribbean women's voices illustrates how the ethic was put to use differently for purposes of migration and early adjustment to Canada.

Olive: I came to Canada because I didn't know anybody here. I came to get away from a life which had become very kind of nightmarish. And I wanted to go somewhere that I knew nobody and nobody knew me. I came with 300 Canadian dollars, as that was all they asked for then. When I got off the plane and the man asked me my name, I gave him my maiden name. Nobody looked at my passport, and I went to the YWCA and registered in that name. (Interview 6, 1 September 1994)

Kamla: My mother died and my brother and I were obliged to live with relatives in the Caribbean. The domestic problems were unbelievable and devastating to me. So I thought my only recourse was to leave home and come to Canada. I lived alone in a single room and got a job in a factory. (Interview 38, 5 September 1995)

Saida: I was tricked by my husband here in Canada, so I had to become a domestic. I was very much treated badly. I didn't like that! One evening on my way home, I met a girl who worked in a nursing home. She asked me if I would like a job, and I said yes, and the next day she called me....I left the housework right away, and went to this nursing home, staying for eight years. (Interview 17, 8 June 1995)

Ariel: In those days when you spoke up, having come under the Domestic Scheme, you are risking it. Anyway I went to Manpower and Immigration, and I said, "Look, I need a job. I have qualifications, I have skills. Please give me a proper job". They sent me to a place to do sewing. Remember, I don't like sewing! Plus they are paying nine cents an hour! So I left there in a huff and puff....Well, I had power and I used it again. They got me a job in a factory, little better, you know, and I stayed until I was employed at Expo 67. (Interview 17, 8 June 1995)

Aita: When I came I got a job with the government. I looked around, saw there was this pool of White women doing the most mundane, numbing kind of work. They said they had been there ten to 15 years. I thought if I had to move up, I would never make it. So the first thing I did, after a short time, is to apply for another position I saw and got it. Then I said to myself, "I am going back to school!" (Interview 20, 14 June 1995)

Zindzi: At times, I remember my mother and the reason she told me she moved from M. I think a lot of how her independent spirit influenced the choice I had made. Because my elder sister went to the University of the West Indies, I wanted to go to a separate university elsewhere. I was trying to see how far I could go without familial props. I wanted to see how good I was on my own. So, in a way, there was a move up to my own independence that got me to come to Canada. (Interview 9, 23 September 1994)

In all these cases, the actions of these Caribbean women were in resistance to domination and were challenges to patriarchal rules that subordinate women. Olive indicates that only total physical changes could help her escape the certain oppression she was experiencing in the Caribbean. Thus, she changed her appearance and almost erased external evidence of her middle-class background. She opted to be recognized as a person associated with the radical politics of the time, Black Power, and duly became involved. She then casually landed herself a librarian's job, for which she was well-qualified. The Indo-Caribbean traditions, preserving chastity and purity, that coerced Indian women to live with their families, did not deter Kamla from migrating alone from her Caribbean home to Canada. She envisioned her self-sufficiency away from the religious ideologies that suppress Indo-Caribbean women. Saida's and Ariel's defiance to subjugation was to manoeuver their skills around immigration rules stipulated for domestic service workers so as to redefine themselves. Neither of them allowed limitations of class to inhibit their goals for self-enhancement. Aita, having come to Canada intending to seek increased self-improvement, immediately recognized the dual effect of being both Black and a woman and proceeded to change her course to avoid victimization. Finally, Zindzi, in having chosen a Canadian university, liberated herself from familial control to begin her own self-defining.

૭ Outcomes as a result of the use of independence

These Caribbean women are a sample of those who choose to employ independence because of their consciousness of the ways that systems of colonialism and patriarchy work. These systems generate subsystems creating issues of race, gender, and sexuality which breed oppressions. In turn, there is a hierarchy which, with its complexities, maintains superiority as a standard attributable largely to Whites and White males. Thus, universally, the position of women, in particular "Black" women, is in the least denominator where it can be engineered and manipulated by these systems. These premises that define ideologies of race and gender only stifle and obfuscate Caribbean women's potential as politically and intellectually active individuals. The stories they provide about coming to Canada indicate that their knowledge of the use of independence was instrumental in breaking barriers and in exploring their need to create strategies for ongoing survival.

Consequently, those quoted above are among many whose lives depict an understanding of how to survive. Olive moved away from librarianship into more than one corporate management and government executive position, both in the Caribbean and Canada. Kamla upgraded her education and became one of the directors of a hospital that was slow in recruiting her when she first applied for an entry level position during her early months in Canada. Saida chose to establish her own business, based on her nurturing skills, as both a foster parent and a home decorator. Ariel pursued her interest in community and social services as a career and acquired university degrees that landed her a profession in social work, where she held a senior and leadership position at a relevant agency. Aita moved on to the tertiary level in her education and became a university professor in social work. Zindzi, who is also a university graduate of the same level, occupied top management positions in education in Canada, and, at the time of her interview, she was an international consultant in anti-racism.

Ways we are known in Canada

Many Canadian scholars who have critiqued the discourse which produce an "immigrant woman" identity, applicable to women of colour, do not go beyond the point of entry to recognize the historic legacy Caribbean women have for dealing with domination and oppression. Hence this identity that I explore is not recognized for migrant women. On the one hand, non-Caribbean Canadian feminist studies focus more on race and gender discrimination, embracing the stereotype "immigrant woman" identity, and less on agency and resistance (Macklin 1992; Boyd 1991, 1987, 1986, 1975; Ralston 1991; R. Ng 1982; Seydegart and Spears 1985; R. Ng and Ramirez 1981; R. Ng and Das Gupta 1981; W. Ng 1982). On the other hand, Caribbean-Canadian feminist studies deconstruct the stereotype "immigrant woman" as inappropriate for a Black woman's profile and provide a significant focus on the discriminatory effects of the interlocking systems of race, class, and gender for Caribbean women migrants (Calliste 1993, 1989; Silvera 1983; Brand 1984). Calliste's (1989) study on Caribbean domestic service workers introduces us to the agency used by some of these women who resisted the stereotype of "immigrant women" as passive and accommodating to embark on work careers of their choice. My own story authenticates her analysis, as within 11 months of the start of my contract, as I wrote earlier, I became a library assistant at the Faculty of Law Library, University of Toronto.[5] Yet scholarly or popular thought persists in portraying the image of a Caribbean woman as victimized and dependent, controlled by a hegemonic meaning of migrant women. This image is very different when Caribbean women's social research and fictional writings resist the controlling and stereotyping to explore features of courage and resilience at sites of activism.

Ways we are known in the Caribbean

၄

၄ Social research

The Women in the Caribbean Project was one of the first main initiatives to focus on research on women of the region distinctly. In 1986, the report was published in the Caribbean journal, *Social and Economic*. The studies — by Christine Barrow in Barbados; Dorian Powell in Barbados, St. Vincent, and Antigua; and Stella Odie-Ali in Guyana — demonstrate the theme of how some Caribbean women survived economically. Their findings display features of agency, independence, and resistance at sites of acute economic repression. Yet, the resistance and survival of Caribbean women can be linked to their ambivalent attitude to autonomy in gender and social relations. Thus, the findings tell us of the multiple contexts in which women in the Caribbean region negotiate their survival. It does not clearly indicate that they are conscious of their own empowerment. There is a gap between the desire for autonomy and the impossibility of gaining equality with men to challenge the idea of independence. Yet, I argued earlier, independence, as suggested in Odie-Ali's study of African and Indian women (1986), is neither monolithic and static nor a trait of permanence[6]: *it can be employed.*

What fiction tells us about ourselves

In Caribbean women's fiction, I draw on Joan Riley's (1987) *Waiting in the Twilight* and Patricia Powell's (1993) *Me Dying Trial* as testimonies of resilience that reflect some Caribbean women's experiences of survival in the diaspora. I am mindful that not all Caribbean women are able to cross the dangerous boundaries established in both colonialist and patriarchal systems. But, from time to time, depending on the context, many Caribbean women may become self-assertive and can resist oppressive practices. Characters in Caribbean fiction represent that form of identity. For example, among the characters in *Waiting in the Twilight* are two Jamaican migrant women who reside in England. One of them rationalizes her presence there by saying "Girl, ah like me freedom!" Freedom, for her, is a life of self-reliance, a life where being an economic provider is sustainable. To achieve a viable economic base so as to provide caringly for her children, she had to leave them in the Caribbean. The character Gwennie in *Me Dying Trial* maintains ambivalence towards an extremely unsatisfying marriage, yet she is motivated to improve her education and to develop profound relationships with her peers. A teacher in her hometown, she is meaningfully active in the struggle against domination in her profession. She believes in unionizing and mobilizing against unfair labour practices and assumes a leadership and productive role. At the point when she is overly exasperated at the responses her husband makes to her strategies to hold their marriage together, she accepts an opportunity to migrate to the United States of America. Firm in her promise to her mother, she sends for her children after she has bought a comfortable house there from her earnings as a domestic service worker. Even though she experiences racism on the job and has had her teacher's qualifications nullified, she remains in the safety of domestic employment, so that she can attain her goal of ensuring her children the university education that has evaded her, although she cultivates herself intellectually. Thus, the use of independence is manifested in this Caribbean woman's intention never to lose sight of what she holds within.

These are a few of the many examples provided in Caribbean women's literature that speak about agency which fosters consciousness and, ultimately, independence. Many stories portray a self which takes the power to act wisely in a private sphere and which retains that wisdom in the public domain, as I will discuss further in Chapter Seven.

Although a Caribbean woman's identity remains stereotyped and homogenized in Canadian literature and society, Caribbean women writers in the diaspora chronicle an identity with a difference. Their female characters use independence to distinguish an identity which has emerged from a historic struggle against race, class, and gender in imperialism. For instance, in Dionne Brand's (1988) short story, "Priestess of Oya, Goddess of Winds, Storms and Waterfalls", the protagonist, Blossom, defies being stripped of the value she places on herself when she orchestrates utter embarrassment for her employer, a doctor in the White community, over an alleged assault. Sexual harassment is often her experience in her private life; therefore, to reduce the pain of this challenge, she accepts an opportunity to become a married woman. When marital stability appears to deepen gender exploitation, she takes responsibility for herself and demands a separation from her husband. During her time as a single woman, she withdraws into intense self-evaluation and emerges as woman filled with spiritual power. Once more, it might appear that she is a victim — divorced, single and unemployed. She struggles, however, with a new self-definition that allows her to continue her use of independence and that will have her reconnect to her community. Blossom reconstitutes her identity as a night pub owner and a spiritualist, "Oya, Goddess of Winds, Storms and Waterfalls". It is from this position that she gains respect from "Black people in Canada", because she has arrived at "prosperity" and is an Obeah woman (Brand 1988: 41).

Sometimes in issues of gender, penalty, a corollary of independence, can manifest itself violently, as Althea Prince (1993) illustrates in the short story "Body and Soul" when she writes of Delores, an independent, Black Caribbean female character: "She had gone after and got the right training, the right house, the right clothes, and the right car. She had gone after the right man, too, only to meet him when it was too late. She had bought the right home only to have an intruder destroy her feelings of peace" (101). Delores's life story serves as a counter to the denigrating images of being Black and Caribbean that some women bear. Her romantic history is plagued with failure; her familial relations are no less painful. Yet, as Prince says, she has done the right thing in every way. When she finds a White male stalker sprawled over her skylight, staring at her as she lies in bed, she is utterly devastated, because the confrontation reminds her of the loneliness that independence has brought her. It is an intense loneliness that progressively engulfs her: she has degrees, a house, a career, and a car. She needs no longer to be objectified, yet she is. The alarming contradiction forces her to commit suicide. This means that the use of independence, even as it makes the responses to domination effective, can also be disempowering. In Brand's story, Blossom emerges triumphantly, while in Prince's, Delores' triumph is overturned. Thus, strategies of survival for Caribbean women to escape subordination and violence have to be seen in terms of variant negotiations and manipulations.

Ramabai Espinet (1992), in her characterization of Caribbean females in a complex short story, "Barred: Trinidad 1987", also deals with the use of transformative practices of resistance. She explores the identity of an Indian-Caribbean woman through stream-of-consciousness vignettes about female experiences. Their contexts are in the Caribbean (home) and Canada (foreign) as well. In the first vignette, the female character is protecting herself in a room at "home" for which she has lost her keys. Though she is experiencing fear about what may be an adverse result of this, she recalls the time in Canada when she "suddenly" found "the mad urge to fling all valuables down" into a river (80). Thus begins the construction of a radical subjectivity. The act is a metaphor for the abandonment of that responsibility imposed on her as woman in order to control her. "Meagre" valuables can be barriers in the route to acquiring personal freedom. She is thinking of defining herself differently, outside the gendered construct of "woman" as passive victim, dependent on the male. Espinet draws this character in a vulnerable state, grappling with a loneliness that ought not to be, in terms of the definition of an Indian woman coupled with a man. This woman, however, is intent on thinking that she could deconstruct this static image. She confesses, "that impulse [to change] has resurfaced over and over". This suggests the thought itself is empowering her. She knows there is strength to be attained in being independent-minded. The irony lies in the potential consequences. So Espinet has her wonder, "but what would I have done without them?" (1992: 80).

The woman is haunted by the trauma of being alone as she faces this predicament in the current location. She knows she has to be responsible for securing her body. She knows that male sexuality produces power in terms of her own desire, so she can understand the implications of the return or arrival of an unwanted man. Hence, she strategizes how to guard against this intrusion, and this, symbolically, is resistance to the appropriation of her personal space. She is resolved to take up whatever available choice there is to prevent any total victimization. She plots: "I have no idea, but under my bed I keep a tin of insect repellent which I am told is good for spraying in their eyes. I also possess an old walking stick, a rape alarm with a light on it, and some candles and some matches" (Espinet 1992: 81). It is her belief that she has the courage to eliminate the aggressive intruder.

This is the courage that goes with the vision of self-reliance that is valuable to her, because she wants to "possess a spirit of independence" (Collins 1990: 109). What damage will it do to her integrity as a person if she opts to be on her own? How far will she go to show she wants to be left alone? However, dawn breaks, and we meet her envisioning the strategies that will bring her hope, suggesting that shifting to a new self is never complete.

The sequence of reminiscences moves on to another aspect of an Indian-Caribbean woman's identity. This vignette portrays the memories of indentureship, its hardships, humiliations, and suffering. The narrator speaks: "I am Indian, plain and simple, not East nor West, just an Indian. I live in the West. My travel across the water to this land has not been easy and many a time I have squatted in the dirt of this or that lepayed hut[7], a few coins knotted in the corner of my orhni, waiting, waiting-waiting to make the next move" (Espinet 1992: 81). This woman has to make the choice for the "next move" to destroy her husband's life, or else he will destroy her. Here again there is that urgency to claim the right to survive that I associate with the use of independence. As the wife of an alcoholic and abusive husband, she has the strength to examine the experiences that restrict her in a sickened condition. As a result, she feels she can no longer continue to let herself be victimized and subordinated.

In other words, she is conscious that imperialism has made both herself and her husband victims, but his current identity shows he has succumbed to domination. She seems to have not felt similarly victimized, but empowered to transform her condition even though she may experience the loss of her life. She says: "Who is the enemy? Is it rum? The boy I married turns into a strange man who hits and curses at night. I bear much and one night I squat on the dirt waiting. ..." (Espinet 1992: 82). Since she cannot negotiate a resolution to this situation, her musings seem to say, she has to challenge it to find a space outside domination that can provide her a sense of self. Thus, she draws on strength to act for her survival: "the cutlass by the fire, I chop some wood up this evening to cook the food. He on the bed and quick quick I chop him two, three times, me ain't know how hard. He give a lil sound and then he stop quiet" (Espinet 1992: 82).

The final interpretation I draw from Espinet's complex short story is that responding with independence can produce fewer gains and more struggles. The last vignette is of an Indian-Caribbean woman who chooses to liberate herself from dominance and deprivation by running her own business, like Cooper's (1992) mother did. The patriarchal system that constructs men as breadwinners has failed the Indian man. He is frequently out of work. But this same system did not valorize Caribbean women's worth, particularly in regard to their labour. Hence, this woman's resistance, in order to survive, challenges the stereotype of inferiority in a Caribbean woman's identity, which includes dependency and passivity. When the opportunity comes to act creatively for the survival of both herself and her family, she accepts it. She tells us: "One morning I got up. Dass had gone for the day already. He had forgotten a full pack of Anchor cigarettes on the table. And right where the window faced the road, I put an empty Klim tin, and two empty condensed milk tins turned upside down on either side of the Klim tin. It wasn't long before a man came and bought a packet of cigarettes. He was my first customer" (Espinet 1992: 84). It is the beginning of her route to economic independence. As well, the story makes us conscious of the interconnectedness of Caribbean women's histories and the interrelatedness of their social conditions. This Indian Caribbean woman's first customer is a "Negro gentlemen", and next was, as she says, "a Creole woman down the road [who] showed me how to make sugar-cakes and tamarind balls" (Espinet 1992: 84). Espinet's imaginative piece shows how boundaries of post-slavery and post-indentureship overlap as Caribbean women forge an identity in resistance.

Moreover, this "interdependence between women is a way to freedom" as Audre Lorde (1984) suggests; it enables each woman in Espinet's short story to be and "not used" (111). Rather, they act in participatory and creative ways as Espinet's Caribbean women do in the story.

How we come to know ourselves

Independence was employed by some Caribbean women in the study to challenge "the rules governing our [their] subordination" (Collins 1990: 155). Their consciousness about colonial domination, social inequities and injustices inspires their activism and political stance. For example:

> **Nikki**: When the powers realized what Development Officers were really doing, the axe started swinging. They found all kinds of ways across Canada, and especially Ontario, of dismissing us. But I wasn't dismissed. I let this bureaucrat know that he paid lip service to helping people. I made the mistake, I suppose, of laying blame on him at a staff meeting. I felt I might be the next to be fired, so I heard of the expansion at the Human Rights Commission, applied, had an interview and got the job and left Indian Affairs. (Interview 22, 17 June 1995)

Similarly, Alice speaks of her struggle against racism and homophobia at the YWCA this way:

> I ran for local President in the union — a very, very interesting experience. White women were getting up to speak against my nomination even before I was nominated. And I wasn't sure if it was because I was Black, or they felt I was younger, or I had dreadlocks, or I was a lesbian. Anyway, whatever I, Alice Dougherty, meant to them, they had to create opposition towards her. It was surprising how overt racism and homophobia was within this women's organization. But you know we were able to push and push and push until the whole thing erupted. They suspended me. We went to the press and the Board eventually stepped in and fired the Executive Director. (Interview 30, 8

August 1995)

Lena challenges a health institution:

> In England I had been used to a professionalism at its very highest
> in the nursing field, and such things as bedside manners, protocol,
> and stuff like that. I had a shock when I started work in Canada;
> they had removed all those barriers and straight laces from the
> profession. One day I was on the neurosurgical ward, where there
> was this guy whose neck was broken and spine paralyzed, so he
> was on a striker plane and as such required a bit more care. So I
> was talking to this patient, and the staff nurse said something
> like, "Why don't you get to work" — well, I just freaked out,
> and began telling her all sorts of things about her not being a
> nurse. So they transferred me to another ward and blacklisted
> me. That's funny because that didn't encourage me to stay in
> nursing, so I said to myself I will leave and go in the arts. (Interview
> 27, 28 June 1995)

Radika relates her setback in the workplace this way:

> I had studied hard the Human Rights Code before the interview.
> After I went to a high-powered seminar with Americans from
> the EEOC, I recognize the job they gave me in Canada was
> classified as a clerical job, but that I could refine it to be more of
> a professional job. I applied a higher analysis than what was being
> used by other intake workers and developed a new intake process.
> I tried to railroad them into a decision, and kept hearing no, no,
> to everything I ask for. That made me more agitated to become
> more of a change agent, and it is what has driven me on to what
> I am today. (Interview 11, 31 May 1995)

All these stories demonstrate that independence is an oppositional ethic.
The agency to maintain self-sufficiency is tenacious among many Caribbean
women in the study. These quotes show that these women project
themselves as survivors who may, though sometimes temporarily, claim
personal triumph over aspects of the capitalist system that manifest
oppressions of racism, sexism, and homophobia. As I intimated earlier,

individualism may seem apparent when some of the stories illustrate how the women directed and controlled their personal journeys, rather than let their identities be totally engineered by systems. But independence involves the need to remain conscious of the insidious nature of the capitalist system that produces interlocking oppressions of race, class, and gender. An often-used expression of Mama, my adopted mother, applies: "Life is not a bed of roses". The confidence that comes from having independence derives from observing the results of the effects of strategies of survival against patriarchal ideologies. Yet embedded in those strategies are two things: one, a conflicting message that indoctrinates Caribbean women to believe in male dominance, both in the private and public spheres; and, two, a fostering of mutual dependence among their communities. Many Caribbean women resist being "manipulated objects" because they would rather be regarded as agents who choose, within limits, to reconstruct subjectivities between and within the terms of gender discourses and of the patriarchy that constitutes them (Davies 1990: 344).

❧ We struggle for self-definition

The discourse of respectability that is fundamental to bourgeois society prompts Simone's use of independence to struggle for a self-definition in Canada and a rejection of the typical Caribbean female image. Migrating independently, she claims, was initiated as an adventure to avoid her father's fixed ambitions for her to pursue a respected profession:

> I remember sitting with a friend and saying, "You know what I want? I want people to know my name!" And we couldn't figure out at first how we were going to do this. Both of us had this thing, and I said let's go on TV. So she and I both made a proposal — she is a White girl — she got on TV and I got on TV. I phoned up Channel 47, and said "Would you like to have a storyteller?" and they said, "No!" and I said "Can't I audition?" and they said "Okay". And that's how I got on. I think people then got to know me. (Interview 23, 22 June 1995)

Another similar case is Roberta's reflection of how the thrust to "respectability" may have influenced her choice to find her self-definition and independence outside the Caribbean.

> Prior to leaving — it was just the beginning of the Black Power movement — and we came into our Afros and the African-styled shirts and whatnot, and countries getting political independence. But I do not think we did a lot of internal searching and valuing, because we were still obsessed with what it is to be decent. It meant you didn't go dancing, you stayed at home and prepared yourself to be, if you were a woman, a housewife, or some women worked as teachers or nurses, some in the bank. But you didn't talk back; you didn't question the status quo. I saw in myself I couldn't accept that lifestyle; that is one of the reasons why I left home. I think the way things were gave me the impetus to search for my own identity and despite, I would say, sometimes the confusion within the family and among friends I needed to go through a kind of purging and throw off that colonial "suppression", as I call it. It was my mom who would secretly admire me, but only when we were together; and she encouraged me — go, go, go — type of thing. Momma was a very independent woman. (Interview 18, 7 June 1995)

Roberta arrived in Canada with dreams of liberation. As she imagined, in a metropolitan community in Canada, wider opportunities for profound growth exists. She, however, found that she had to use independence to continue her self-definition and enhance her self-reliance.

Many Caribbean women have had to be self-reliant in a Canadian society that racializes and marginalizes them. It is a common and personal struggle, but it does not mean individualism. I demonstrate this argument in Chapter Seven, when I discuss the community activism that distinguishes these women's identity in sites of oppression. Here I introduce Lucinda's story to further illustrate my definition of independence, as she is among those who display that sense of responsibility and purpose which these Caribbean women direct to others in their families.

Lucinda: I had a goal, a real strong goal for myself and my kids, as I was the only person they had to depend on. I had to make sure I had a job and a place to go, and I had to be busy. You see, when my husband left me, I lost a house, heavily indebted. When someone suggested I go on welfare, I said it is bad enough that I am living in Metro Housing; I would feel I would die to be living on welfare! So even though the money was small, which I got at...college. I decided I would buy a house only when I moved out from the Housing, because foremost I wanted to see my third child finish university. I could say with perseverance and a lot of hard work, all fell into place in the process. (Interview 26, 26 June 1995)

Lucinda's management skills manifest agency to successfully accomplish her goals at the time of the interview and, like the other Caribbean women, she constructs her self-definition independently.

As individualistic as these narratives of assertiveness — self-sufficiency, resilience, and creativity — may sound, it is, nonetheless, evident that when these women talk about survival they understand it in terms of community. As Lauretta explains:

For me, there is independence: inner freedom, even individualism. The thing is the entire creation is interdependent and interconnected, so you can never be totally independent. So, I say, assertion of self within the context of the community — this is very, very, very important as a child growing up, and it became affirmed and confirmed in Black Theatre Canada of those days. (Interview 21, 14 June 1995)

In modern western culture, two essential attributes of identity are autonomy and agency. To be adult and human, people must come to see themselves as achieving a sense of agency, that is, they must see themselves as having responsibility for making choices about what they do. At the same time, these choices must appear as rational and acceptable to structures of decision-making within the community, the society to which an individual belongs. Feminist literature has critiqued humanist discourses which considered agency as equivalent to being fully human, being a rational, universalized subject. In contrast, poststructural theory points to the way people are subjected by discourse, claiming, therefore, that agency is an illusory concept. Feminist poststructuralists see another possibility and that is to claim a subject who can understand how discourses subordinate her/him, and who can know ways of existing and negotiating between and within discourses, using that knowledge to change, manipulate, or modify terms of one discourse with another. Any act or refusal to act exists in terms of how one's experiences have constituted subjectivities and how individuals are in relation to the subjectivities of others (Davies 1991: 343). Neither agency nor independence as its tool is an individual matter. While it is carried out singly by some Caribbean women, it encourages them to make political statements about society's persistent sexism, racism, and homophobia.

❧ We sometimes pay the price

Thus, the use of independence carries a price to be paid, sometimes dearly, as these experiences indicate. Mother Del, the Archbishop of the Shouter National Evangelical Spiritual Baptist Faith (Toronto, Canada):

> **Del:** When I started going to Bible College, doing music lessons, running programs in the community, my ex-husband literally sat me down and said, "If you move any further is either the ministry or the marriage". We had other problems as well. I chose the ministry. I said, "You met me with it and you won't stop me". (Interview 46, 7 August 1997)

> **Haniffa**: I went for a year to university, and met my husband there. He is African, from...; as you could see, I am East Indian and no one wanted to accept that. There was difficulty for me to finish university as I had no support from and no interaction with my family. He and I got together and we decided he would finish school and I would work. Yet, I think my having not finished school was a turning point in my life. Although I did not pursue higher education, I got jobs continuously, and in each case the next job was better than the last. I got a job organizing an African Studies Conference that held a lot of political meaning for me. (Interview 4, 25 August 1994)

In each case, these Caribbean-Canadian women's experiences with family life forced them to provide spaces for their own liberation and self-definition. The penalty for use of independence is loss of traditional family life—a spouse in Del's case, and parents and siblings in Haniffa's. In Mother Del's story, her choice to follow a direction in which she can realize her own goal, caused her to lose an imagined marital harmony. For Haniffa, her cost was the loss of the biological family, if only temporarily, yet her gain was to establish use of independence in a racially mixed marriage.

Conclusion

I have argued that independence is *not* a quality, but a response to domination. We find it within a Caribbean woman's identity when we examine her subjectivity to understand what she does in order to survive in human ways. A Caribbean woman can value the use of independence as a distinguishing symbol of her self, even among the misperceived identities that colonialism has produced and modernism has retained to devalue her true worth. Unleashing that agency for self-definition in social, or even political contexts, is a mark of who she is within. I have found that, in the collective subjectivity of this group of Caribbean women, the tendency towards the use of independence is defined in their understanding of domination and resistance. But this does not mean that independence essentializes nor homogenizes any oppressed group, particularly Caribbean women. It means that identities, which colonialism constructed through gendered practices, are not immobile. The history of the struggle for Caribbean women's liberation shows that some Caribbean women have instituted a legacy of resistance which in the twentieth century was passed on to the next generation. This transition has been taking place at home, a site of learning resistance.

Thus, when Caribbean women migrate to Canada, like the group in this book have done, they bring *home* with them. The following chapter demonstrates how the impact of historical activities has defined home for Caribbean women, enabling me to link it with this definition of independence and to further theorize that home is a site of learning, the significance of which enables some Caribbean women to survive in Canada.

Notes

1 Standard English translation: *Epistemology.*

2 Erna Brodber's sample, consisting of Jamaican women, was part of the Women in the Caribbean Project (WICP). Forming households without males as heads, the women could act outside the norm of gender relations. Yet, they showed dependence on men for particular tasks and for information about the outside world.

3 Feminist ethics is a derivation of the "explicitly political perspective of feminism" (Sherwin 1992: 16). It addresses women's experiences that are politically unacceptable. This ethics constitutes the basis upon which women's creation of diverse strategies was used to combat subordination.

4 This idea brings to mind the stories of Mary Prince, who freed herself; of the legend of Nanny of the Maroon wars; and of Mary Seacole who, in spite of rejection, went to the Crimean War, where she saved lives.

5 I recall that two of my close friends ended their contracts in three and six months respectively.

6 Guyanese women farmers in the Caribbean performed multiple roles, including decision-making and agricultural management. They are self-reliant, on the one hand, but, on the other, they are vulnerable dependants of male relationships.

7 "Lepayed" means the structure of the walls of the hut which is made with mud plaster over a wooden and grass frame.

FIVE

Imagining Home:
Home full o'cankala[1]

The social and economic diversity of the plantation society, with its attendant forms of dehumanization, produced certain theories of "home".[2] Home, in the Caribbean, is not a fixed place, as Caribbean-Canadian women's stories inform us, because it may entail many geographical locations and creations of spaces that can be mobilized. As well, home does not mean homogeneity, either as in a nation, or as in a nuclear family unit. The subjects in this book have no concerns about home as producing nationhood, nor do they consider the diaspora as not home, therefore a displacement (Grewal 1996; Puar 1996). For them, home is inextricably tied to a notion of survival and community, which is connected to Caribbean women's resistance to exploitation in issues of race, class, gender, and sexuality within imperialism and patriarchy. Therefore, my discussion, which establishes home in a Caribbean-centred way, explores some historical factors that have produced rootlessness, fragmentation, and stratification as part of the process that institutes a collective Caribbean women's subjectivity.

Caribbean theories of home

Caribbean feminist scholars address theories of home to reflect its complexities, either by theorizing its usefulness as a teaching element (Springfield 1997) or as a bridge for identity (Boyce Davies 1994). Even though traditionally it is not uncommon to regard home as a private sphere, it can be viewed as "a site of communal wisdom or a place of sexual oppression" (Springfield 1997: xiii). Among the Caribbean-Canadian women in my study, however, community wisdom was accepted, but stories of resistance superseded the objectification of Caribbean women in sexual oppression or domestic violence. Home, for them, is a site where they learn to resist. Home is the place where they observe strengths in older Caribbean women. It is, at best, an imagined construct that enables them to survive. Hence, they suppress the negative and perhaps romanticize home holistically, while recognizing a wide range of mixed experiences that identify it: violence, race (colour) discrimination, and economic deprivation, along with communal sharing, affection, and so on. All of these elements do not prevent us, Caribbean-Canadian women, from constructing home both as a site of contradictions as well as an empowering space, a space that taught us to strategize survival.

This group of Caribbean-Canadian women appears to have no need to interrogate the protection of "home". They know its weaknesses, they know its strengths; hence, they can dismiss it while respecting it for the capabilities they derive from it, as Kamla relates:

> My mother instilled in us values — principles that she followed. As a result, I feel strongly about that. I was raised in an environment where you don't get things the easy way. I've seen the struggle which she went through, and I have seen how she died because of the struggles that oppressed her. So I feel those are the reasons that made me a super strong person—I will not fail her, no matter what, I will not fail her! Really that's why I ended up here [Canada]. (Interview 38, 5 September 1995)

Thus, Carole Boyce Davies (1994) writes: "The rewriting of home becomes a critical link in the articulation of identity. It is a play of resistance to domination which identifies where we come from, but also locates home in its many transgressive and disjunctive experiences" (115). Her statement reflects the position of African-Caribbean/African-American women in the United States of America, whose writings indicate a connection between identity and home. In particular, for example, they explore cultural and sexual politics to articulate shifting identities from the Caribbean to the United States, or from female to Black, or from African to western values, and so on. These writings reclaim an identity, or a reconnection to it, by exploring family history (Boyce Davies 1994). That is, African-Caribbean writings certainly romanticize home by naming it as a space in a rural area where grandmothers live and pass on wisdom. Yet, when some of these writers describe home negatively, they remember it as an alienating space due to colonizers' exploitation of it. For this, I refer to Jamaica Kincaid's (1988) *A Small Place*.

Caribbean-Canadian women, in my study, rely on similar meanings of home, but they cannot all imagine a connection to an historical African identity as they comprise a "racially" diverse group. Yet, collectively, their visions of home are similar in multiple and diverse ways, especially when they conjure up distinct memories of resistance and survival. Canadian experiences that challenge how these women sustain either racial or lesbian identities can be readily associated with the exercises of resistance acquired in learning to survive at home. They believe that home surrounds their lives to the point that oppressive experiences in Canada do not always surprise them. In the past, home taught them methods that enabled them to aim at winning, as they learned to assess challenges and to search for solutions. Roberta, whose story of her childhood is one of poverty and racial discrimination, speaks of her period of adjustment in Canada this way:

> I think my transition into Canadian life and racism was perhaps facilitated because I had already dealt with those kinds of disparagement at home. (Interview 18, 7 June 1995)

These words are manifestations of many of these Caribbean-Canadian women's knowledge of how colonialism, with its ravaging ills, differentiated identities in the region. They were able to understand unwarranted experiences of negative issues in Canada because of the resonance of a Caribbean experience. Home, for the entire group, remains firmly on their minds as a sorting ground for a number of processes to challenge and resist domination, even though some of them may not often have agreed with all of its resolutions. As a result, this imagined home, as part of their subjectivity, helps them to redefine their identities in this new geographical and economic space: Canada.

Defining "home" in the Caribbean region

My picture of home in the Caribbean provides a subject, Caribbean woman, as an almost full participant of an evolutionary system that locates her in several cultural and geographical spaces rather than as a victim of social constructions of gender exclusion. That is, the world of home, which the Caribbean women in my study imagine for themselves, includes a private sphere, where they were socialized to resist, and a public sphere, where they learned to fight national degradation.[3] There is this permeable boundary that enables both these areas to overlap, merge, and yet remain separate and complex. Thus, home can provide Caribbean women with opportunities to self-actualize. As both Nancie L. Solien Gonzalez (1986) and Christine Barrow (1996) have argued, the reality of home and/or family is often a complexly interwoven set of relationships in which exist sets of conjugal relationships and non-biological ties. My own experience of family resonates with having an "auntie" who is not of my bloodline and, later in life, my being an "auntie" to some younger people with whom I have no biological ties. When we group in this way, it culminates into a "family" within a "home" that is multifaceted and shifting. Home, therefore, may include a diversity of people that encompasses a network of geographical spaces, cultures, and heritages without clearly defined boundaries. For example, this is how Amanda told me of her memories of home:

> **Yvonne**: Amanda, what do you call home?
> **Amanda**: Home for me is Pointe-à-Pierre where I was born and grew up for some time in the oilfield camp. Then, I don't know why, we moved to Tunapuna. I also grew up in San Fernando and went to Naparima High School (Trinidad and Tobago). I recall that in Tunapuna, I was adopted by the entire neighbourhood.
> **Yvonne**: How would you describe the people that made up your community?
> **Amanda**: Mostly Black, Indians, and a few Whites, but more Black mixtures. My grandmother, my aunt, and my mother lived each in one of three houses in a row in the district. All of them

were responsible for us, so that if we did anything at all, my
mother would know about it before we got home from school.
(Interview 44, 11 February 1996)

I am well aware that, for Amanda, home encompasses a range of
experiences from the more hierarchical space of race differentiation,
White/coloured privilege, upper class, and degrees of foreign intrusion
(Pointe-à-Pierre) to a communal and more indigenous space of interracial mixtures within a middle- to working-class milieu (San Fernando,
Tunapuna).[4] Thus, Amanda can occupy multiple subject positions
contextually, because home provides disparate influences, stimulated
through class shifts. A bit contrasting is Abena's description of home as
she says:

I grew up in a community where everyone knew everybody
else's business. It was like a grand family. If your mother is going
to the market, then she could pass you over the fence to a
neighbour and so on. (Interview 29, 11 July 1995)

Her description articulates a singular and somewhat homogeneous position,
identifiable as working class, where economic survival and social safety
readily produced a tightly knit community, thus confirming that home
embraces people outside biological ties.

The Caribbean family system, within the Caribbean region, which
brings a major meaning to "home", is sometimes regarded as having
ties to ancestral countries, mainly Africa and Asia, from which
descendants of the enslaved and indentured have never lost the
essential qualities of community (Barrow 1986; Brodber 1986; Odie-
Ali 1986; Powell 1986). For many years in Caribbean history — that is,
perhaps, up to the 1960s — both African and Indian descendants in the
Caribbean have retained the predominant custom of extremely close
and interdependent households. The contiguous interaction between
members of a family group was sometimes preserved in separate
households.[5] Continued postcolonial dependencies on the western world,
together with modernization, might appear to have eroded some of the
enchantment of the extended family. Yet, for the generation of Caribbean-
Canadian women in my study, those indigenous family patterns have to
be reconstituted in Canada so as to retain the strengths of home, as Aita

emotionally says:

> ...like everybody who leaves that support system that they have home, and does what is called migration, which is a real rupturing of your identity, of everything that is familiar to you, because it turns your world upside down, coming to a place like this. (Interview 20, 14 June 1995)

Other Caribbean-Canadian women, however, saw how the retention of home as a place of strengths can be transported to Canada. Mabel recalls her period of adjustment:

> In the sixties, I find there was a sense of community, that is, Caribbean people pulled together more at that time. They were not confused about what the dominant culture called "privacy", as we knew this concept was different in the Caribbean. Today, I wonder how our three families lived in the same house and got along! There may have been one washroom! There was definite sharing and scheduling work time. My uncle would work nights; another one in the family would work days, so there was always an adult around to look after us, the children. That is how I know our culture was inculcated. (Interview 33, 23 August 1995)

Thus, the extended family system is crucial in making home an institution. This system fosters an interaction through to a deep commitment among blood relatives, friends, and neighbours. It enables home to be perceived as a space for racial and ethnic plurality. In the diaspora, as in the Caribbean region, this system defines home according to circumstance and need.[6]

But memories of home also reflect restriction and discipline, contained in the striving for respectability, as some of these Caribbean-Canadian women recall when their parents expressed the dynamics of their own gender relations to institute rules of sexual propriety.

> **Clarita:** ...you essentially used to come from school, sit, and read. You met friends somewhere else. It was a kind of schizophrenic arrangement, quite frankly. I wasn't allowed to even go to parties or any place which would cause my parents to worry about me. (Interview 19, 18 June 1995)

Yet, it was crucial for home to make links with community at macro levels because it was constituted as an integral part of nation-building,[7] though, from a gender perspective, Caribbean women may not be readily facilitated in the nation-space that appears to be the domain of Caribbean men. Some Caribbean-Canadian women, nevertheless, seem not to have internalized that difference.

> **Alice**: It now occurs to me, after 20 years, I haven't taken out my Canadian citizenship. This is interesting, you know! I have yet to become a Canadian citizen. As I always think—I would never become a Canadian. I want to go back home and finally become a part of the government, even though now, as I am older, those thoughts have changed. (Interview 30, 8 August 1995)

Conceptualizing "home" the way these women do produces an accordion-like concept. Home is a world that socially produced their identities through movements between accommodation and rejection of dominance. They think of home as a personal connection to family and friends in one breath and, in another, it is their community or nation where their contributions count. In addition, they configure it romantically to be the space for cultural integration and harmony.

> **Sastra**: I am listening to music with Jeremee, who is from Tobago, and we get so excited about that music, you know! He, an African, and I, an Indian! We both agreed that it is only the Caribbean can produce that music, because it is the only place with that rich mixture. That is the meaningful part of being from the Caribbean, and that is why I will never give up that identity. (Interview 40, 19 September 1995)

Thus, their ideas of belonging to home are real, in spite of the contradictory experiences that might tend to displace them as women. Home can always help them in redefining their identity and in giving a sense, in the way Gayatri Spivak (1993) puts it, of the "things without which we cannot live" (4).

Home is a product of resistance to the major historical patterns of social and political development in the Caribbean. That is, in the construction of socially produced identities, Caribbean subjects may have developed a pattern to circumscribe home within these features:

(a) *rootlessness*; (b) *fragmentation*; and (c) *stratification*. These features can be confirmed by examining the historical process that created the sense of home synthesized in the stories of these women.[8]

First, *rootlessness* is conceptualized in the deracination and displacement, and subsequent relative isolation, of the Aboriginal peoples of the Caribbean; of the enslaved from Africa; and, to a lesser extent, of people whose origins are in Asia and Europe.

Second, *fragmentation* refers to the fractional economic systems that survive mainly because of external dependency. According to Lloyd Best (1985), in the formation of a Caribbean nation, multiple plantocracies guaranteed many "cleavages and contradictions" in imperialism (135–38). As a consequence, constructions of class are based on a "catch-as-catch-can" system.[9]

Third, *stratification* is a structure that responds both to the issues of economics and miscegenation. The combination of these issues has established hierarchies of colour and achievement to rearrange and destabilize identities. I will now further define these three features to show how Caribbean thought on home is grounded in a history of affirming, through resistance, a process of a collective Caribbean identity.

๛ Home is always shifting: Rootlessness

Rootlessness is a paradigm of resistance to historically produced social and economic oppression under colonialism. It is earliest reflected in the genocidal consequences of Aboriginal resistance to enslavement. Amerindians fled from the institution of slavery and religious conversion which White adventurers tried to enforce on them. These original peoples of the Caribbean fought bitterly to maintain a strong hold on their islands, which they called home, while forming communities in other places, like mainland Belize (Beckles 1992). Those who assumed ownership of the islands, the Europeans and, to a lesser extent, the Jews, never regarded the Caribbean as a place in which their lives could be rooted, as they maintained economic, social, and political ties to Europe and North America.[10] For example, consistent imperial rivalries often resulted in the change of authorities and produced instability over time in some colonies.

The effect of colonization was disastrous on the lives of Africans, who remained for an excessive period as victims of imperialism.

They could not experience home as rooted because of enslavement, brutality, and dehumanization. Yet, there were many Africans who strongly indicated that the plantation was *not* their home as, in resistance to European domination, they created separate Maroon communities (Craton 1982). Individual stories (Montejo 1968; Prince, in Ferguson 1993b) illustrate that some may have engaged in constant migration among plantations and across islands. Establishing a home outside the master's domain was a means of entering, as fully as possible, into the struggle for their then-limited rights in the Caribbean. The persistent terrorism by the White minority, together with the inferiorizing of African/Amerindian culture, provided neither a foundation of permanence for the oppressed, nor a real reason for entrenching roots. Given the instability of plantation life, home could not be standardized in modern terms. Brutal oppressions through human sale, torture, and punishment, and other cruel whims of White plantation owners resulted in fleeing as a strategy of resistance among the enslaved.

During indentureship, the Chinese and Indians were also noted for deserting the plantations and integrating into a Creole life to escape the harshness of the planters' brutality (Mangru 1996; Look Lai 1993). Later, descendants of enslaved Africans yearned or were persuaded, by people such as Marcus Garvey, to return to their countries of origin (Higman 1984; Gouveia 1965). As well, for indentured Asians, reports of repatriation were quite substantial (Ramesar 1994; Look Lai 1993). Thus, we see evidence of rootlessness in the back-to-Africa, back-to-India movements, which are mapped on to the twentieth-century history of resistance (Singh 2001). Plantation, as well as postcolonial economies, on the one hand, benefited the White elite and stabilized their colonial strongholds (Beckles 1989a; E. Williams 1970); on the other hand, there was no comparative and substantive economy to enlist the loyalty of very many Caribbeans caught in the trap of capitalism (W.W. Anderson 1993; Bush 1990; Higman 1984; E. Williams 1970). Rather, this economic system instituted unwaged labour through slavery, with no respect for mortality; cheap labour through indentureship, with offers of either repatriation or settlement to the emancipated Africans and the freed Indians. Thus, in the early twentieth century, the dynamics of migration, regionally and internationally, created degrees of insecurity mixed with autonomy around issues of exile and return for a diverse group of people who had experienced the results of economic depression in the region. Caribbean peoples, men in particular, had to leave to find work in places like Panama as a solution to economic uncertainty (Chamberlin 1997; Lamming 1953).

Rootlessness became even greater later in the twentieth century, when a climate of underemployment or unemployment persisted in the wake of structural adjustment in the Caribbean. This region's economies have continued to be precarious and dependent on capitalism, supplying the elite with material excesses and denying the working class of rights to bare essentials. Therefore, Caribbean-Canadian women, like some in my study, experienced these effects drastically; they were and are almost forced to repeat the cycle of migration to move to metropolitan western countries, like Canada, as a means of orchestrating forms of economic survival (W.W. Anderson 1993). As a result, the structure of home encounters dualism, mainly for many Caribbean mothers in Canada: first, they send supplies to the Caribbean, where "barrels"[11] and remittances enable children to live with their extended families; secondly, they work in Canada, where the multiplicity and availability of menial jobs and possibly new domestic arrangements seem to give a semblance of roots. Thus, their experiences reflect a notion, peculiar and common to the lives of many Caribbean-Canadian women, of making and unmaking home. Boyce Davies (1994) reminds us of this in her mother's story, which tells how she converts anywhere she goes socially and culturally into home and vigorously either commends or criticizes each new "home" where applicable. Thus, home is not a fixed place, but rather a place which can be fixed to become home.

⌘ Home is a number of small pieces: Fragmentation

Our Caribbean society has never been homogeneous, as Lloyd Best (1985) stresses. It has been constructed in fragments. After the collapse of the plantation society and the end of colonialism, no single economic pattern emerged; rather, the various historical systems of labour have resulted in a mixed contemporary economy. Added to that, no one but the minority elite has capital; hence, masses of people have been faced with diverse economic disparities from which they have taken various routes to implement their skills to survive. Fragmentation, therefore, means the many political, economic, and cultural elements which have been, and continue to be, in co-existence and which have never made the Caribbean society whole in the western sense (Brathwaite 1974; Best 1985). In exploring Caribbean identity, we find that the idea does not exist of a homogeneous, yet dichotomous, society of Black and White. But these terms are co-opted from time to time as a matter of convenience. Caribbean society has been, and continues to be, a construct of fragments: ethnicity, colour, demographic difference, religions, specialized interests, and so on. Thus, Brathwaite (1974) suggests that it is difficult to have a majority of people readily accept any fully recognized leadership, in the traditions of a western society.[12]

The idea of home, therefore, is opposed to conventional ideologies that construct it as a critical mass of people who are not otherwise distinguishable in their ties to ancestral and mostly mixed heritages. Fragments, as the foundation for social and racial divisions in the lives of these Caribbean-Canadian women, can often regulate their subjectivities. Marise's story portrays this when she says:

> I think of myself, first of all, of the things that were major cultural influences for me as a child in Guyana. I realized early of the several different heritages in my environment. In my family was the Portuguese, then African and Chinese. As well, among my close friends were nearly the same: Africans, British, Indians, Chinese, and Portuguese, of course. There was a sense of exposure to differences, so that I grew up with a kind of appreciation for what contributed to one's being worldly. (Interview 41, 27 September 1995)

But she is aware that racial intolerance exists among these multiple identities because of her mother's abandonment of home on these grounds. Yet, the marriage of her mother, "Black and Jewish heritage", born in St. Kitts, and father, "Madeiran Portuguese", born in Guyana allows her to imagine a unified culture.

Class, as it is prescribed, like racial heritages, produces fragmentation and defines home.

> **Sumanta**: I would describe "home" as working class, though my mother was a teacher. Yet, it is hard for me to define that because of the difference. First, her roots were in gardening, as she worked in the rice fields and sold stuff in the market to pay her way to go to school and, after, to Teachers' College. Then

my father worked in the land: we were semi-urban people. But my mother's family was rural. Pa did their gardening. (Interview 40, 19 September 1995)

In a similar fashion, here is Haniffa's story:

My parents' marriage was an arranged one. That was common in those days, whether it was Indians or Africans. My father was an only son. His stepmother did not produce any boys, so there was a lot of rift in the family around him. Then when my Mom married my Dad, she inherited that rift. Though my grandparents had a lot of property, because of controversy, they did not want to inherit it. We lived in a one-room flat, and my Dad cleaned gutters, fixed things to build up himself, so when I was born, they had just bought a cinema. (Interview 4, 25 August 13, 2002)

These discursive practices that differentiate Caribbean peoples mark their survival and regulate their identities, in spite of the fact that little of the history of these fragments is known to the holders of these identities.[13] I hold the notion that there is a social reality in which the cultural and racial heterogeneity of a Caribbean identity forms, in an imaginative way, a tapestry. This view enables Caribbean individuals, on the whole, to appreciate differences internal and external to them. Thus, they can coalesce to form various types of communities and societies. There is neither one permanent culture nor continuous inheritance of class. Added to that, the Caribbean region embraces hierarchical structures that often first reconstitute then rupture into further fragments, producing levels of homogenization and divisiveness. These levels sort themselves in a stratified way so as to recognize the differences that do exist in any Caribbean society. Stratification, therefore, is an integral component of home.

✑ Home is layering identities: Stratification
While the fragmentation evident in racial mixing is in part responsible for instituting stratification, stratification itself is linked to the social dynamics of race and class. That is, historically, miscegenation produced, in strict terms, a basis for layering colour and differentiating identities, broadly speaking, into White, coloured, and Black. These broad layers of the slavery period had their purpose in social and economic terms.

Therefore, they regularized a continuing colour/class differentiation in the Caribbean region.

> **Mabel**: As I reflect, I wonder how people who were of lighter skin colour than me had the privilege, a better chance at everything. The island was racial: separate clubs for Whites. These things did not bother me, for you see, outside the school, when you went into your community, it was very cohesive, and so you didn't feel inferior, unlike here [Canada]. There were no racial slurs nor slights from people that make you feel you aren't any good. (Interview 23, 23 August 1995)

While recognizing that White privilege was appropriated to enforce Black inferiority in a similar demographic, Mabel appears to be in denial about the effects of racism on her subjectivity.[14] Consequently, she constructs subjectivity with the consciousness that home exists within two worlds: the insider, family/community which affirms and the outsider, White schoolmates, which rejects her identity.[15]

But Caribbean identity is about survival. Thus, home, in race discourse, defines a means for adjustment and accommodation to the stratification experienced. In other words, those who are given an inferior status experience the interlocking systems of race and class and resist them, sometimes by paying for the privileges associated with an assumed superior status.

> **Roberta**: It made such a big difference when I went to high school. Where at elementary school there were few White people preparing to go to high school, at the high school there were more White people than Black people. There were few Black students at the Convent. One, because it was a private school, and you had to pay; and two, at that time, they were restrictive, since you had to be Catholic. Some Black students even change their religion just to go there. That system, however, changed over the years.... (Interview 18, 7 June 1995)

Yet, for Blacks, the sharing of class privilege with Whites does not preclude covert racism and barriers to achievement later on, as Roberta continues her story:

> Since I was interviewed with the Barbados Ministry of Education, I realized that I stood a chance for a scholarship in Medicine. The

questions I was asked really teed me off, even now! Something made me realize that I would not get a bursary, or a scholarship— not that I was not eligible, I did not have the right connections. One person, who got the scholarship that year, was not from Barbados, but her family owned stores on Broad Street. I wouldn't deny she was bright: she was also White! I didn't get the schol. (Interview 18, 7 June 1995)

Having a "connection" is the means of "beating the system", though the consciousness that racism, emerging from colour and wealth, is not uncommon. I recall observing the privilege that Caribbean women with lighter skin experienced when I worked in the Trinidad and Tobago Central Library system during the fifties. Their connection to "Whiteness" stemmed from both the historic colour stratification and the fact of their fathers' social status. These were Caribbean men who either held public service positions or were doctors or lawyers. As a result, these women were rarely, if at all, scheduled to give service at bookmobile stops in rural areas, which occasioned staying overnight at government rest houses.[16] Yet, in the contradictory nature of home, the reversal roles of race and class can be realized, as Lucinda, earlier in Chapter Two, told us:

My Mom, who is much fairer than I am, went through a great deal of discrimination, because she was poor. I remember her telling us a story that she went for a job once as a housekeeper, and the woman looked at her and said, "We can't hire you, because they wouldn't know who is the servant, who is the master" [laughter]. (Interview 24, 21 June 1995)

Experiences of the interlocking of race, class, and gender systems vary among the Caribbean women in my sample, according to their stories. The scale upon which serious economic disadvantages and related inequities is measured indicates that home is experienced by a majority of Caribbean peoples whose phenotype is labeled Black/ African, a homogenizing social construct. This does not exclude the presence of poverty and the struggle for rights among people of Asian and other heritages. Hence, home can also be known through variations in consciousness that might create stratification as acceptable.

Lena: Back home, Trinidad, me? Not an ordinary middle-class person. We were poor! Therefore, we did not have such a thing as an identity. I, as a young person, did not consider myself to be anything special. The best thing that could happen to me is when my boss at Imperial encouraged me to go into nursing. (Interview 27, 28 June 1995)

The consciousness of the negative reality associated with a Black Caribbean (woman's) identity and its contingency on an attainment of a status quo go hand-in-hand in this story. In the fifties and the sixties, her tale was typical for many Black Caribbean women. It was a common story then and resonates in my own experience. That is, some of these women, aware of their potential as capable individuals, held on to ambitious goals, which they believed could be attained only through secondary and then tertiary education. Opportunities to materialize these goals were weak because of lack of family finances. Success, as Lena relates to us, often came through chance encounters.

By comparison, other Caribbean women of colour could experience their privilege in terms of social and material wealth. This was the case of Abike:[17]

My mother had died. I was alone with my future. I never thought of myself as university material. I didn't think of myself as exceptionally bright, really. I didn't have great ambitions. I thought I would train to be a nurse in a hospital. But the nuns of the convent in Grenada, which I attended, wrote the nuns in St. Vincent University, Halifax. They replied immediately that I could start the semester the next week, and I left. (Interview 18, 7 June 1995)

The stories of Lena and Abike show different outcomes for ambitious young Caribbean women, because material success can be dependent on the ways in which race, together with class, operates to produce superiority/inferiority in society. Yet, this difference does not preclude the suggestion of their commitment to resist either marginality or subjugation. The point is, these women seek to self-actualize.

In parallel is the situation of those Caribbean women who are engaged in struggles to survive due to experiences of inequities created through class. As Abena explains, her knowledge of the terrain, home, in which she grew up:

I don't think the kind of experiences I had here [Canada] could have given me the kind of strength that I drew from the past. I grew up in a predominantly African community, the east end part of Jamaica. I grew up among Rastafarians, and those who supported Marcus Garvey and who the system treated very, very badly. Rastafarians were not embraced by Jamaican society…not in those days! (Interview 29, 11 July 1995)

In other words, for Caribbean societies, resistance to marginalization and material deprivation produces a particular identity of socio-economic difference and oppositional politics. Poverty, which is the cause of differentiation in a capitalist society, is the fundamental weapon of oppression, which perpetuates powerlessness and violence (Young 1990). As well, inequities emerging out of marginalization present a strong reason for oppositional politics and activism. Abena's reality of home involves public confrontation with dominant ideologies. It contrasts with those other Caribbean-Canadian women who saw their older Caribbean people struggle against race/class ideologies but with some level of empowerment because of their class positions.

Simone: For me, class was one of the big issues in my home. You are supposed to do well because you are a Wollanka,[18] whatever that meant. In my family we had judges, we had alcoholics, like any other family. My father worked on the road in Kingston. It is not that he was always used to a life of privilege. He worked his way up to a white-collar job in sales. He believed very strongly in treating people fairly. At the same time, he believed in people knowing their place. And God knows! That is something that distresses me. (Interview 23, 22 June 1995)

Her story suggests that for some Caribbean peoples there is an attitude to resist marginality by asserting respectability through associating with a higher social class. Also, there are ways in which some Caribbean peoples find themselves being co-opted into the class system as a means of becoming creolized and, therefore, acceptable. Marilyn tells of her identity change when she was growing up:

I remember being baptized in the Catholic Church in order to get into a good school. So my Dad named all his daughters "Mary" [laughter]. For us, it was always a struggle to fit in, just like you experience here [Canada]. We were struggling from birth to fit in, and my parents added to that by saying: "Our Chinese people built a Chinese Association so that young people would go and meet each other". They did not want us associating outside of our race. We knew that those who didn't obey were bad. Yet, it happened — a lot of people intermarried. (Interview 39, 29 August 1995)

The opportunity for this family to gain social mobility came through the dominance of the "standard" religion. It was an affiliation they made so that children of Chinese heritage could be educated and be accepted as creolized, while they learned to retain some semblance of Chinese heritage. Yet, integration did not preclude the racism practiced by those who were marginalized. That is, Marilyn's story shows that Caribbean peoples with a distinct ethnicity found ways of maintaining exclusivity, like establishing social organizations. This indication of double consciousness substantiates Christine Ho's (1991) point made in Chapter Three about the Chinese creation of separate spaces, while integrating Creole food, music, and so on into their lives.

In another part of the Caribbean, Guyana, the situation was not so benign, as the politics of race exposed the violence of racial intolerance between Africans and Indians imported there under colonialism. Sastra observes at the personal level how social and cultural integration has taken place:

In my parents' home, you see, my mother's friend was an African woman of social class. She was a Christian and a teacher, and she and my mother were bonded. My mother had no formal schooling, but had learnt to read Shakespeare, novels, and poems because of this woman, Miss Mattie. She got the respect, the China teacup, and she passed through the front door. But, the relatives from the rice field came through the back door and got the enamel cup. (Interview 36, 29 August 1995)

This story establishes the interplay of the dynamics of interracial relations. Steeped in European traditions, the private sphere works to transform identities, to produce privilege, and even to divide people of the same heritage. Yet, in the public sphere, the differences are polarized, as Sastra's story continues:

> Later on, as an adult, when our country went into revolution, I witnessed slaughtering that went on, and the Indo-Guyanese were being attacked. I was in a mining town and my neighbour, who was an African, called out to me and warned me to leave. She said, "They are going to kill every East Indian person they find". She offered to carry me on the boat that night. We also heard from Miss Mattie that we should leave. So we got on a ferry and it was an Afro-Guyanese who put his jacket over our babies. So, at the personal level, you have these deep relationships, and then, at the national level, people are killing each other. (Interview 36, 29 August 1995)

Both Marilyn and Sastra, through different subject positions, can relate that, in a Caribbean society, social stratification is not rigid; it can produce flexibility for survival. People can move between the prescribed layers so as to combat the intentions of social systems. They can lift barriers, or disrupt clear divisions, or maintain exclusions, as social conditions allow.

Thus, social stratification also manifests the complexities that are recognized in the concept of home. Caribbean-Canadian women of diverse heritages — African, Chinese, Indians, and Mixed — experience issues of race and class differently.[19] Class may not only be defined by a stratum of occupation or income. The social class that includes respectability or power may also be attributed to difference, that is, to the attainment of an indigenous identity, a Creole identity, which enables people to position themselves by ethnicity, grades of colour, and still portray features of a European identity. Yet, these Caribbean-Canadian women did not consciously recall that these pliable hierarchical systems constituted overwhelming barriers to their success. Instead, they articulated their survival beyond such tensions to self-definition.

❧ Home shapes identity

When we examine the features of rootlessness, fragmentation, and stratification that are integral to the concept of home, we realize how home itself has shaped a Caribbean woman's identity as she comes to understand her Caribbean society at the micro level. Reference to home means a series of complexities: a foundation for identity (roots) is not permanently planted; detachments from ancestral heritages (fragments) co-exist diversely in class, culture, and ideologies; layers and hierarchies (social strata) are movable and can be challenged. Yet this is not a monolithic picture; it represents different clusters of social, political, and cultural practices in which traditions can be recreated, but in which the political hegemonies of the West can be pervasive.

Many of the Caribbean-Canadian women in this study believe home was the source of their strength through the everyday practices that framed resistance and constructed their subjectivities. I argue that home exists in the imagination as a site where they believe they have a right to belong. This group has not constructed home in their minds as a place from which they have been displaced, or one to which they have no desire to return. They recognize home as a place of belonging, in contrast to the unfamiliar and alienating climate that surrounds their identities here in Canada. "Black", "South Asian", "visible minority" are handy labels to support divisiveness in the dominant system of Canada. Consequently, some of these women feel they must return home for self-affirmation.

> **Sumanta**: In my twenties I started going back every two years. It was a part of my finding myself, and reconnecting with Trinidad helped a lot, taking in the culture, and the mixture and the religion. Connecting with my grandmother made me connect a lot with myself. (Interview 40, 19 September 1995)

Self-affirmation is also most desired during the period of adjustment and settlement in Canada. The search for community, which is a vivid part of home, also constitutes a re-connection.

> **Kamla**: I remember reading CONTRAST and seeing there is a Caribbean Catholic Centre. So I went to their services regularly and even became a member. It is the first place that felt like home. (Interview 39, 5 September 1995)

In concluding this discussion, I ask myself why referring to "home" was so important to these Caribbean-Canadian women. Is it because they seek the source of their survival? I can only provide an answer by arguing, as I do in the next chapter, that *home is the site of learning resistance*, and it comes to mind every time each of these women encounters domination. It is not a delusion of being in a situated, fixed, and safe place. These Caribbean-Canadian women believe it is a place from which they derived values to oppose victimization.

Notes

1 Standard English translation from Trinidadian language: *Home is a complication consisting of mixed elements, for example, compassion to bitterness; humour to seriousness; affection to hate; support to control, and so on.*

2 Home is mainly understood as a dichotomy—that is, as a birthplace and belonging and as not-home, in the sense of the powerlessness, displacement, and alienation experienced with migration and travel.

3 I use the term "fight" in the context of Trinidad and Tobago to mean engaging in critical thinking and doing proactive work for a system which may "guarantee rights without prejudice". See Rennie (1998).

4 This analysis is derived from my direct knowledge of the social terrain of Trinidad and Tobago as I can tap into my social/geographical experience of this country.

5 Arranged marriages, followed by newlyweds taking up residence in the home of the groom's family, created extended households and a Caribbean Indian ideal joint family, and is an example of instituting a community, particularly when each nuclear family took up separate residences close by (Barrow 1996).

6 The works of Christine Ho (1991; 1993) demonstrate how a majority of Caribbean migrants to the USA have recycled the family system transnationally. Practices such as depending on "minding children" (child care) are still in vogue, and are samples of resisting western styles of individualism.

7 Freed Leeward Islands Africans settled as peasants in the post-emancipation era and, in resistance to domination, initiated systems of exchange for labour, so that land tenure was based on kinship and community (Besson 1995). Similarly, indentured Indians gained capital through planters' benign control in the offer of land as opposed to return passages, thus instituted similar patterns of kinship and community (Look Lai 1993).

8 These features are explored in various analyses depicting Caribbean society (Nettleford 1979; Thorpe 1975; K. Brathwaite 1974; Gouveia 1970).

9 This is a post-independence expression to symbolize the status of people's response to Caribbean economic systems, which are often unstable, producing poverty that allows people to barely eke out day-to-day living.

10 Europeans, who were engaged in the slave trade, maintained links with imperialist countries, traded with and colonized Africa and India, and were also absentee landlords in the Caribbean. Jews as well were supported from Europe and North America in their industry and commerce. These connections lessened considerably the possibility of their permanence, that is, being rooted in the Caribbean.

11 Caribbean immigrant women who work in the industrialized world, North America and England, have created an economic phenomenon in the region's history. That is, they have institutionalized the shipping in barrels, with regularity, non-perishable

foods, clothes, and other necessities, to their families and friends who, generally speaking, have very low incomes or are in poverty. The arrival of barrels from abroad often becomes a community event.

12   In the twenty-first century there has been a polarization of politics on the basis of race/ethnicity of Indian and African heritages, particularly in Guyana, Jamaica, and Trinidad and Tobago. Political changes in governments run along these lines and mirror an either/or divide, in spite of the multiplicity of cultural differences. These changes create a horrendous amount of debate to present a binary syndrome of rejection/acceptance, yet the reality of the political climate—particularly in Trinidad and Tobago, the most complex of the three—is a rich and vivid picture of collaboration and conflict.

13   Chapter One illustrates diversity and discusses the lack of knowledge of its parts.

14   See a film screening of Richard Fung's, *My Mother's Place*, where Mrs. Fung suggests an acceptance of stratification and thus endorses Mabel's words.

15   For a critique of Caribbean racism, see Ford-Smith (1994). He argues here that race structures the desires of individuals.

16   These locations, sparsely populated in the fifties, were either in the most northerly or southerly parts of the island of Trinidad and Tobago.

17   Abike's father, as she describes him in her story, was a White American who was once owner of a large plantation in a Caribbean country. Thus, race and class set off many privileges for her, like attending a boarding school in another part of the Caribbean region (Interview 18, 7 June 1995).

18   I replaced the subject's family name with this imaginative word. She is describing how some members of her family chose to use the surname to enable them to bring a distinction to themselves through class association.

19   Briefly, the two largest populated areas in the Anglophone Caribbean show that, in Jamaica, there is an indication that social mobility may frequently shift between class and status inter-generationally (Gordon 1987), and that in Trinidad and Tobago, an individual's promotion in the system may depend on academic achievement and various forms of wealth (Ryan 1991).

SIX

Home is the Site of Learning Resistance:
Yard tallawa[1]

Lena: I think that some of my strength and character came from my mother. My mother was father, caretaker, doctor, medicine woman, and everything. She taught in a Hindu school, and spoke Hindi fluently. (Interview 27, 28 June 1995)

Claiming "home" as a site of learning resistance

Expressions, like the one quoted above, were repeated often in the stories of the Caribbean women in my Canadian study. Therefore, collectively it proves that, in the Caribbean, home is an educative institution — *a site of learning* — and, in particular, it teaches *resistance.* As we know, home may have diverse meanings, but for the Caribbean-Canadian women in this study, it is the place where they acquired a knowledge that enabled them to meet the challenges of life and that prepared them to resist any threats endangering their identities. These Caribbean-Canadian women memorialized the tremendous strengths of independence demonstrated by mainly older Caribbean women — those who were mothers, grandmothers, aunts, or guardians — as well as, sometimes, Caribbean men. The memories are of relationships which provided models for learning and opportunities for relaying strengths. For example, older women were described as moving forces who were "advanced" in their thinking or who were "feminists" as they mostly taught younger women rules of survival through a sometimes unique pedagogy. Mabel explains:

> You learn by seeing how people do things, and sometimes by
> anecdotes. The Anancy stories that they tell you! You learn your
> culture indirectly. It is still so even now for my brothers and
> sisters who were born here, because my mother, though she has
> been here for a long time, she is very much a Barbadian. (Interview
> 33, 23 August 1995)

The "Anancy stories" Mabel refers to are African folk tales, much told in
the Caribbean and often controversial. Anancy is resourceful and famous
for acts of deceit and mischief that hoodwink or outsmart his victims.[2]
According to Richard Burton (1997: 63), he is a "disrupter of structures",
operating with tricks to favour the "*existing* order of things". He can
partly both confirm and subvert given the limits of his subversion. That
is, Anancy can make himself the victim or can victimize others, but his
manipulation of the White man's power is the act that makes him a model
of strength. To western ideology, it is difficult and near impossible for
Whites to be victimized by Blacks since that would be a humiliating
experience. Thus Burton (1997: 64) speaks of Anancy as a "hero, scapegoat
and object of opprobrium". He adds that he is "in short a polyvalent
symbol of the strengths and the weakness of a slave community".

I suggest that the Anancy tales portray the structuring of adaptive
strategies, and these were used by my Tan Georgie and many other
Caribbean women like her to survive. Adaptive strategies include,
in modern terms, critical thought, forms of complicity, wit, and even
conspiracies to enable the oppressed to surmount domination.[3] Thus,
planned acts taught this group of Caribbean women, in their homes,
about survival and resistance. It is on this social terrain that they
learned *independence* as it relates to domination and subordination. Younger
Caribbean women have seen the extensive contributions many older
Caribbean women have made to the status of the economy and social
life in their region, contributions that may have been totally unrecognized.
Caribbean studies now inform us that the process of national development
depended significantly on Caribbean women's creative energies to strategize
survival. Yet, their activism has been largely ignored (Barrow 1986). The
Caribbean-Canadian women in my study observed a range of
contradictory behaviours in their elders, from assertiveness to powerlessness
in order to cope with patriarchy and the inequities of the colonial system.
The values that emerge from these contradictions are harboured in their

consciousness and, according to their stories, have been applied to current experiences of oppressions.

Home, the social environment resulting from a colonialist structure, is the context in which identities are engineered so as to set up independence as a response to control and domination. Caribbean women, irrespective of race, class, or sexuality, learned to negotiate their identities in situations of domination before their migration to Canada. In these negotiations, they acted as agents aggressively or sometimes humbly, and connected themselves, as subjects, to discursive systems which otherwise would have degraded or victimized them. They were able to display agency in acts of resistance. Resistance is to be understood as a set of specific cultural or political responses to everyday life experiences when individuals, families, and the community are oppressed by dominant and exploitative systems. As I discussed in Chapter Three, resistance is a historical legacy through which people have accommodated or outrightly rejected systems of domination to suit their levels of comfort. The experience of learning resistance, often referred to as socialization, is an activity that took place in the Caribbean home. It is structured in six parts: (1) *the value of education*; (2) *the means of gaining economic independence*; (3) *the perpetual striving for self-definition*; (4) *the continuous consciousness of community*; (5) *the recognition of race and class oppressions*; and (6) *the significance of spirituality*. These are the components that create a syllabus for teaching resistance when home is used as an institution of learning.

Learning the value of education in resistance

∂

Values surrounding class and heritage in Caribbean ideologies made no difference to the way the Caribbean women in this study recognize the tremendous significance of education. They all emphasize the persistent encouragement they got as children to acquire education. In the words of Mighty Sparrow, they could have heard: "Children go to school and learn well, otherwise later in life yuh bettah off dead".[4] As a result, Sumanta, claiming that home for her was a mixture of "playfulness" and "violence", remembers the emphasis her mother placed on education:

My mother always pushed me to school. My mom was a teacher... she would take me into her classes and she used to encourage me to learn. Both my parents did, my mother more. She valued education a lot. (Interview 40, 19 September 1995)

Education was continuously stressed by older Caribbean women and defined as a transformative tool to support a wide range of activities, personal and political. I recall the frequency with which I heard this idiom, "Education opens doors to life", and the meaning it bore is reflected in the approach I took towards my career (see Chapter Two). Yet, as this summary discussion shows, it can enunciate its role in gender and class:

Toni: Education was tied to class at home. We were taught that education would broaden your mind and lead you to upward mobility.

Marylin: My Dad was very protective. His attitude was that you get the best education, be as ladylike as possible.

Sastra: Education for me was a word for my age group of Guyanese women, especially East Indian women. Education was not for my agenda, it was for my brother.

Aretha: Education was key, extremely valuable, and more important than to earn money. I knew I had to get this education. I came late in the family: everyone else had gone off and done great things. I had to follow suit. (Focus group meeting, 29 August 1995)

Education, therefore, was taught at home not only as a strategy of resistance for social mobility, but also as a tool to distinguish identity though the dynamics of gender which were sometimes in conflict with this notion. In Sastra's case, this gender bias delayed her fulfilling a personal yearning for education; however, years after migration to Canada, she acquired a university education.

Gender ideology, together with colonialist repression, inhibited Caribbean women's progress often significantly. Given the legacy of resistance — first, the struggle of slaves and indentured servants and, then, of women, for equality — older Caribbean women had internalized the importance of education and accepted it as an identifying force in their quest for independence. According to Olive Senior (1991), the formal colonial education system dates back only to 1835 and was marked by an elitist structure that served to reinforce race and class biases. Education for the masses was a civilizing process meant to enforce loyalties in master/servant relations on plantations, and the system paid little attention to women, except for women of elite status, for whom it was used to produce good wives and mothers according to Victorian stereotypes. As Senior informs us, a report of 1875, produced in England, indicated that the patriarchs of the day had not deeply considered women's education as a priority in the colonies. A system of gendered unequal provision of education prevailed in the colonial system up to the 1960s. However, during the middle to late twentieth century, in phases that prioritized women by race and ethnicity, the numbers of educated women have been on the increase (Senior 1991: 46–50). Rhoda Reddock (1994) rightly puts it this way: "colonial education, therefore, was not meant to liberate the colonized, but rather the means whereby the values and interests of the colonizers and masters would be internalized by the colonized and perceived as their own" (48).

Even in the twentieth century schooling was differentiated between boys, who were taught military drills, and girls, who were taught sewing and housewifely things. Patricia Mohammed (1988) makes the point that during colonialism the patriarchy "thought it was unwise to educate girls" (389), an ideology adopted by the two largest ethnic groups in the English-speaking Caribbean: Africans and Indians. Olive Senior points out that educational opportunities for girls have increased dramatically over the last few decades and have changed the picture. However, these changes have neither reduced economic marginality nor produced equal status in career-building with men, as numerous women remain in low-paid occupations and routine jobs. As Senior writes, to explain the paradox: "At the individual level, women are achieving breakthroughs and in some cases approaching numerical equality in some of the formerly 'male' professions. Yet, for the broad masses of women, educational advances have so far not been reflected in substantial improvement in their status in the world beyond school. The majority of women are still to be found in domestic labour, or in white-collar jobs such as teaching and nursing, both low-paid occupations" (1991: 45).

But education, as Senior also argues, contributes to a Caribbean woman's empowerment, which in turn enables social mobility and, of course, a remunerative income (Senior 1991: 44). Many of the Caribbean-Canadian women in my sample remember how learning this value as a strategy of resistance took place.

> **Mabel**: A lot of values were instilled in us. Like it was important for us to get a good education, which was not questioned. It was not like you have to, here in Canada, get a degree! It was more you have to learn something. They weren't too sure how far you could go. (Interview 33, 23 August 1995)

> **Alice**: I think the greatest influence in my life, and it is true even today, has been my grandmother. We talk together all the time. I think one of the things she gave us was ambition. She was determined her children and her children's children were going to make something of their lives, and so education was certainly the most important thing to achieve. (Interview 30, 8 August 1995)

> **Yaa**: I think, based on my grandmother and my aunt, I would say the prescription would be getting yourself a good education and stay off the street. (Interview 10, 29 May 1995)

Finally, Lena introduces the notion of gender in education, and says:

> **Lena**: There isn't that much of a consciousness to follow a role. It was not that you had to do this. We just took it naturally that we had to go to school, and we had to be educated, and become something. Where men could do many things; they could go off to Pointe-à-Pierre and become architects, draughtsmen, plumbers, and the many careers allotted to them, we women had either to be a nurse or a teacher. (Interview 27, 28 June 1995)

Caribbean women's historical experience of gender subordination and the struggle to secure educational provisions have become a political legacy that these Caribbean-Canadian women learned at home. Older Caribbean women, conscious of this, emphasized its necessity. They may have regarded the lack of education as a great loss to their potential for self-definition and empowerment. Perhaps they recognized the power and recognition that Whites and sometimes Caribbean men generally received because of education. So they coveted education as a means of increasing the value of their development and activism. Generally speaking, a Caribbean woman's thinking of education as a strategy of resistance focuses on its liberatory effects and its significance for the use of independence.

Learning to respond to economic oppression

Capitalism, historically, equalized the status of Caribbean women and men in slavery and indentureship; that is, women, regardless of race, did field work on the plantations, and they have been known also to have done male-dominated jobs, such as loading and unloading ships (Beckles 1989a). As Christine Barrow (1988) points out, capitalism was different in regard to the treatment of Caribbean women, because it did not always confine them to "home and domestic affairs, allowing a measure of equality of the sexes" (165). Hence, Daisy in my sample can confirm: "Jamaican women have always had to work" (Interview 16, 7 June 1995). Continuing structural adjustment policies in colonial and neo-colonial times have occasioned the out-migration of males and encouraged an increase in the number of female-headed households in the region (Massiah 1983). As a result, these policies have forced many less-educated Anglophone Caribbean women to empower themselves by becoming entrepreneurs in gender-segregated jobs such as domestic work, higglering, and wayside vending. Therefore, the fact of Caribbean women as workers and, at times, earners is not a strange phenomenon, as these memories tell:

> **Mabel**: I look back at the period of my grandmother, who died at 92, and she never seemed old to me. She worked very hard, because cooking was an all-day job. I guess your life is defined by your work. She used to sell pudding and things off the land. I remember at a young age I'd help her do that. (Interview 33, 23 August 1995)

> **Roberta**: Momma was a very independent woman. She was able, even though she stayed at home, she did work from time to time, raising pigs and turkeys. So she had her own money and

135

a bank account. She would play the horses, and so she won some money at the horses and so she bought the land and two small houses which she rented. So she *taught* us how to spend money and how to make money. Also two of my aunts worked. One took in washing for rich people and my other aunt worked in somebody's house. (Interview 18, 7 June 1995)

Zora: We had a bakery which collapsed when my father gambled. My mother then baked out of home, and she had these little shops she used to supply with cakes and pastry...She would try any little thing. I see her turn around money in one day like nobody's business. She said she wasn't going to let pride get in the way of trying to get money to make sure we went to school. (Interview 31, 10 August 1995)

Lena: I don't know about laziness. I watched my mother work hard into the night. It worked to my advantage, because that stamina, that doing! She worked for several people all week, starching and ironing...and so this is how we got money. Since 1973, I have always had two and three jobs. I mention I used to sell mutual funds. I also used to sell Holiday Magic, a makeup system, while nursing [laughter]. We are very productive people! (Interview 27, 28 June 1995)

Lucinda: I think that for me, over the years my strength was derived from my mother's power to be independent and to maintain high standards. My father moved back to England and left her with two kids, so she had jobs like sewing, even housekeeping, to make sure that we were independent of anybody. (Interview 24, 21 June 1995)

In these stories, we can clearly see that the source of learning to strategize economic independence, which came mainly through the use of nurturing skills, was centred in the home and the work of women. The activities they undertake in order to survive, however, indicate their ability to employ agency and that reflects their potential for "beating the system".[5] For Caribbean women, this means eliminating both victimization under colonialist economic policies and dependency on the system of patriarchy.

Thus the claim, "No man could put me to sit down and wait 'pon he" (Barrow 1986:13), as expressed by one of the respondents in the Women in the Caribbean Project, resonates with Abena's story of her mother:

> My mother went and looked for a job because she did not like having constantly to ask my father for money. There used to be constant arguments because she liked to go to the Hall to dance; and one day she said to him: "me na badder wid you, me gwan look wuk". She did a lot of domestic work and had her own cook shop downtown. (Interview 29, 11 July 1995)

There is popular thinking that Caribbean older women's use of adaptive strategies is a display of aggressiveness and a need for them to "wear the pants". This is refuted by my theory of independence. My respect for a Caribbean woman's assertiveness stems from my adopted mother's approach to save herself from abject poverty. In a time of economic distress, she capitalized on one of her assets — professional nursing — in order to make sure that I would have a high school education, which at the time had to be paid for:

> Mama usually raised an alarm [her style] when she found some extraordinary news in the daily press. This day, her shout was somewhat more boisterous: she read of her husband's resignation from the public service where he worked as a pharmacist. He was to become a writer! I remember the silence at home that lasted for some days, until she told us that two of our four bedrooms were to be converted into a "nursing home". She mumbled something about the "wasted space" to be used to accommodate the sleeping areas for our family of ten. After the nursing home was set up, we weren't allowed to use the phone freely, we had to keep our voices subdued, and a host of other restrictions. Yet, I liked being a receptionist to the visitors, and I used to love to hear the first cries of newborn babies, particularly in the early mornings.

I have internalized this experience. Like many Caribbean women, I believe I am permanently conscious of the insidious nature of subordination. Thus, I interpret the actions of earlier generations of Caribbean women, such as those previously related, as creating a link between independence and the promotion of self-worth and self-respect. I often feel I am drawing on some invisible armour that would save me from victimhood or from experiencing martyrdom. The legacy of resistance from these older Caribbean women shows us that there is also a twinning of economic self-sufficiency and self-reliance when, as Caribbean-Canadian women, we engage in a process of re-examining our identities and re-imagining ourselves as having the power to bring about social change.

Learning the process of self-definition to empowerment

African-American scholars bell hooks (1990) and Patricia Hill Collins (1990) identify the emergence of a "radical black subjectivity" as a product of self-definition. That is, they are of the view that "Black" women have to transform their consciousness so as to bring about social change in the ideology of dominance. By working through identity constructions of gender and race, Black women discover self-knowledge and liberate their own consciousness. As hooks writes, "part of our struggle for radical Black subjectivity is the quest to find ways to construct self and identity that are oppositional and liberatory" (hooks 1990: 29). For Caribbean women, much the same meaning is obtained by radicalizing their positions as victims. For example, Rhoda Reddock (1990), in looking at the historical experiences of Caribbean women, argues that the meaning of Caribbean women's activism is embedded in a general definition of feminism. That is, their activism reflects "the critical consciousness and awareness of women of a subordinated and/or exploited position in society and the commitment to do something to change it" (12).

Therefore, women's activities, historic and current, in the Caribbean region, affirm that they have constructed radical subjectivities. The display of self-definition is observed through personal behaviour as well as through public activities. That is, Caribbean women often self-define through individual struggles or through organizing women's groups. Observing these activities in the home, some Caribbean-Canadian women in my study spoke of "images of very strong women back home", while others spoke of women who "never took things sitting down" and who "questioned things". Although younger women got a generally decisive picture of independent-minded, older Caribbean women, sometimes the behaviour of these elders seemed to be contradictory. That is, forms of radicalism were often shrouded in conservatism that endorsed the tradition of womanhood, as the findings previously discussed in the Women in the Caribbean Project, 1986, have shown (see Chapter Four, page 92). Maya speaks of it this way:

> I found, although she [mother] was dependent on him [father], she had an independent type of personality. Even though she was traditional, that is, knowing her place in the home, she wasn't submissive. So by observing her in relation to my father, I must have absorbed it in my pores, as it is like, I am not taking shit! (Interview 26, 27 June 1995)

Clarita's observation is of accommodation, as she says:

> I am expressing a contradiction here, because, on the one hand, I acknowledge my mother's independence, yet she did not seem to understand, as I saw it, the privileges he got from his job [he was chauffeured back and forth to the base], that his earnings ought to be adequate enough to take care of us; instead, she kept doing all the necessary things to maintain our home. I admit that I repeated a lot of the stuff that my mother did, in mainly trusting men. (Interview 19, 18 June 1995)

In other words, although Clarita's mother did show independence, and self-defined as independent, yet she continued to encourage male superiority as a norm.

While ambivalence about gender relations in the home may prevail in the minds of some Caribbean-Canadian women, others see the previous generation of Caribbean women acting in concert with Audre Lorde's (1984) famous maxim: "the master's tools will never dismantle the master's house" (112). For example, Aita remembers her mother's initiative, when she was three years old, in disagreement with her father, to leave him and move to another island. She, her mother, and other siblings set up a household with her grandmother. Brodber's (1986) research supports this notion that there is certainly a penchant for self-autonomy, proven by the creation of female-headed households.

Yelena: I remember being raised by a man, but my paternal grandmother was strong and independent. She ended up being strong because she had to raise four sons as her husband gambled away the family fortunes. She used to buy coffee beans and grind them and send her sons on the street to sell. My other grandmother, too, who had a Chinese background, also had to raise sons on her own. Her husband abandoned her. Auntie J. taught me how to smoke and gamble. I remember Auntie K. who was strong and independent. They all also taught me to be strong, which means to take care of myself, and be independent yet respectful of other people. (Interview 28, 29 June 1995)

The stories of some of the women in the study validate the roles of Caribbean women in constructing ideologies that spring from the intersection of class and gender, as Rebeka claims:

Like many, many Caribbean families, there were different levels. My mother was a proprietor in a shop. I got daily mothering from Dada, my nanny from the day I was born. My great-aunt was an extraordinary person. I think she was a lesbian, and she ran a business with my uncle. Then there were the nuns who didn't give me any sense of womanhood except in the religious sense. So it was a mix: on the one hand, my mother and Dada, although she was a bit subversive with being a girl and getting married, and my great aunt who had a different view, not that she preached it. Even my mother had a sense of independence, although accepting quite a lot. She had her own circle of friends, including male friends, and did not depend on my father, socially. (Interview 43, 11 December 1995)

A summary of the ways in which these Caribbean women see how other women radicalize their subjectivities in the home might be appropriately understood in these simple words of conviction from Saida, when I asked her how she survived:

I always have a goal to go forward. I got it from my mother and my grandmother, because they always tell us: you know, you never sit; if one thing fails, you don't just sit and give up. (Interview 17, 8 June 1995)

Her story is a reflection of that Caribbean female legacy of which self-reliance is a part. When I met her in Montreal, another of her life's challenges had come to an end. She was at a social service agency expressing gratitude about her success in adopting three children. She had been a foster mother many times as well, since her arrival in Canada as a domestic service worker. Saida had been frequently victimized as a Black woman in the variety of paid and unpaid jobs that she had done.[6] In addition, at times her status seemed dubious — foster mother? married woman? — as her husband's conflicts with the law often diminished her gains. Why is it that she never gave up? Why did she never let herself become a statistic? As she said above, she believes her strength comes from the example of her mother and grandmother.

Caribbean women in the region taught their daughters to persist in self-empowerment even when race/gender hierarchies, planted by colonialism, attempted to regulate their lives. Self-empowerment is an elusive form of the infrequent and temporary control they bring to lives that are often subordinated through colonialism and patriarchy. This is a skill that can be applied in many political spaces. For instance, Zindzi learned from her mother what it is to be politically conscious.

> **Zindzi**: It was in the days when the colonial inspectors were there...she [mother] always used to say, "You have to let these White people know their damn place"...and she never said what exactly that place was. But the way she said it, I knew exactly what she meant. I remember, I couldn't be more than six or seven years old, when the Anglican vicar did something to upset her, and she asked him whether he thought he brought the school with him from England on his back, and told him that as long as she was headmistress there, he would not be crossing this threshold to give religious instruction. (Interview 9, 23 September 1994)

Interestingly, many women in my study, regardless of their heritage, claim never to have seen older Caribbean women in prolonged positions of subordination, but would often see examples of liberated women who broke patriarchal barriers.

> **Radika**: I saw my mother in total control of her life. It was a sort of matriarchal family: the women always made the decisions; the men talked politics. My mother would always challenge the men's arguments, while my aunts would try to divert the topic. (Interview 11, 31 May 1995)

Sastra: For some Indian women, being in the presence of men is not allowed, so this woman, my mother, with her strength of character, always felt, if the conversation was good, she would be part of it. You see, my father was a coward, no doubt! (Interview 36, 29 August 1995)

My study, therefore, reveals a significant discourse that provides us with an understanding that a legacy of self-will has been handed down from an older generation of Caribbean women to the present one, forming part of their identity. These older Caribbean women are the unsung heroines of the mid-twentieth-century Caribbean.[7]

This knowledge about older Caribbean women establishes that self-definition and empowerment were tools of survival that were perpetuated in the domestic practices of a great many families. The agency to display these strengths of survival has influenced the construction of the subjectivities of younger Caribbean women who participated in this study:

Annzinga: I don't think I thought of it at the time; it is later on through reflecting, I thought the person who had most influence on me is my mother. Thinking of it now, she was a feminist long before the word became popular! (Interview 45, 1 October 1995)

Daisy: My mother was strong and devoted to her family. I remember there were times when she would go without things so that her children would have what they needed. (Interview 16, 7 June 1995)

Caribbean women in this sample see self-definition, as practised by older women in their communities, as a means of employing agency to locate themselves beyond rules governing race, class, gender, and sexuality. Class did not seem to be a deterrent either for the use of agency or for encouraging interdependence among women. I assume the philosophy of survival in subordinate gender positions was cross-class. As Rowena says:

G. was my nanny from when I was four years, and she too influenced who I am as a woman. I loved her very much because she was my mother in the sense that she was the person who taught me a lot. She was a strong, opinionated woman who was not afraid of anybody, so her position in the house was quite clear. My mother went out to work, and G. ran the house as she see fit. She did not like housework and she was a housekeeper. (Interview 37, 31 August 1995)

Caribbean women who had social and economic privilege were in the struggle to empower themselves as well. In those homes, younger Caribbean women also learned how to subvert gender roles and to transform the home to create gender equality, particularly in authority.

Abike: My mother took over the plantation when my father died. She was very busy seeing that things went well. My mother often shuttled between two places. We had two homes, one in P. which was across the river from the town. We lived there during school days and during the holidays we went to the plantation. At seven years old, I was sent off to boarding school. (Interview 13, 7 June 1995)

Hence, in Abike's story, her removal from the estate remains in her consciousness as evidence of the rootlessness of *home*. Yet, she did not remember any experience of deprivation from this, but rather how her mother's agency brought a new structure to the family; that is, the replacement of the male role on their family estate by a female remained as a model for Abike's future.

In the Caribbean home, some Caribbean-Canadian women learned how their mothers empowered themselves to structure class and family relations, which is another way of self-defining, and of resisting the social gaps produced by colonialism.

Sastra: I think the strongest of values I got from my mother was her sense of self. She was really grounded in her own identity, and she never forgot her roots. What I learnt from her in this groundedness, is her dealing with a social class split. My father was a landowner, but she related to the peasants who were still barefoot in the mudfield, in the ricefield, in the same way as she did to her sister who was an aristocratic in G. known as Anglais-Indians — they were more British than the British, you know! But Mother would let the rich and the poor pass through the same door. (Interview 36, 29 August 1995)

Yet, the learning experience was not homogeneous, as a few Caribbean-Canadian women had different experiences of their mothers' relationships with colonial systems. For example, Ariel, a community activist who has challenged institutional systems on racism in Montreal, claims her independence might have developed in resistance to her mother's conservatism. Looking back, she does not attribute her independence to her learning at home, where the role of a Caribbean woman was traditional.

> **Ariel**: The way I was socialized is the woman is supposed to be at home taking care of the children, taking care of the family needs, and the husband goes out and brings in the money. I sort of rebelled at a very early age. From that little pigeon-hole my grandmother took care of the home, and my mother, to this day, is doing very, very well. My mother is the traditional wife, at age 80, [and]still looks after her husband. (Interview 15, 6 June 1995)

Thus, Caribbean women have not always learned to reject the status quo from this module of teaching self-definition and empowerment. Yet, they may be motivated by other conditions to think critically when they choose to become oppositional. Therefore, regardless of the contexts in which home operates, it projects qualities to be displayed outside its walls in the public sphere or community.

Learning community
through social consciousness

Home, like community and nation, is an *imagined* construct (B. Anderson 1991: 6).[8]

Regardless of the inconsistencies that prevail within the home, individuals believe that they belong to it as an entity that embraces safe relationships and nurturing among several and diverse people. Perhaps home, as I pointed out earlier, is also romanticized by my subjects, who recall an inclusionary culture with no sense of racial divisiveness most of the time and who emphasize the commonality of communal living. Yet, home imagined in this way enables a social consciousness within a Caribbean-Canadian woman that allows her to hold herself responsible first for herself, then for the community that defines her. Home is the embodiment of knowledge that was passed on to her so that she may apply independence when the need arises for the liberation of self and community from acts of subjugation. It appears to be less difficult to build and maintain a community because home *is* with her; that is, she is aware of a reality that induces her to employ agency to conduct acts of resistance. Why did this all begin?

On the whole, Caribbean women, over the centuries, have developed a consciousness of the ongoing processes of racism and sexism within capitalism and patriarchy which may put their chances of progress in jeopardy. They have learned, however, to construct a meaning for community which sustains it as a viable site from which they can address the need for strategies based on the legacy of resistance. Aretha, who has lived for 37 years in Canada at the time of her participation in this study, notes how she sees this legacy:

> I see being a Caribbean woman as being from a strong background, where I always have worked in a community, even though I was little [young]. I think that continues in me. Sometimes, when I look at it, I see what I am doing, I see the need to do because my mother did it. (Interview 34, 29 August 1995)

Just as Aretha can see a link with community through her mother's doings, Evelyn, another Caribbean-Canadian woman of best years,[9] endorses this idea with narratives of her own activism. Her story exemplifies directly the employment of independence to disrupt the traditional images of "Caribbean woman". She was a left-wing political activist, who defines herself also as Indian/upper-middle-class/radical/businesswoman.

> **Evelyn**: [Back home] I was involved in everything, church, town council (I always called them Town Scoundrels), member of the Police Commission. I thought I was going to save my country in 1961. Things were happening. If I thought I was Joan of Arc, the people thought they could burn me up.... (Interview 1, 17 August 1995)

Like other Caribbean women, Nikki speaks of how she formulated her understanding of community:

> My mother was undoubtedly strong, not confrontative. That is one of things I have from her. She, too, was involved in community work. She was an active member of the Anglican Church, and she was involved in the Mother's Union, and this and that, so I think that influenced some of my community interest. (Interview 22, 17 June 1995)

This idea of home collapses any separation between the private and public spheres because of the extent to which community and domestic issues were placed together on the everyday agenda of many Caribbean women in the region. Their activism produced an experience in which they used class privilege for the purpose of both advocacy and service.

> **Nisa**: I think I was related to everyone. It was a narrow community. We all had to work in the basic school, which was ours and which was training ground for my sisters and me. My mother pretty well started it, because, looking back, it was the principal that my aunt and the elders didn't particularly like. This is why they pulled out the children. Also, she was a pretty open and generous woman who showed the strength of independence. She founded a women's group which was cross-age, and she acquired pensions for older women. When anyone was ill, she would take linen to them. She felt a change of linen was refreshing. She belonged to a small church which had opened up and they weren't doing well, and she got together with the community, held a party, and used the proceeds to give to the church, as she was convinced they were good people, whom she wanted to stay in the neighbourhood, so she helped them. She was that type of person. My father was basically the tough one who clung to what he had. (Interview 14, 5 June 1995)

Her story describes how middle-class privilege enables people to differentiate themselves, as well as to display forms of altruism, which, according to Honor Ford-Smith, is symptomatic of the "Lady

Bountiful" syndrome. This behaviour has historical precedents that indicate how a colonial or Creole White or coloured woman could use her subject position to mobilize communities and to voice issues on behalf of other Caribbean women, particularly those in working-class positions (Ford-Smith 1986; Reddock 1994).

Yet, I remember my experiences with Tan Georgie and Mama, who separately engaged in providing a minimal level of community protection and support, in spite of limited income. Thus, boundaries of economic and social status overlap and conjoin in ways to make many Caribbean women agents in differing class positions and to radicalize their public responsibilities.

Heterogeneity and contradictions, fostered through community, are markers of the subjectivities of Caribbean women. Those of the previous generation found the building of community a useful reprieve from situations of domesticity. In carrying out those activities that were mutually beneficial to themselves, as women, and to others in their physical environment, they taught younger Caribbean women political consciousness.

Lauretta: I learnt by doing. My mother was very people conscious, very political over what the government was doing, so she went to those meetings. We were there. When she had dances to raise money, I was a part of preparing for the dance, and running the dance. When she went to visit the poorer people, we were there. Well, she didn't take us to visit the leper home; she was afraid we might become infected. Of course, we were too young for the Mother's League. Oh yes! I was learning, because all those things I'm talking are things I do now. So, I know I picked them up from her. I learnt more about race from my father who was very interested, at the time, in the civil rights movement in the United States. (Interview 21, 14 June 1995)

Alice: I think that I developed social consciousness — I was saying the other day to a friend — at a very early age, because of the role my grandmother and aunt played in the community in Grenada. It was they who were concerned enough to ensure that everyone in the neighbourhood had milk for the children. They would ensure that Mrs. F.'s children, up the road, had shoes, because a daughter was bright and entering high school. I think I saw that growing up and I knew, you know, sharing and sense of community and community responsibility is a very special value that I received from them. (Interview 30, 8 August 1995)

Other Caribbean-Canadian women learned as well that the presence of gender control did not constrain their mothers' voluntary activism.

Anne: My mother was a moving force in the family. She was involved in things outside the home — the church groups, the youth group — and I remember seeing her involvement without having to receive anybody's permission. Once she decided to do something, she went ahead and did it. I was influenced by her, as I know that many times it scares me because I am so much like her. (Interview 12, 7 June 1995)

Caribbean-Canadian women's stories contextualized in a working-class background present a different experience with community activism. These women learned how to face Caribbean neo-colonialist hegemony directly so as to combat social marginalization and economic deprivation. They saw community activism as intense political involvement beyond the altruism which Caribbean middle-class women, discussed above, often provided at that time.

Abena: I became involved politically at a very young age, because I grew up in a poor community, not at all protected by the system itself. And to this day, we have a close bond. I grew up in a community where everybody knew everybody else because of the struggle. That history is so strong. It is where I got my first exposure to activism when I was very, very young. I became socially conscious very early as a teenager. (Interview 29, 11 June 1995)

Her experience of social and economic inequities created a space from which she learned that struggle in her community was to be hers, totally hers.

The stories by Caribbean-Canadian women of Chinese heritage reflect a different definition of community. Their learning about community is predicated on their marginal status among Creole societies in the Caribbean, even in the mid-twentieth century. They saw their elders constructing separate communities to mobilize independence against discrimination. Yet community meant, as in the cases discussed above, the individual's link with others to form a site for collective resistance.

> **Kim**: I was not in a community-minded group. I left that to our parents because they had a sort of Chinese club: Chinese Benevolent society. There was a Chinese name as well. It was the older ones who went there. Just like the Chinese-Caribbean Association up here. It is only the older ones who participate: you see the similarity. (Interview 8, 6 September 1995)

Marilyn, who comes from a similar background, describes a strategy the church initiated to get the Chinese involved with the Creole community. She saw that Anglican and Roman Catholic clergy, respectively, solicited her parents' interest in either of these religions at different times. This was reminiscent of the colonial evangelizing process designed to civilize indentured workers and migrants to the Caribbean. While her parents responded in order to ensure that their children would receive a high standard of education, there was also a need to cope with marginalization and secure their heritage in another way.

> **Marilyn**: For us, it was always a struggle to fit in, just like the experience here [Canada]. We were struggling from birth just like you might experience here. My parents did not want to associate with people outside our race. They said they built a Chinese Association so that young people would go and meet each other. Yet we were brought up by the neighbours. That's how we were named [western-style]. (Interview 39, 6 September 1995)

Learning to signify community in the Caribbean region is different for some Caribbean-Canadian women of ethnicity. In the diversity of the region, identity is framed with colonial issues that label and inferiorize cultures and heritages so that there is a tendency to form isolated communities. That is, ethnic groups, Chinese or Indian, as descendants of the population of indentured workers, were initially forced to bond in their own cultures. The domination of European culture, together with African culture, had established a Creole root, which could be considered mainstream even after the abolition of indentureship in 1917. A syndrome fostered by capitalism, both to exploit the indentured peoples and to diminish the economic strength of the emancipated African, slowed the process of integration. Thus, as these stories of Caribbean-Chinese women indicate, learning community at home meant constructing a difference that would enable Chinese in the Caribbean to resist relations of race and class. Thus, they saw parents in various forms of struggle coping with marginalization and the layers of dominance, though the idea, for them, was that their community had to be segregated from the larger society in order to continue to exist. Learning community consciousness assisted with both resistance and survival.

Learning to resist oppressions of race and class
☙

The economic structure of the system of European colonialism has itself institutionalized race and class oppressions in the Caribbean. This system has promoted the layering by colour as a marker for achieving Whiteness, hence privilege.

> **Abike**: The Dominica of my youth is where I must say that I learnt there is racism in the Caribbean as well. Because, if you were light-skinned, more privileges and opportunities would be accorded to you, for example, you could work in the bank, or be a public servant. If you were dark-skinned, you would be a clerk or less in the store. If you were really, really bright, and they couldn't keep you down, they would let you teach, but teach in district schools, in elementary schools. The people who taught in the Convent seemed to be light-skinned with long, blow-away hair. And there is also racism in the Caribbean-based family. Who you were, the name, the class, the economic status of your parents...that's Caribbean racism! (Interview 18, 7 June 1995)

Abike's frank statement summarizes many of the views that Caribbean-Canadian women have on the subject of race. This critique problematizes any romantic notions of home. Yet, they avoid making a profound critical comment about the issue of race in the region. Maya's experience is an example of this withdrawal:

> I certainly didn't have a sense of my identity in terms of being Black growing up in Dominica. I think that sense developed when

I was in Canada. What helped to bring that forth was the sense of not belonging in this society. (Interview 26, 27 June 1995)

Like Maya, Fern also experiences consciousness of race only when she encounters racism in North America:

I never felt any distinction in Trinidad. There [in Seattle] the majority of Blacks lived in the middle; the Chinese in another area; and the Caucasians in another — so different from the way I knew it to be back home. We made friends because we went to the same school, or we were neighbours. For me it had nothing to do with whether we were Chinese or not. It was quite different to the way we were brought up. (Interview 7, 6 September 1995)

Kamla and Sumanta claim that cultural integration exists and ethnicities are not polarized:

Kamla: I really identified with both Indians and a lot of mixed friends, or what you term "Black" today. My mother was very liberal; she never curtailed us in anyway. I related better to my mixed friends than to Indian. I never liked the Indian culture because it is too restrictive. (Interview 38, 5 September 1995)

Sumanta: I couldn't characterize my family as having a single attitude. It was just a continuum of Hindus, Catholics, and Muslims. My Mom and Dad married in the Hindu religion, but because they needed to get jobs, they officially changed their religion. That's colonialism! (Interview 40, 19 September 1995)

The strategies of resistance against race and class oppression that these Caribbean-Canadian women were learning may have heightened a sense of belonging. The oppressed could, from any class or ethnic position, seek ways individually or together to accommodate difference, in spite of the glaring effects of race discrimination in their societies. In the Caribbean region, some of these women do learn how identities are formed through social relations and how pigmentocracy (the colour system) works to give or deny privilege to some. Because Rowena is light-skinned, she was among a few I selected with whom to have a dialogue about the significance of race and class in her childhood.

Yvonne: Did you socialize with Black working-class people other than your nanny?

Rowena: Yes, in high school.

Yvonne: Did your family have a problem with that?

Rowena: Actually no! You see, I went to a girls' school....

Yvonne: So colour was not a problem?

Rowena: Not until ah bring home a Black boyfriend, me mother get vexed. She would go on about colour didn't mean anything, but it mean something to her. To my understanding, my father didn't seem to have a problem around class; he was totally different to she ["she" in reference to Rowena's mother is a measure of her aggravation]. (Interview 37, 31 August 1995)

Although a large majority of these Caribbean-Canadian women claim for the most part social consciousness through the impact of colonialism on their identities, they have differences in their "routes to political and critical consciousness".[10] Some even see class as a major issue in discrimination.

Radika: My earliest recollection was like living in a very secure environment and always, sometimes, feeling a sense of longing, even as a child; and being confused about why some people had a lot to eat and drink and some people hadn't. For example, beggars would come to our house and we would give them money. (Interview 11, 31 May 1995)

However, Radika's confusion did not stop there. She learned to understand survival in a household that was diverse in many categories: shifting levels of poverty experienced by a "new" class following the abolition of indentureship, internal discrimination because of racial mixing of Indian and "Spanish",[11] the missionary influence on her grandparents, and the tensions produced through land tenure issues of indentureship. These are some of the many factors that have created untenable connections within families. Historically, issues of domination often created a kind of triple jeopardy; that is, they helped to structure the power around race, class, and gender to create the multivalence of a Caribbean identity. Yet, some Caribbean women have learned that there can emerge "alternative visions of power" to self-actualize based on human values, as Collins (1990) has reasoned for African-American women (224). Older Caribbean women showed persistence in making responses to challenges of race and class through strategies of independence, which helped to bring liberation to younger Caribbean women. For example, the older women tried to empower themselves by means of hard work, the results of which they deemed could be effective in crossing class boundaries. They also often theorized that education would be the tool to erase class inferiority and could, perhaps, cause the next generation to experience equal opportunities, reducing race as a marker.

> **Yaa**: My mother was in the States, my grandmother worked in a hotel, my aunt was dressmaking, and I had another aunt in England. We were dirt poor! I did the 11-plus exam and won a scholarship. In retrospect it was so funny they chose for me a school that was really beyond my reach in terms of class structure. The school was very White and middle class. The kids had access to things I didn't have. It was a struggle for me to buy textbooks. But there was a financial need for me to go to that school, and I remember how painful it was as well. (Interview 10, 29 May 1995)

Her story shows how faith in self-power, coupled with defiance, can transform the degradation of poverty and its link to colour (Blackness) to achieving a future of greater comfort. Yet, the experience of some Caribbean-Canadian women of colour provides a contrasting situation:

> **Lucinda**: There was a struggle when I was a child, because of our poverty. My mom, who is much fairer than I, went through so much discrimination because she was poor. I know I do it consciously now to tell people I am Black, as my grandparents are Black. We are all mixed race: Irish, English.. my grandmother is a Maroon! I could focus on the Spaniards, the Africans, or any other of them. (Interview 24, 24 June 1995)

Black is her political consciousness. It is an evident claim because of the interconnectedness of histories discussed in Chapter Three. Other light-skinned Caribbean-Canadian women see that the assumptions around colour may have enabled them to gain privilege.

> **Marise**: I am trying to think of the first sense I have that there was some racial tension in my own family who were [of] Black

heritage and, say, East Indian heritage. I am trying to think of my first knowledge of race: probably in school, maybe around seven years old. I had an East Indian friend, and she made some comment to me about Blacks, as she didn't want Blacks in the school. (Interview 41, 27 September 1995)

School as an extension of home is a site where experience of racial tension can become real. In this case, we do not know whether or not the tensions were resolved, but when I further asked Marise how she then identified herself, unlike Lucinda, she was ambiguous:

> Well, I think obviously at that time, she saw me as light-skinned of Portuguese heritage, but not of Black heritage. In that context skin colour was important, and that's why I was picked to be a friend. (Interview 41, 27 September 1995)

I interpret her reply to mean that she learned to choose to construct a racial identity so as to protect her privilege.

But for other Caribbean-Canadian women, the denial of the role that race played in signifying identity in a colonial society can be expressed in these words:

> **Aretha**: I didn't even know that being Black was not a good thing. I didn't even know I was Black. I was just me. I was red! I was all kinds of other things, but you see, "Black" growing up for me meant that your skin was very, very dark. My mother was a "Black" woman; my father was not a "Black" man. Black had to do with the way you looked. Now I know they are two Black people. I wasn't thinking of life in those ways at the time. (Interview 34, 29 August 1995)

Olive, however, recalls the Caribbean and colonial society as setting a tone for divisiveness: "White girls standing by the school gate combing their hair and waving at boys, while Black and brown-skinned girls skipped relentlessly". This was an observation that enables her to define herself.

> **Olive**: I went to Bishop Anstey High School, which makes me a particular brand of person. I have an innate relationship with women in Trinidad who sound like me...who, while we have an

awareness of class and colour in Trinidad, we don't have an awareness of the limitations that class and colour placed on us. But, in spite of that, I think, as we made our way through high school, the people who emerged as leaders were bright, articulated Black girls; either brown-skinned, Black, or whatever we [were] "high school" girls. (Interview 6, 1 September 1994)

Since this school environment is familiar to me as a former student myself, I endorse Olive's notion that the spaces that "Black" students occupied were regulated by informal, artificial boundaries of difference displaying the privilege of lighter-skinned girls; yet, as darker skinned "Black people", we persisted in defining ourselves positively.[12] Educational oppportunities, however, irrespective of class or colour, can segregate Caribbean women in club style, as Olive describes. The consequence, though, is the development of the ability and understanding to reject those notions that perpetuate stereotypes which objectify and dehumanize us (Collins 1990). We have a responsibility to apply our formal education in a critical way.

I knew I was Black, since my brown-skinned adopted siblings never let me forget that, in contrast to themselves. They subscribed to Eurocentric aesthetics of beauty, which allowed them to search for features in me that would elevate my "Black" identity; thus, for instance, they warned me to avoid marrying a Black man to ensure that my children's colour identity would be enhanced.[13] However, I found ways to approach my self-definition through my adopted mother's open-mindedness and sense of justice. I learned from her how to resist negative images, search for myself, and nurture an inquiring mind. I observed as well that her light skin colour did not appear to cause her to act in a discriminatory manner to anyone regardless of race, colour, or class. Today I feel I am still influenced by my observation of her in relationships with others.

This discussion about social learning around issues of race, colour, and class exposes some of the problems of identity within a Caribbean womanized system of resistance against domination. My analysis suggests that there was no clear deconstruction of racial issues taught at home, as resistance practices did not fully challenge the dominant discourse of race, which contained colonial terms of race and divisiveness. While my argument is focused on how individual actions formulated collective resistance against domination, I recognize the limits of proof placed on this form of social/political activism because, from our stories, the strategies used in resistance to racist oppressions did not really undermine oppressive ideologies. There seems to be some permissiveness: in learning to survive race, we were allowed to construct bodies in racial terms. That is, in the stories from these Caribbean-Canadian women, opposition to racism was not as overt as it was to poverty, and no one seemed to learn about the impact on well-being if one experienced racist practices, even when they were not too uncommon. The important thing, however, about learning resistance is to know how to strategize so as to avoid evidence of victimhood.

Learning spirituality promotes self-empowerment

ॐ

Lena: I watched my mother work hard into the night. She read the Bible when Catholics were overtly forbidden to do so....While she was ironing, I used to hear her saying things like "Lord, help me...." (Interview 27, 28 June 1995)

Lena's words reflect another module of learning resistance at home. That is, like many others of the group, she observed that older Caribbean women used a link with a spiritual being to develop a work ethic. Interestingly enough, in the twenty-first century, thinkers who explore the meaning of spirituality provide a set of criteria through which individuals may integrate spirituality into their everyday lives. The use of spirituality deepens intellectual capacities that can be directed towards survival. This group of Caribbean-Canadian women, who tell their stories of survival in Canada, speak with a sense of amazement at the magnitude of their commitment to redefine themselves as migrant women, in spite of the very many risks involved. I conclude that their use of, and reliance on, notions of spirituality was dependent on their intellect as much as it was on their practical need to take initiatives.

Modern critical and cultural studies, both in the western academy and among research on Caribbean women, have privileged reason or secular thought, and, as a result, "spirituality" is rarely an object for intellectual analysis. Yet, in feminist thought, which includes experience spirituality, cannot be denied in cases where we search for an understanding of identity.[14] However, there has been tardiness to develop this theme, even among African-American feminist scholars who recognize the place of spiritual biographies in the history of the liberation of African-American women (Wade-Gayles 1995; Moody 1994; hooks 1993; Peterson 1992). Although some scholars have spurned spirituality in religious persons as "bovine or asinine", they have done so as a way to achieve status in White male academic discourse (Moody 1994: 30). Others, equally conscious of the importance of religious backgrounds, recognize that introducing spirituality into their works would be in dissonance with western thinking of "dualism of the body and soul, but also elevation of the body over the soul" (Wade-Gayles 1995: 3). I found that some notions of spirituality are associated with Christianity as espousing the need for feminist spirituality (Praetorius 1998; Chittister 1998; Ochs 1997). Other sources, quite popular, indicate that spirituality ought to be defined around one's psychological or emotional needs; yet, few relate spirituality to the life force which prescribes a motivational energy for activism, as described by the subjects of this book.

In the Caribbean, a spiritual life is known for its relevance to the conditions that either destabilize or affirm people's lives. In general, Caribbean people often feel at risk: notions of underdevelopment and undercivilized — "*us*" — contrast their lifestyles with "*them*" — developed and civilized. The continuous reinstalling of systems that create an unequal divide is a historical and hierarchical legacy of foreign domination. That is, for many groups of Caribbean peoples, situations of persistent poverty, underdevelopment, and unjust distribution of income can engender feelings that living is precarious.[15] How then, do Caribbean women survive? The question becomes an enigma, as presented in these stories, when disparity of income and scarcity of services, together with an erosion of identity, do not seem to provide scope for survival. No wonder I have often heard proclamations of faith that glorify a divine being beyond earthly limits of one's own vision as an enabling entity in survival.

> **Aita:** I am not a religious [person] in the sense of practising religion, but I have a deep sense of spirituality that traces itself way, way back. (Interview 20, 14 June 1995)

Other members of the group indicated some studied approaches to finding meaning of life in their spirituality.

Doreen: I am still part of the "Assembly of Spiritual Awareness", that is, we deal with the spiritual…the authentic part of our ancestors' spiritual tradition where we believe there is a God, we believe in our ancestors, and in the method of spiritual worship, not the distorted way that Europeans projected us. (Interview 5, 13 May 1995)

I myself have grappled with a meaning based on observation of how Mama "did her thing":

You see, Mama [adopted mother] a slightly bohemian-type woman, did not set an example herself as a church-going individual, yet she often sought solitude in reading, sometimes philosophies, other times fiction or poetry, which we were supposed to be too young to understand. She removed herself somewhat briefly from the hustle of household/nursing routine to do this and remained alone and quiet. Whenever I asked her what she was doing, she muttered something about meditation. Later I could hear her remarking that her confidence was renewed, she had been given strength and courage to continue working towards the family's survival — getting the food, the clothes, the school fees, the books, and so on.

On looking back, I have kept following that path; that is, I am not active in religious affiliation, yet I hold a strong belief in a spirit, a divinity, which enables me to strategize my life around a series of five-year plans. In a similar way, other Caribbean-Canadian women's stories refer to prayer, to a belief in a god or some other deity that indicates there is something beyond the material that helped those in the previous generation to maintain self-sufficiency. Lauretta was convinced that her recovery from race and gender crises, which threatened her life in Canada, was due to the place she occupied in her community working for God (Interview 21, 14 June 1995). Her work was not in the tradition of a religion, but it was a continuation of what her mother had taught her to do at home.

Ethnic differences do not preclude Caribbean-Canadian women from experiences of spirituality as part of the socialization process. Sumanta, for example, learned the value of religious mixing of Catholicism and Hinduism in her family. This was an action that she claims "kind of brought everything to me and placed everything in me and helped me to determine my spirituality" (Interview 40, 19 September 1995). Yaa, who experienced Africanized Christianity in her home, also connects her family's survival to spirituality and, in particular, to prayer.[16] Describing home as one of extreme poverty, she emphasizes spiritual beliefs as instrumental to the empowerment of the women in her family.

> **Yaa:** I think one thing, the spiritual, other than religion, was very important in our family. I was raised an Anglican, my grandmother was a Spiritual Baptist type of thing. I remember there was emphasis on praying. When there were hardships, you resort to prayer to work through things. I remember there was emphasis on praying and thanking God for whatever came our way. (Interview 10, 29 May 1995)

Audre Lorde (1984) makes two crucial points in "Uses of the Erotic", a chapter in her text *Sister Outsider*, which support my analysis. She says that it is incorrect to separate the spiritual and the erotic, and it is false to dichotomize the political and the spiritual. First of all, the erotic is defined as a force that can help women to explore intellectual potential without fear of being radical. Thus, the erotic is not understood as sensation, or as a component of the romanticized sense of the sexual self through gendered dominance. It is to be examined as "an assertion of the life force for women" (55). For Lorde, the erotic functions to share joy in relationships, to retain a sense of self, and to be convinced that a woman needs to respond to an inner voice which requires her to do what she ought to do (56–59). In postmodern terms, how can this notion relate to socially produced subjects? Does it mean that spirituality is yet another discursive position in which subjectivity shifts? Caribbean women in the study tell of experiences that lead them to act, experiences that suggest the presence of a life force engaging their capacity to make reasoned and evaluative approaches to situations that threaten their stability. They realize that positive outcomes are often inexplicable; hence, they resort to belief in higher degrees of power, which I term as their spirituality. How can Lena, constituted as a "Black immigrant woman", explain her capability to establish and sustain an alternative theatre for 18 years in the city of Toronto? How much can her words help in understanding that reach to spirituality?

Lena: I think God had something to do with it. I think he gave me strength to persevere. I think there was something inside of me that always wanted to express it. (Interview 27, 28 June 1995)

As I discussed earlier, the group of women in my study, irrespective of race, class, sexuality, and religion, are constituted as Caribbean women by learning to have a political consciousness toward anti-subordination. I am reminded that Lorde (1984) asserts that there is a necessity, as women, to keep politics and the spiritual together. This is one of the ideas that validate the relationship between the conscience and community activism, as it has been a Caribbean female ideology to be guided by the intellect, as it emerges from within, to act against social injustices. Other postmodern feminist thinking helps us to understand why spirituality is of significance to one's self-identity. For example, bell hooks (1993) admits that she has "sustained a spiritual life" and a belief in "divine spirits" is often referred to as "higher powers" (183). Her association with spirituality, however, is more related to issues of healing and self-recovery than strategies of resistance for survival.

Many Caribbean-Canadian women are socially constructed in identities that relegate them to remain within boundaries of race and class. These constructions often lock them in positions as "immigrant women". This is the space in which they mainly experience being othered, victimized, and inferiorized. Therefore, their assertiveness on foreign terrain can appear to be acting "out of place". Some of them interpret the effects of their resistance as an emergence of faith and hope, which reside beyond the practical effects of life. For instance, Saida, in her story, depicts her life through folk knowledge as this helps to simplify the mystery of how she has survived a variety of oppressions in capitalist systems. I was curious about her courage, and how she understands its source. She replied:

Oh yah! I had the courage to do it myself, because I had a goal, yuh know, I just have to go forward. Don't look back if one fails. God is there to provide the next one, because he provides for the birds and the bees, and he provides for me. And that's just the way I feel, so....Ideas like that come from my mother, and my grandmother too. (Interview 17, 8 June 1995)

Interestingly, Hazel and Deloris, who are professionals in religion, have a similar prescription for spirituality outside their respective doctrines.

> **Hazel**: I think you have to be yourself, and have a deep faith and a deep trust in God. That is what helps me through, because a lot of things weren't always easy and smooth flowing, even when we came here to a Black congregation. (Interview 16, 7 June 1995)

Her story conveys the faith she had to deconstruct the traditional gender role for women in the Christian religion. Defining herself as a "strong Black woman", she has incorporated the routines of being a mother and wife with her role as a missionary both in Canada and the Caribbean. Her position at the time of the interview was Outreach Director of the Union United Church in Montreal.

Deloris is Archbishop of the National Evangelical Spiritual Baptist Faith in the Diocese of Canada and has had the courage to struggle for, and to acquire, public recognition in Canada for the Spiritual Baptist movement, a marginalized religion even in the Caribbean region. She claims this is due to her religious and spiritual background in the Caribbean, where worship and sharing in her community were significant aspects of her life.

> **Deloris**: I was very religious as a child. I had to get up and pray at 5 o'clock every morning. My mother stayed up at nights praying ....Her first strength was spiritual. My Dad was a community person, so I had to get involved in the Church. (Interview 46, 7 August 1997)

These stories blending religious doctrines with community activism complement the arguments made by those who are laypersons, that "spirituality" is significant to our well-being. Lauretta's words seem to sum up the notion of spirituality as having been learned:

> Humility is in my family, and people have become my family. But the reason I've been able to remain sane and healthy is because I genuinely believe in God. I believe the only reason Theatre in the Rough[17] is around is because of God. (Interview 21, 14 June 1995)

Home is in the mind; it came with them

When these Caribbean women in Canada "make two ends meet" in the diaspora, or when they connect in their networks to laugh together, *home* is the imagined construct that makes them reconstitute their subjectivities. Home is not "four walls", as we say; it is the history of resistance to multiple oppressions; it is not unified in these Caribbean women's thoughts, because they experience it in a variety of ways. They know that home is the reason they could act beyond the boundaries set for them in race, class, sexuality, and gender, even though certain discourses of nation may exclude them. Home is certainly a constant site where they see older women address issues in their communities and where they observe the acts of resistance to survive oppressions of domination. They imagine themselves within this site called home, as part of the nation learning to perpetuate resistance. Collectively, these stories indicate the possibility that the past can filter down to the present, and, therefore, that families can construct home as a learning institution.

Caribbean women brought "home" with them to Canada, because they were prepared for the contestations they would face as immigrant women. Their memories of home embrace a range of experiences, from negative to positive, through which percolate strengths for resistance. They see home as a place where older women negotiated boundaries between the private and the public. These women established ties with the community in social work, in teaching, and in the politics of social or racial upliftment. *There is no place like home*, because even if, or when, they experienced psychological or physical violence there, it is remembered most for communal sharing and for diversity. Also, it is remembered as a place where women seem to be independent enough to challenge and resist racist and patriarchal oppressions. They claim that going back home, for instance, enables cultural renewal that energizes them to continue in the diaspora. For some, returning is a form of continuing education as they revisit ways in which Caribbean women in the region work to survive. As well, it keeps home in their minds as a particular reality to maintain a sense of their own security in Canada. For example, Lucinda's confidence about the appropriateness of revisiting, in spite of her 27 years in Canada, is clearly an expression as belonging to *home*.

Lucinda: I think where I was raised and where I was born, the type of parent I had, gave me strength to achieve my goals in Canada. I can go home, back now, today, and you can ask anybody who knows me back home. It's like I never left. (Interview 24, 24 June 1995)

Home is where a whole range of experiences and oppressions are gendered. It is, then, a space for Caribbean older women to perform resistance assertively in domestic and occupational roles. We see these women, not in the colonizer's stereotypical images of strengths that debased women but as endowed with strength to be consistently resourceful.

Finally, I find that these women's stories of their learning resistance, all at different homes in the Caribbean, suggest how prepared they were to address challenges that they confronted during their periods of adjustment.

Sastra: My experience of being raised in my parents' home — the subtleties of race and gender, class and religion — we came with that history to Canada. (Interview 36, 29 August 1995)

Younger Caribbean women were forced to be a part of many of these community-based activities and were influenced by them, thus acquiring an "emotional expansiveness" (Brodber 1986: 25), which engenders an ability to relate to multiple sources from which distinct or overlapping values spring. Movement in and out of spaces called home constitute the multiple subjectivities of women, as their stories briefly address these different positions (Mama 1995). Multiple subjectivities are produced from experiences of numerous relationships with parents, relatives, and paid care providers, relationships that blend or overlap. Emerging from almost all these relationships were lessons that confirmed that Caribbean older women were teachers of survival skills and providers of strategies to understand how to act against subordination.

Notes

1   Standard English translation of Jamaican language: *The home is full of strengths*.

2   Anancy is a character which developed in the storytelling among enslaved Africans. As a leading character, it took several forms, mainly as the spider, but often as an animal. Anancy was a fantasy about the subjugated Africans in the Caribbean to empower themselves in imagining that their conditions could be reversed. The interesting thing about this character is that it was contradictory: a winner and a loser, sometimes being both in the same story.

3   African-American women working as domestics gave incorrect names and used to appear slow-witted and submissive when they were objectified by White women. Their work was well valued regardless of poor performance when they acted obediently (Collins, 1990: 55–57).

4   Dr Francisco Slinger, Calypso King of the world and composer/singer of very many social commentary calypsos, was born in Grenada, but his rise to career achievement took place in Trinidad and Tobago.

5   A Caribbean expression that indicates a person is finding ways to combat social and economic repression.

6   In spite of limited formal education, Saida deflected the harshness of discrimination through her tolerance and her willingness to provide insights into how residents in a metropolitan area can live communally.

7   Caribbean women in the region, regardless of race, experienced difficulties such as vulnerability at work and full responsibility for child care. In spite of this, they used their resources communally from "their own economic activity" and were able to meet "familial and personal needs" (Anderson 1986: 291–324). Read Austin Clarke (1999).

8   Benedict Anderson's (1991) notion of home is appropriate, as, collectively, Caribbean-Canadian women construct a communal sense of belonging to the geographical spaces in the Caribbean regardless of the diversity in the region.

9   Using the word "best" to describe women over 65 is to deconstruct the stereotype of "senior".

10   I gratefully acknowledge Professor Sherene Razack's insight here.

11   Refer to Chapter Two, page 29.

12   See also the movie by Richard Fung, *My Mother's Place*, in which Mrs. Fung suggests that racism was accepted because everyone in the community knew the place to which they truly belong.

13   Their racism is fictionalized in their father's short story (Carr 1996).

14   I am mindful of Joan Scott's (1992) notion of "experience", in which she argues that experience does not originate in individuals alone. It is related to the historical process in which discourses are produced and reproduced.

15   Western and capitalist intrusion has perpetuated the images of European superiority in public administration, culture, science, politics, and so on, as an ideology that mostly destabilizes and disempowers Caribbean peoples.

16   In the popular magazine *O*, an article discloses the power of prayer. A few studies

have been done in the USA to prove that people in a prayer group experience less severe symptoms and require less medication than those for whom no praying was done. See Davidson 2002: 260–63, 287.

17   The initiative for this theatre will be discussed in Chapter Seven.

SEVEN

Strategies to Make
Canada Home:
We does get troo, bonjay![1]

Home is imagined to have taught the Caribbean-Canadian women in this study to survive oppressions. Therefore, on their arrival to Canada during the fifties to the eighties, they were prepared to confront the issues of racism and sexism that challenged them. These issues arose at all levels of society because of the dominant discourse that had shaped their identities as subordinate: "Black" and "immigrant women". On the one hand, Canada, on account of its nation-building strategies, had offered these women many opportunities; on the other hand, its societies generally opposed or belittled their presence. For instance, the Domestic Scheme of the fifties, which appeared altruistic,[2] had typecast and homogenized the identities of women of variant social backgrounds as permanent "domestics". As well, through a nursing program, Caribbean nurses and nursing assistants who were qualified under the British colonial system in the Caribbean were de-skilled and demoted in health institutions in Canada (Calliste 1989, 1993).

The reduction of Caribbean women's identities as immigrants to Canada began at the level of this country's immigration laws, which were promulgated to fulfil a shortage of specific types of labour. That is, regulations from 1914 to 1966 stipulated a preference for which countries would supply immigrants, prohibited immigrants on the basis of certain categories,[3] and limited access to admission.[4] The ideology pervading these regulations measures immigrants from "underdeveloped" countries, like the Caribbean, as being less qualified, less civilized, and so on. Therefore, Caribbean female migrants who, in general, refused victimhood as a permanent choice, as they demonstrated in specific cases of activism, disrupted systemic racism in Canada's immigration policies and in institutions of labour and employment arrangements. Caribbean women, in the period of the late fifties to early sixties, countered victimization through breach of the Domestic Scheme contract and through proof of their qualification as nurses that they had "indeed exceptional" skills exceeding, in many cases, those of their Canadian counterparts (Calliste 1993: 93).

This chapter argues that Caribbean-Canadian women strategized their survival through the use of networking and education in Canada where, by and large, they were ostracized. It illustrates how these strategies developed community activism as a force to construct a social movement in defiance of their exclusion from mainstream feminist organizing and their diminishing roles in Black community organizing.

What did Caribbean women do in the fifties and sixties?

Caribbean women's adequacy for skilled and professional jobs, together with their tendency to use independence as an ethic, without essentializing an identity here, remains a contradiction to the ideology of victimhood and passivity. We are reminded that, mainly in the twentieth century, "home", with its unstable economies, pushed Caribbean women into Canada where many of them were able to gain some financial support for themselves and even to contribute to Caribbean national economies through their remittances to families left behind. Therefore, when we focus on the majority of Caribbean women who seized opportunities to survive, we cannot ignore how their actions were driven by a spirit of independence. In many cases, struggles against race and gender discrimination generated a variety of personal skills, which began with a preparedness to leave their respective areas of the Caribbean. After these Caribbean women passed the point of entry into Canada, it was necessary to adjust to new challenges of living in relative strangeness: climate, population, and cultural differences. Some challenges, of course, were acceptable, yet the problems of discrimination that precluded their integration into a new society were perpetuated widely by employers, landlords, schools, and health services (Henry 2002; Bakan and Stasiulus 1997; Head 1975) For instance, Zora was sensitive to the racist positioning she experienced during her period of adjustment:

Zora: In retrospect, I felt that file clerk position was kind of a racist selection of me to do that work because I obviously was capable of more. I mean, when I took the test, he said nobody has ever gotten such a high score. (Interview 31, 10 August 1995)

Also Aretha, who assumed that her privilege as a student might defy the experience of racism in housing, eventually faced the distorted image many Canadians held of Caribbean peoples.

Aretha: When my roommate and I were told over the phone that it was fine to get a place on Avenue Road, we went up there to look at it. The woman who we met said to us, "'I can't rent the place to you, your people". And I said, I don't have any people. It is just my roommate and myself here, and we talked on the phone and you said we can have this place." She got confused, took our phone number. When we got back home, she called us and said she was just the landlady, and it is the people who owned the place that said so. It is only when we sat down and talked about it, we realized it was racism. (Interview 34, 29 August 1995)

Networking as a strategy of resistance

It was necessary, then, for Caribbean-Canadian women to see racism as a reality and to explore their memories of survival at home in order to cope with its damaging impact. Through their stories, I realized that the principle of community was integral to their use of agency in resistance to their identities being nullified on the Canadian scene. That is, it was crucial to resuscitate an ongoing connection with the "extended family" pattern so frequently experienced at home. Their lifestyle, which consisted of reciprocal movement among families and neighbours, created an organic definition of family, on which basis a shared knowledge of domination and subordination was sufficient to perpetuate community action, often on an everyday basis.[5] Therefore, community is linked to networking.

Transported to Canada, networking retained its effectiveness as one of the main strategies of resistance against marginalization, powerlessness, and avoidance. It may very well have been the intervention that gave meaning to what otherwise would have been lives of lonely individualism, the mark of the lifestyle of metropolitan societies. Networking has historical significance for Caribbean peoples who have been economic targets under the capitalist plantation system of forced labour, whether during slavery, indentureship, or colonialism. They repeatedly had their original kinship ties broken and their family structures replaced, particularly in slavery, through miscegenation and the high mortality rate that created changes in relationships continuously. Networking entailed making new contacts based purely on internal plantation relations and had no connection to lineage, ethnicity, or other social dynamics. This act of connecting and bonding replicates the construct of home, in which Caribbean peoples' interdependency, outside a tradition of biological family, includes others who may identify as friends and neighbours. Thus, in Canada, networking is conceptualized by many Caribbean women as an opportunity to re-enact home as a place where one finds strength in multiple and variant activities with people who share a cultural identity. It would appear that home, in the diaspora, bears no apparent structure, but carries with it a reciprocal responsibility by persons participating in the network. That is, Caribbean women and men in Canada were more likely to become "aware of occupational and/other available opportunities" during the fifties and sixties through networking (Turritin 1976: 306).

Networking, as it was known historically to do, subverts the oppression of marginalization which gives the state power to both materially and socially deprive the oppressed. It is a strategy that deconstructs the nuclear family and develops a material and psychological bond among Caribbean-Canadian women and men. It also embraces circumstances which range from celebratory to needy within groups.[6] Networking helped to diffuse, for these Caribbean-Canadian women, interactions with Canadians that produced cultural racism. That is, their cultural practices could be expressed without chance of being exoticized or ridiculed. Of course, for many of these women, it was a way to make a connection and an appropriate commitment with each other so as not to lose "home" — the place that defines food, language, laughter, music, and other forms of communication (Ho 1991a). Therefore, in the period of the early sixties, it was necessary for Bianca, who first resided at the YWCA in Montreal, to transform networking into community.

Bianca: One Sunday morning I met a young woman in the cafeteria in the YWCA where I lived. She smiled when she came walking towards me, as though she thought she knew me....She was from Tobago. We went to the campus and met another Black woman, Jamaican, and we began to hang out together, as the kids would say. They decided to move out of the "Y". I stayed because my mother felt I was safe there. They, however, found a room close by [it happened so naturally] like we had a place to cook, we took it in turns, and then later on two guys joined us, so there was a community. (Interview 2, 18 September 1994)

This is one of the many instances when, in order to reduce the effects of marginalization and racism, Bianca and her friends reconstituted home. Discovering that racism in Canada was often repetitive and covert, she saw the need to anchor her identity among people whose identities were equivalent to her own.[7] The interconnectedness of their histories under colonialism brought them to Canada where they were exposed to incidents of subordination in a society which often invalidated who they were. Bianca, at the point of entry, had the experience of racial stereotyping of her Caribbean identity when Canadian officials discounted her achievements as a high school graduate from Jamaica. The next incident was that of prejudice, which objectified her difference as a Black woman in the church where she tried to worship. Faced with these experiences of racism, Bianca recognized the value of networking as she was socialized to do at home. She realized that since it was a way of surviving events at home, therefore, it was crucial to use it if she intended to survive her life in Canada. Her story is repeated by others in the study, with slight variations.

Some Caribbean-Canadian women employing the ethic of independence opted for integration into the mainstream culture through networking. Evelyne was an upper-middle-class woman who retained this status in Canada because she had no need to be reduced to menial jobs, so was frequently assigned to new Caribbean and other immigrants. Her "home" experience, on the one hand, was at leadership, decision-making, and influential levels where she used her self-reliance and assertiveness effectively. However, she also had been a target of political/racial discrimination in her country due to her political views. In Canada, however, on a casual job search, she was asked for "Canadian experience".

Evelyne: I did not have anything to do now, so I went to the YWCA and said I'd like to do some work. They asked "paid or volunteer?" and I replied I didn't care. The woman said, "A lot of older women think they could make a comeback". So I pulled out my papers. (Interview 1, 17 August 1994)

An integral part of racism is impolite and unethical behaviour, such as that recognized in the unwarranted comment by the person who interacted with Evelyne. However, having her background verified, she gained entry into mainstream organizations which suited her to perpetuate a self-image of her Caribbean past.

Evelyne: She then invited me to a coffee morning for nominations to the Board. I went and they introduced me and nominated me to the Board. I then joined the Women's Guild of Craft in Yorkville, and I was on the Mental Health Committee, and I began mixing. But I can't say I picked up one thing new. And I went on and did volunteer work. (Interview 1, 17 August 1994)

Relating this story was a nostalgic journey for her of the "good times" in which she describes her power to negotiate her skills and her identity within Canadian mainstream society. Evelyne introduced African musical instruments to the Royal Ontario Museum and devised a program of education around the use of some of them.

Cultural integration was not always an adequate ploy for Caribbean-Canadian women to deconstruct everyday racism in Canada. Sometimes these women, in strategizing, had to opt for a "rejectionist perspective" (West 1992a: 27) in which networking within community activism reflected independence and scepticism of Canadian social mores. This occurred to me when I first lived in Canada. I experienced the bigotry and intolerance of Canadians towards migrants, along with the claims of the denial of racism in this country.[8] As well, I was perplexed that there could be such a hypocritical and demeaning process that established tokenism by sprinkling Caribbean and Black people on the face of Canada only to intensify their marginalization. My particular interest, at that time, was in the work of Canadian-based Caribbean artists and writers who struggled to secure their rights as citizens and residents but needed space to articulate their creativities and identities. Thus, I relate what was done to overcome some of the powerlessness and marginality of this group of people:

It was the fall of 1964. Austin Clarke, a now famous Black and Caribbean writer in Canada;[9] Charles Roach, lawyer and radical activist; Amba Trott, Ernest Tucker, and Howard Matthews, writers; Lennox Brown, playwright; Salome Bey, jazz singer; and Romain Pitt, lawyer and judge met with me in my apartment in Toronto to consider alternative strategies to resist the frequent discrimination artists of colour experienced in mainstream society. There was a consensus to form an organization named the Ebo Society,[10] which would exclude White people in management and whose emphasis would be on exposing the artistic talents of our people. Each of us made a $25 contribution to the Society to help defray costs. We rejected naming ourselves Negro, coloured, or Black, so we chose Ebo after a proud African tribe in Nigeria.[11] My apartment, my home, became the weekly meeting place of this group, and I served in more than one capacity as Secretary. During the year 1965, we were able to produce bi-monthly a newsletter *Ebo Voice*, that I edited and published with the help of the Canadian Council of Christians and Jews.[12] We also staged a Canada Council award-winning play by Lennox Brown at the ROM, which I produced, together with a poetry reading. And we felt we had excelled when we curated a collection of 18 artists from African-Canadian and Caribbean peoples across Canada at the Fine Art Gallery, Toronto Public Library, for a month.[13] We continued our resistance to marginalization when we organized a reception in November to honour the works of Lennox Brown, Austin Clarke, and Wallace Collins, having received only $25.00 from one publisher. On the whole, we considered our year's work as a vindication for the misrepresentation of our identities as Caribbean and Black people.

There were other Caribbean-Canadian women whose agendas were similar to my own, that is, to reduce the level of powerlessness imposed on Caribbean and Black communities by systemic racism. We were dedicated to removing the stereotypes that retained misinformation and politicized "Black/White" relations in strategies of resistance in community activism. One of these Caribbean-Canadian women was Abike. She acknowledged her class position of privilege in the Caribbean, but recognized that it was her social consciousness that was instrumental in leading her to reject an estate inheritance while the colonial plantation inequities were still in vogue in twentieth-century Dominica. Her choice to attend university in Canada was her journey to her own self-liberation.

Abike: In Canada when I left Mt. St. Vincent and came to Montreal, I became more fully involved with the Black community. I was involved long before "Black was beautiful" to the extent that my brother once sent me a message indicating when I come to my senses, I will be welcomed back home. I was co-founder of the National Black Coalition; I worked with the Negro Citizenship Association in the late fifties, when we tried to integrate the Diamond and the Lasalle taxi industry; I went with Black groups to Quebec City when we were asking the province for Human Rights legislation; I participated in demonstrations for opportunities to rent houses, for employment; I went regularly to Toronto to participate in Liberation Day marches, taking my children and their friends and renting a suite at the Royal York Hotel. I can't tell you how many times I became the first Black female to do x, y, or z. For instance, I was the first Black female in Quebec on the Immigration and Refugee Board, and so on. (Interview 13, 7 June 1995)

Thus, community activism, as these stories and many others exemplify, was Caribbean female-driven, though not female-centred. The actions of these women are reflective of their learning resistance at home where the boundaries between the private and the public conflate in the struggle to reduce subordination. This paradigm was repeated here in Canada among the activism of these Caribbean-Canadian women. Thus, networking into community activism during the late 1950s to the early 1960s became a foundation of future organizing by the Caribbean-Canadian women in this book. Yet, I recognize that there are many other eventful occasions of activism against racist and sexist oppressions in Canada, only some of which are recorded and which my work is unable to embrace. These have all made an indelible impression on the memories of Caribbean and Black peoples in the community.

What Caribbean-Canadian women did from the centennial year, 1967, to the seventies

This new era for Caribbean-Canadian women introduced the struggle on two counts: one, the continuous battle with racist immigration policies, and, two, the politics of exclusion in feminist organizing and in Black community organizing. I repeat, racism and sexism are inherent features in Canada's immigration policies. For instance, new regulations at the time offered resident security on application for landed immigrant status after women had served as domestics for two years. I refer to the changes in these policies during 1967 because Caribbean-Canadian women were threatened by an irreparable damage to self-esteem if the state repatriated them to poverty in their countries of origin.[14] In the seventies, Canada's revised immigration legislation removed the criteria of educational achievement in favour of occupational experience, specifying three classes of immigrants: family, independents, and refugees. These revisions made the Domestic Scheme redundant, thus cutting off the opportunity to emigrate for many Caribbean women, who did not have the qualifications to meet the new requirements, but were desirous of coming up to "foreign". Added to that, the severity of racist practices by Canadian officials in the exercise of the state's immigration polices was nightmarish and was not countered in the dealings many Caribbean women had with employment agencies and housing landlords and landladies. While these experiences were prioritized in the minds of Caribbean migrant women and men, Canadian feminists at that time still had not addressed the issue of race (I will explore this in greater detail later). However, Caribbean women, affected by their learning resistance, which included a specific mandate for education, strategized accordingly.

Education as a strategy of resistance

Caribbean-Canadian women used education appropriately as a strategy to survive the contexts of race and gender oppressions in this period, the mid-1960s to the 1970s. They remember, with much fascination, the messages that older Caribbean women sent them, particularly when the message spoke of being educationally deprived. It was a message that raised an apparent contradiction: resistance to White domination, yet adopting White customs, White knowledge as a means of liberation. Fern recalls how her emphasis on education in her own life falls back on her parents' perspectives of its significance.

Fern: I picked up the way people looked at me, the way they talked to me, the way they even fathered me. That is what motivated me to break barriers of a woman, educationally. I went to university and schools and got diplomas and degrees in business, banking, as well as finance. (Interview 7, 6 September 1994)

Aita's memory is her observation of how well her mother in domestic service employment "picked up every piece of information she could get from the White folks in terms of dress", and how consistent she was in reading the *Reader's Digest* (Interview 20, 14 June 1995). She also respected her mother's ability to organize herself and her siblings around homework requirements, instilling in them that education was essential. But education for Caribbean-Canadian women in this study moved beyond "getting a piece of paper" (Aita, 14 June 1995) from a university to enhancing one's critical consciousness that would progress into an activism of revolutionary politics among Black women and men.

Aita: The first study group I know of in the seventies was with Franklyn Harvey, who brought us the New Jewel Movement. The study begins with Caribbean politics, including Walter Rodney's writings, which gave me grounding.[15] The next was the Black Study group in which there were 12 of us. This was a focus on PanAfricanism. It enabled me to understand where colonialism fits into the struggle, and our link to Africa. These events made up the groundwork for community organizing. Everything in my professional or community work I do today takes me back to those study groups. (Interview 20, 14 June 1995)

Maya: I am doing courses at the University of Toronto and to talk about issues like apartheid was taboo, just as much as talking about racism; even then it was worse. These are the issues which had impact on my everyday life, and I was denied talking about them. Therefore, the study groups gave me an avenue for a discourse that would give a kind of support to my survival in Canada. They helped with my own personal development, as we would read, discuss, and draw from the strengths of those great names like Malcolm X and others. These were activities that grounded me and made me feel more centred, so that when I was experiencing racism, it was not as damaging psychologically as when I had not been grounded. (Interview 26, 27 June 1995)

For other Caribbean-Canadian women, the early seventies was a period in which to resuscitate their longings for the strategy that would enable agency to maintain the ethic of independence. Ariel is one of those whose journey in Canada from domestic worker to single mother to welfare recipient because of ill health to director in a social service agency served to make her understand self-responsibility and the means required to survive.

Ariel: But there was all this nagging: I had to raise my boy; I had to still go to school. How could I do both? At 42? My life came crashing down with bad asthma. By the time I got this asthma under control, my son had graduated from high school, and then I applied to Concordia and McGill and got accepted at both. (Interview 15, 6 June 1995)

Many Caribbean-Canadian women understand how the system minimizes their worth, so they pursue higher education in order to compete and acquire positions of authority. From these locations they can initiate and establish liberal reforms in the hiring practices and client services of institutions. They also recognize that the hierarchy will frequently place a White voice at the top. They are, however, convinced that education is a sufficiently empowering strategy to reduce subjugation. Using it as a strategy of resistance, they design non-racist institutions to oppose the collusion of Whites with systemic racism.

Yaa: I was working in the assaulted women and children's advocacy Counsellor two-year program to train women for jobs in shelters and rape crisis centres. Just the nature of the course I was teaching was one way of resisting. I taught [White] women race, class, and intercultural communication, bringing many Afrocentric perspectives into it. For me, that was one way to challenge, if not undermine, dominance. (Interview 10, 29 May 1995)

Yaa's approach to social justice education did not totally eradicate racist and stereotypical biases of Whites towards people of colour. Yet, in a way, she was empowered to reject hierarchical relations and to reverse consciousness as she assumed authority in her role as educator, thus redefining her image. Zindzi, another woman in the study, found that she had to continue the role and responsibilities she carried out successfully in the Caribbean as an educator and facilitator. To continue here in Canada, she began by depending on solidarity with one White woman who had access to funding and who had an interest in community work. Zindzi's series of speaking programs facilitated the engagement of Canadians in the change to a multicultural demographic society through education.

> **Zindzi**: She [her White colleague] would set up these speaking engagements for me for which I used to be paid. The audiences consisted of people like those who belong to the Imperial Order of the Daughters of the Empire. (Interview 9, 23 September 1994)

Zindzi's activities were necessary at that time as a way to reduce the hegemonic arrogance and ignorance in Canada towards Caribbean peoples. This form of activism enlightened Whites about a Caribbean reality of which many people were proud. Therefore, Zindzi's speaking engagements developed into an initiative for the establishment of the first cross-cultural centre in Canada. Established in London, Ontario, it branched out to other cities, including Toronto, as an attempt to confront racism with information and education.

> **Zindzi**: Another thing that took up much of my time was what was then known as "international education" and "development education". I was a co-founder of the first cross-cultural centre in Canada. It became a major vehicle to address social issues. (Interview 9, 23 September 1994)

Community activism as a strategy of resistance

&

This period, therefore, is significant as one of those in which Caribbean women, engaging in a feminist approach, were empowered to act for social change in Canada. That is, they dealt with social issues mainly from a consciousness propelled by a Caribbean legacy of resistance. Yet, their activism was not primarily based on women's issues. The use of education, in the broadest sense, as a strategy of resistance seemed to clearly anticipate the more radical activism that was carried out during the period of the seventies and eighties, a period significant for the birth of multiculturalism and growing diversity. Then racism became more overt, for with the increase in numbers and the designated category of "visible minorities", migrants' experiences of prejudice and intolerance accelerated in social and cultural services institutions, and many were marginalized, including Caribbean peoples.[16]

Political consciousness, which grew out of the ideological beliefs and the determination of Caribbean peoples to resist domination, has led to historic and current rebellions and other forms of physical resistance (Meeks 2000). Thus, in the seventies, in spite of the soft-spoken attitude on race, Canadians witnessed at home a growing militancy, which had already developed among African ethnicized communities in the Caribbean and the United States. Caribbean-Canadian women and men indicated that they would no longer be passive in their urgency for social justice. Canada, therefore, saw the convergence of a socio-political movement around two streams: the riot at Sir George Williams (Concordia) University, which was a revolt in response to discriminatory practices towards Black students, and the African Liberation Movement, which articulated broad issues ranging from anti-colonialism to a commitment to the principles of Black Power. Members of the Black and Caribbean community embraced the tenets of Black Power and engaged in mobilizing and organizing groups to establish and name for themselves working services and projects to counter racism and marginalization. In Toronto, the more prominent and familiar organizations were the Library of Black People's Theatre, the Home Service Association, the Harriet Tubman Centre, and the Black Education Project. Many Caribbean-Canadian women in this study spoke of contributing volunteer time to both the "Centre" and the "Project".[17] In Montreal, the frequently remembered organizations which provided space for activities to challenge racism in that society were The Negro Community Centre and the United Negro Improvement Association, which also had a Toronto chapter.

It is mainly in this context of urgency and radicalism that some Caribbean-Canadian women in Toronto gave voice to a movement to deconstruct discursive barriers in racism and to lessen the weight of Eurocentric hegemony in education. They joined with other women and men to respond primarily to "West Indian" parents who were outraged at the possibility that their children in the Toronto school system might have been "understreamed" and "overlooked". Most of the programs they devised were carried out at city locations where spaces could be dedicated to the projects. Yet, volunteer teachers also went to the homes of children who found difficulty getting to program sites.[18] Rebeka, who was a co-founder, speaks of the Black Education Project (BEP) in this way:

> I recall a lot of impetus came from Black students at the University of Toronto. They got their Students' Union to give a grant for a couple of years, and Black students from York got heavily involved as volunteers. (Interview 43, 11 December 1995)

Another Caribbean-Canadian women, Zora, who was an undergraduate at that time, describes her involvement with the Project like this:

> I was recruited as a volunteer by a Guyanese man to tutor kids, who had come up from the Caribbean and needed help. I started tutoring twice a week. Some students came alone and left by 7 o'clock to go home; others were picked up by parents. (Interview 31, 10 August 1995)

BEP formalized the networking strategy significantly. As a result, Caribbean-Canadian women and men could solidify their commitment in the struggle against racism with regularity, specifically in areas where issues were extremely oppressive: immigration and education. This Project became a strong initiative in the history of Black community organizing, which drew other individuals to develop other frameworks of social activism against racism in Canada.

> **Rebeka**: This movement with the Black Education Project precipitated the Transitional Program at York University for one year. Then the University of Toronto took it on and it was established there. (Interview 43, 11 December 1995)

Other stories show how individual consciousness continued to develop among Caribbean-Canadian women in a radical way so that they were able to participate in a Black movement that was in unison with other such communities worldwide.

Maya: I came to Canada in 1968. I started getting involved in 1970. As a student on the U of T campus, I belonged to the Black Students' Association, which provided us with links to community organizing around various issues; for example, immigration was a hot one. I was active in the Library of Black People's Literature and the Home Service Association on Bathurst Street. Through this involvement I gained a sense of belonging. (Interview 26, 27 June 1995)

Zindzi: I lived in London at the home of a United Church minister, from which I got involved with the Caribbean community just like I did at home [Caribbean]. I was connected most with summer programs and activities for Black children. We got local initiatives, like grants from all those 1970 literacy programs...Work for Youth. I then joined other Caribbean students to assist Caribbean youths outside the university. (Interview 9, 23 September 1994)

Olive: I made connections with JK and DG who had just started the Harriet Tubman Centre, which was set up as part of the YWCA. That involvement really helped me to hold on to my life. We started to deal with issues of control there, the kind of thing that got my juices flying again, just the way I used to behave in high school, always fighting authority.... (Interview 6, 1 September 1994)

A few Caribbean-Canadian women spoke with pride about their activism, which included material as well as political support for Black liberation.

Abena: Around 1971 to 1972, the important movers and shakers of the Black Power movement came to Toronto — Angela Davis, Amiri Baraka, and Rosie Douglas, people in the Black Urban Alliance who came from the United States. That was how I got introduced to Black community organizing and African Liberation Day. Many revolutionaries stayed at my home, where

I provided food, etc. Yet, I did all the propaganda work for the NPLA [National Panthers Liberation Association], paying the expenses for posters, sending money to the Black Panther movement, and supporting NJAC [National Joint Action Committee] in Trinidad. In addition, I was giving money to the UJ [Ujamaa] movement, the Angola situation, doing fundraising, etc. I was totally and completely involved. (Interview 29, 11 July 1995)

Anne: I was the secretary of the African Liberation Support Committee, a Toronto-based support group for the liberation struggles in South Africa. I was involved in fund-raising, bringing speakers from the USA for public education. I experienced encounters with the cops and witnessed police brutality, including the derogatory comments they made about us. (Interview 44, 16 September 1996)

Though the level of involvement and commitment was exceedingly high, some Caribbean-Canadian women needed to express their consciousness about the conflict between presumed gender equality and their subordinated positions in the movement.

Rebeka: I was becoming more and more conscious of being in the background, being a woman, doing the "shit" jobs — the maintenance work — while the man is in the front line receiving the glory or whatever. I started thinking more consciously about feminism in terms of what it meant to be a woman, and what roles and responsibilities I should take on. It was a real struggle, as men in the movement here were saying what others elsewhere were saying, that is, "Keep quiet. First we must win the revolution, then we will move on to you. We are not the enemy, capitalism is the enemy". We, as women, said, "No, the same way we can say racism is the product of capitalism we are not going to wait to defeat capitalism, to defeat racism. We mean liberation of women is a priority." (Interview 43, December 1995)

The gross misinterpretation of gender as a category that includes the subjugation of both men and women has to be noted as a stage in the anti-racism movement which was not a site of full liberation for these women. Their motivation to continue working with Caribbean men in resistance activities did not preclude their resentment of the objectification and the continuous devaluing of their worth. Hedy, in Montreal, whose substantial experience in community organizing was ignored, spoke of how she insisted in making her contribution:

> I responded to Black community mobilizing back in the days of the Sir George Williams incident. I was 18 then, and attended meetings at the United Negro Improvement Association, giving support to the students charged. Since then I have not stopped. I was President of the Barbados House for two years. It was important to show members that a female could really head an organization. Certainly males dominated the Executive Committees of many meetings. I often had to stretch myself to attend them. They went on until midnight, but I stayed even when I was called at the last minute. But I did! (Interview 12, 7 June 1995)

Other Caribbean-Canadian women displayed their consciousness of oppression that went beyond their prescribed communities of Black or Caribbean. Unfair rental practices and persistent domination in a downtown Toronto building in which Annzinga lived is the object of her story.

> **Annzinga**: What I saw was a building full of immigrants, Chinese, Latin American, and so on. We were doing everything in English, so we frequently got a core group of people to attend meetings. People were reluctant to do something with the differences manifested at the meeting and among the tenants. For example, there were tenants, women, who could not make decisions; they had to wait until their partners, who spoke and read English, got home. I began having all circulars translated into Chinese, Greek, Spanish, and other languages so as to prepare ourselves effectively for a class-action suit. The tenants feared for my safety, as apparently the landlord had a reputation which could have been a serious threat. I work hard and a lot at that, voluntarily; plus, I had my full time job. But we successfully formed a Tenants' Association, which went on to do amazing things: the reduction on the rent increase of 19% back to 7%. (Interview 45, 16 September 1996)

A few Caribbean-Canadian women acted outside the framework of "Blackness" as a target of oppressions and were similarly involved in working for the liberation of other oppressed peoples in Canada.

Cheryl: When I first arrived, I notice Caribbean peoples were ghettoizing themselves, saying they want to belong to this group or another. I wanted to be seen as a Canadian: a citizen of this country. I found a weekend job in which I was responsible for giving advice to alcoholic and retarded women in my own little way. (Interview 3, 22 August 1994)

Nikki: Now, with First Nations peoples, I was put to the test over a long time, especially by the Chiefs, who would run me ragged to see my reaction to their thinking. I guess I passed the test and was able to help with an empowering program I developed in workshops with women and men. As I worked closely with them, they saw I was from a group that was oppressed, although not as oppressed as they were. I felt there was some affinity. (Interview 22, 17 June 1995)

Abike: I received the Order of Canada for my contribution to First Nations education. I was by myself as a coordinator, having got a call for graduates from Vanier to work on the reserve doing special care counselling. I questioned the administrative set-up, and got permission from Vanier College to deliver the program on the reserve, which I did, volunteering myself for three years. This distance program I undertook resulted in the first-ever graduation of First Nations peoples on a reserve in Canada. (Interview 13, 7 June 1995)

Social consciousness sometimes affords some Caribbean-Canadian women an opportunity to explore identity issues; that is, they can refine some of their ideas about the difference they experience in a White society. They therefore chose to become involved outside the Black and Caribbean community, perhaps in order to become socially integrated, yet their open-mindness does not preclude racism.

Simone: I wanted to be a volunteer during my first couple of years in Canada, so I went to the Central Volunteer Registry, and they sent me to the Central Neighbourhood House, which supports mothers who are upgrading their education. They gave me one White kid, and the mother was furious. (Interview 23, June 1995)

The standing issue of ethnic/Creole difference in the Caribbean region is perpetuated in Canada. Chinese-Caribbean women, recognizing double marginalization, became active with the Caribbean Chinese Association, because their experiences of trying to get involved with either an Asian-Chinese or a Caribbean (Black) community was negative. This association, while initially established for social and cultural activities, had to become politicized in order to support its people on the perennial issues of immigration, housing, jobs, and education. Fern and Kim became members immediately on their arrival in Canada during the late 1970s.

Kim: It was the time when there was a need to get together to give each other moral support, to give each other information and sensitize ourselves about our rights in Canada. We had to find ways to get through the bureaucratic tape, and to help each other financially, because we had members who went through some hard times. (Interview 8, 6 September 1995)

With regard to sexuality as a category for oppressive practices, Yelena experienced similar urgency on her arrival in Canada to get involved with community work. Her moment of liberation came when she announced her lesbian identity to her family. She was then better prepared to initiate her activism around issues of race/sexuality discrimination with which she had become totally familiar.

Yelena: I just immersed myself on the lesbian scene in Toronto to do critical work around oppressive practices. One night I was on the phone line at LOOT,[19] and a woman called, who was just pushed out of her home. When I told her I was from the Caribbean, she came to the House. Her parents were from Barbados. I also quickly met women from Jamaica and St. Lucia, and we formed a network and we used to "lime"[20] regularly in lesbian bars. (Interview 28, 29 June 1995)

These stories, told by Caribbean-Canadian women whose identities diversely range in class, privilege, colour, education, demographics, and so on, yield a collective identity for use of agency. How they made their contributions pointed to a reality where responses to racism in particular were not essentialized in the dichotomy of Blackness/Whiteness. All these women spoke of their preparedness to act according to conscience and to compatibility with issues that plague humanity. The practice of strategizing resistance with the use of education, networking, and community activism helped them to form an ideological base for the 1980s, in which they could validate their identities in Canada as survivors, not victims.

Much has been discussed about the substantial changes in migration patterns during the 1980s, as Canada made another shift in immigration policy which stressed training and entrepreneurial skills. This was not a deterrent for Caribbean peoples, as many of them invariably met the points system as long as it was applied without discrimination, as Wolseley Anderson (1993) suggests. Yet, Caribbean women who migrated during that period because of their employable skills were placed in low-paying jobs (R. Ng and Estable 1987) that diminished their identities as women who had achieved clear goals, either in education or intellectually rewarding employment opportunities. Thus, they were among the migrant women who were racialized because they occupied menial job positions in the labour market.

Racial tensions were not greatly reduced when Canada's multiculturalism legislation and policies were enacted in 1988. This initiative was merely intended for Canada and its "immigrants" to celebrate their differences and possibly to showcase this country's ethnic diversity from time to time as a construct of Canadian society. Therefore, governments at all levels were active in sponsoring conferences, festivals, and related cultural activities on demand so as to distinguish heritages both in a separate and inclusive fashion. While multiculturalism may have demonstrated a national commitment towards providing multicultural groups an equal access and participation in a Canadian way of life, it did not insulate Caribbean women and other migrants from the pain of inequality within interlocking systems of race, class, gender, and sexual orientation (Gabriel 1996; Fleras and Elliott 1992; R. Ng 1988). Even if this system intended to generate a semblance of national unity, it only served to trigger resistance within a fast-developing multiracial society that contained distinct barriers to many forms of real entitlement as immigrant communities. Yet it was in the 1980s that state funding of advocacy groups grew, mainly because of the pressure of immigrant women's communities (Agnew 1996). It was also an era when labour unions championed the cause of the "right to equal pay work of equal value", and the Ontario Liberal government introduced pay equity legislation.

Caribbean women and other immigrant women, often referred to as "visible minority women", were extremely concerned that in spite of a seeming change in political attitude, issues of race did not disappear, but were more apparent. It was puzzling that the provincial government had bypassed the significance of employment equity and did not seem to be swayed by the federal government's passing of the Employment Equity Act in 1986.[21] It was equally problematic that racist ideologies, which previously influenced the interaction between Whites and Blacks, now served not only to prohibit access to housing, health, and jobs, but to foster a vindictive attitude from the protective services.

Finally, the climate of the 1980s generated ambivalent responses from both the State and Canadian feminism in recognition of the race issues that deeply affected the adjustment of Caribbean women to Canada. Many of the Caribbean-Canadian women in my study spoke of the ideological differences between White feminist organizations and their own, in which the focus was placed both on race and gender equity. These are the Caribbean-Canadian women who became intolerant about the lack of recognition of racism as an issue to be articulated to the State through the mainstream feminist movement. They are the Caribbean-Canadian women who moved with a collective ethic of independence to initiate an *alternative women's movement* for migrant women, Black and of colour.

Notes

1   Standard English translation: *We have succeeded, praise God!*
2   Caribbean women were given one year contracts along with landed immigrant status in Canada.
3   According to Wolseley Anderson (1993), the categories can be defined as independent application, nominations by relatives, and sponsored dependents in which would-be migrants earned points in the immigration selection criteria.
4   Until regulations were amended (1955) to delete "Asian", Indo-Caribbean women were denied entry as independents in the Domestic Scheme (Calliste 1989: 133).

5   See Chapter Six: Learning community through social consciousness, page 144.
6   There is a theory by Christine Ho (1991), which proves that networking, locally and internationally, eliminates marginalization and redefines "family" to resist acculturation in the culture of the USA.
7   Bianca's group, apart from island distinction, consists of women and men who were phenotypically different.
8   See Bobb (1959).
9   Dr. Austin Clarke, having received many distinctions over the years, has won two of Canada's prestigious book awards: the W.O. Mitchell Prize in 1999; and the Giller Prize for Canadian Literature in 2002; and the 2003 Commonwealth Book Prize.
10 The Toronto *Telegram*, a now defunct newspaper, presented the case of the Ebo Society in the last of its series examining the changing role of Canadian society. I was quoted as saying, "after a generation a European immigrant is no longer an immigrant. He is a Canadian. His skin is white. A Negro is always a Negro. His skin is black. A Negro cannot become like everyone else. He does not want to. He just wants people to accept him as he is and they will not" (*Telegram*, 16 August 1965).
11 In 2002, as I reflected on writing this book, the name of the Ebo Society centralized Africa and marginalized other identities in the Caribbean, an ideology which I here deconstruct. Yet those who might have claimed other heritages opted for an African identity at the time.
12 I acknowledge the assistance of Jeane Kotick, Administrative Secretary (deceased 2001), an assistance which was given with her passion and commitment to eradicate racism in Canada.
13 For a mention of *Ebo Voice,* see Winks (1971). For coverage of the exhibition, see the *Globe and Mail*, 10 July 1965, and the *Toronto Star* of the same date.
14 Foreign countries, from a Caribbean ideological perspective, are supposed to provide means for readily acquiring personal upliftment, something denied to Caribbean peoples in the region.
15 The New Jewel Movement had its roots in the Caribbean. I was a member in Trinidad and Tobago, and there I engaged in critical thinking which emerged from regular reading and organized discussion. For Caribbean thought at that time, see Harvey (1974).
16 See the study by Head (1975) for an exploration of the incidents of discrimination, which indicated the rising levels of prejudice at that time.
17 Standard research of Canadian news and periodical indexes of the 1970s could provide no listing of articles related to these projects. The names came from the participants in this study, identifying them as participating in community activism during that period.
18 Taken from the brochure *The Black Education Project: An Introduction, a Free Community Service* (n.d.).
19 Lesbian Organization of Toronto.
20 The Canadian near-equivalent of the word "lime" is "to hangout". A favourite pastime in the Caribbean, it takes place at convenient locations from street corners and bars to patios and poolsides. A lime consists of a group of individuals, often

cross-class and more usually male, informally becoming a centre of social criticism through the information shared; the issues debated; as well as the gossip enjoyed (Rennie 1969).

21 The non-separation of two interrelated social issues — pay and employment equity — would make effective the goals of women's equality, as Linda Briskin and Patricia McDermott (1993) argue.

EIGHT

An Alternative Women's Movement in Canada:
One day, one day, congotay[1]

Caribbean-Canadian women, in this book, proved they belong to those ancestors of the Caribbean region who charted a legacy of resistance: Aboriginal, African, Asian, and, least in numbers of all, European.[2] These women belong to a people whose histories are interconnected and whose experiences under the evil forces of imperialism are interrelated, because they have come from the "nigger yard", the "coolie yard", the "bound yard";[3] often they remain "strangers in a hostile landscape".[4] To this new landscape of Canada Caribbean women brought their resilience to sexism within Black communities and to racism within White feminist organizations. The rejection experienced in these two sites of struggle during the eighties precipitated a strongly aggressive thrust by many Caribbean-Canadian women to find space for their voices to explore issues of identity in race, gender, and sexuality. As a consequence, a Caribbean brand of feminism was adopted to examine comprehensively the oppressions that subordinated them and affected not only their rights, but those of their communities as well. Their efforts crystallized in the formation of a women's movement which was an alternative to White and mainstream feminist organizing.

Caribbean feminism vs. Canadian feminism

These Caribbean-Canadian women practiced a Caribbean feminism which, as Rhoda Reddock (1990) argues, reflects their historic struggle in opposition and resistance to a dual system of capitalism and patriarchy. Their fight for liberation has produced a counter ideology to that of women's roles in western society. This ideology includes seeing Caribbean women fundamentally as workers, who seek female emancipation through proficiency in skills to achieve social and economic independence. As well, it includes their sense of humanity in joining Caribbean men in leadership of anti-colonial and labour struggles.

Thus, Caribbean feminism had some major ideological differences with Canadian feminism. Firstly, those who described themselves as feminists at that time in Canada were White, middle-class women who were often well educated. Caribbean-Canadian women who were active in the struggle against racism were cross-class and had not yet, in numbers, achieved the levels of education nor career-based opportunities that White Canadian feminists had, although they were intellectually active. Secondly, Canadian feminists saw "home" as one of the significant sites of oppression. Caribbean-Canadian women were opposed to centralizing home in a negative manner, because their experiences of home meant nurturing and connection with "family" to support their strategies of resistance against issues of race and gender. Thirdly, Canadian feminists opted for a hegemonic approach to identity; that is, they did not attempt to define or recognize diversity and difference among women. Caribbean-Canadian women comprised a group of diverse heritages, though collectively at that time, they identified as Black. There were others who chose a single identity — Indo-Caribbean or Chinese-Caribbean — who were also engaging at disparate sites in the struggle. Fourthly, Canadian feminists failed to see racism as an issue for White women within their primary politics. For Caribbean-Canadian women, their true lives were submerged under a loss of identity occasioned by ongoing discriminatory practices of the state and the public constituted racism.

Therefore, on these four counts, Caribbean-Canadian women "felt silenced and robbed" (Pierson 1993: 207). Experiences of these differing ideologies amounted to condescension, patronage, and defensiveness in the movement.

> **Rowena**: My initial foray into politics here was in feminist politics, the women's movement, in the late seventies and early eighties, which was extremely White. I dropped out because I was not taken seriously. I was tired of women who weren't getting it. And there were no women of colour. Me was tired of dey tekkin me fuh a nice likkle brown girl.[5] (Interview 37, 31 August 1995)

Caribbean-Canadian women, in particular those who worked in domestic service, usually in White homes, could not see the negativity in "home" espoused by White feminists. As domestic service workers, the experience of long separations from their families made their home their haven whenever they got there and the employers' home a site of oppression. As well, these workers' identities were afflicted with White feminists' insensitivity to race issues, because, in the "historical and contemporary treatment of domestic workers from the Caribbean", White women employers always seem to pathologize a Caribbean woman's identity (Stasiulis 1987: 6). There is also an argument that failure to see racism as a burning issue for migrant women, coupled with many White feminists' denial to apprehend its ill effects, might have been due to their inability to recognize how their social power "revictimized" Black women (Pierson 1993: 189). Therefore, for many Caribbean-Canadian women who were socially conscious and active in the movement towards social change, feminism, under White jurisdiction, was another marginalizing process in their settlement in Canada.[6]

Caribbean-Canadian women's experience of everyday racism focuses mainly on incidents in their workplaces, in housing, in school, and in social and health service institutions.[7] These women applied an ethic of independence and created oppositional activities within community organizing to fight against these experiences. They chose sites of involvement such as immigration and refugee issues, social service practices, cultural production, and, eventually, the politics of women-centred issues. Their repeated strategic efforts in response to issues of discrimination and victimization, which formulated sites of pro-action and reaction, I interpret as a development of a social movement in its particularity. I label this process comprehensively the 1980s Alternative Women's Movement in Canada (AWMC). This movement encouraged individual initiatives to anti-racism efforts in the Black community; it also enabled reform of racist biases in institutions to which these women were directly related. Added to that, it fostered collaboration, inclusiveness, and solidarity among migrant women from Africa, Asia, Caribbean, and the Philippines, as well as with women of the First Nations and of African backgrounds. Like the mainstream movement, it was dependent on state recognition for its funding, as well as financial contributions from corporate and community sources.

However, the differences in gender ideologies between Canadian and Caribbean feminism caused the segregation of the AWMC. Caribbean-

Canadian women who were involved in this movement, recognized a different social reality — that of the Caribbean legacy of resistance, which embraced community, including men and children, in the struggle for liberation.[8] Their responsibility for Caribbean men conflicted with radical feminists, who could have forced them to preclude Caribbean male issues around race and gender. These differences in gender ideologies raised some doubts for Caribbean-Canadian women about the rectitude of adapting fully to White thought on gender and leaving Caribbean men out of their concerns.

> **Maya**: I could see the oppression and, yes, the sexism as the source of violence. Yet it never made me want to do away with men in my community. I recognized they are oppressed on the basis of race as well. So, for me, it became a struggle. I had to think much about an argument from lesbians, in particular, that we can't be supportive of men because we are feminists. It is something I never agreed with. (Interview 26, 27 June 1995)

Aita further clarifies how that brand of Caribbean feminism became operable to produce this alternative women's movement.

> **Aita**: I call myself a feminist — I do! — because I believe in the liberation of women. Believe you me, I don't believe in the liberation of women outside the liberation of the family and the community. (Interview 20, 14 June 1995)

৶ Raising the issue of Black in community organizing

Therefore, a social movement that consisted of Caribbean women who chose to strategize resistance at community sites and then to join like-minded migrant women of colour institutionalized that Caribbean legacy of resistance and inclusivity, which had been historically produced. I stress this point as though coalitions of this nature might reflect a political identity of the Caribbean region when the opposite is true; hierarchies of income, class, and colour, spawned through colonialist structures, are often constructed in mythologies of unification, but they certainly can be distinct and separate.

Thinkers and politicians, in their attempts to eradicate colonialism in all its manifestations, more frequently explore and emphasize the devastating effects of slavery on the majority of people, the Africans, rather than close the gaps created by the intruders who dominated the histories of the peoples of the Caribbean. Very little practical work has been done to reduce the conflicts of identity within countries of the Caribbean as a region. But I want to stress, with respect, that the histories of Caribbean peoples *are* interconnected, and there lies embedded a significant Caribbean ancestral legacy of resistance. This is a resistance that collectively freed the region from the worst forms of enslavement and various types of dehumanization. The issue of diversity and racial identity is a topic that has not been directed in a purposeful way to change colonialist structures in Trinidad and Tobago, for example. Thus, Earl Lovelace (2002) remarks:

> Race, far from being a question to side-step, is our rich, if fragile, heritage, to be rescued from colonial definitions and to be engaged with intelligence and compassion. The excesses that we will encounter are an expression of the human search for boundaries that enable us to impose limits on behaviour and to give shape to our civilization.[9] (232)

In other words, he calls for dynamic action to be taken to address the essentialism that marks difference, so as to be rid of the misunderstanding, erasure, and displacement that are cultivated in ethnic relations in the Caribbean region.

In the diaspora, social relations between different heritage groups appear to be sometimes nullified, particular in political settings, where racist stereotyping has magnified a Black identity as aggressive and troublesome. However, in the alternative women's movement, this Black identity subsumed other identities of Caribbean women, particularly Indo-Caribbean women who attempted to become community activists. Their voices were often near silenced because of the ardour with which Caribbean (Black) activists pursued the struggle politically for liberation from race oppression. When asked about their erasure of an Indo-Caribbean identity, they declared that any disconnection was probably due to PanAfricanism. For example, Aita notes elsewhere, "I was clearly decided on my allegiances at the PanAfrican Congress and developed a closed line with Black Africans" (Interview 20, 14, June 1995). This sensitivity for defining Blackness would appear to be relatively new for many women like Aita. It was not an issue of clear definition when we discussed home as a site of learning resistance, in Chapter Six. Black, however, reflected the global political climate change that surfaced to crystallize an identity that is opposed to Whiteness and is prepared to appropriate the suffering experiences due to White supremacy.

When the term Black, as Avtar Brah (1992) reminds us, was used as a political colour, acknowledging broad cultural differences, it aimed at achieving political unity against racism. Yet, it became very controversial when it referred to "the politics of solidarity between African Caribbean and South Asian activists" of the eighties (127). When Indo-Caribbean women seek to embrace a Black identity or to self-ascribe as Black, their acts of self-definition problematizes Blackness as a representation of people descended from Africa. Also, it raises the question of the geography of identities, when phenotypically different identities occupy Africa as a home-space. A few of the subjects in this book voice their concerns.

Kamla: I have to say the Black community does not include people like myself. I consider myself a Caribbean person and a Black person. I may not be Black as it is referred to on this continent, but I am not White. When you reflect on who you are and what you are and where you fit in with this society, people like us are not identified in any form or fashion. (Interview 38, 5 September 1995)[10]

Sumanta: Now I definitely describe myself as an Indo-Caribbean Trinidadian or woman of colour depending on the context I am in and where my organizing is happening in different areas. I am on the Board of Desh Pardesh, and I try to push that identity. I realize there is little political presence around for the Indo-Caribbean identity, and that is very detrimental to our existence. (Interview 40, 19 September 1995)

Haniffa: I remember when Nelson Mandela was released; we of the African National Congress had just left a meeting when we heard it on the radio. We organized a big rally on the Danforth. A lot of artists gathered there, and lots of people came to celebrate. I was so excited and emotional. Then I heard this Caribbean woman say to me, "What are you doing here? This is not your cause". I started crying openly, for here it is, a person whom I considered my sister, my people, rejecting me, telling me I didn't have a cause to be happy. (Interview 4, 2 August 1994)

Because of the complexities of Caribbean history, as we earlier discussed, issues of identity remained framed by the mastery of colonialism in order to craft dissent. This book attempts to move beyond the issues that polarize a Caribbean identity in order to produce knowledge of the ingredients of a collective identity rooted in a legacy that fights against the subordination imposed by White and gendered oppression. The stories of Caribbean-Canadian women, whose identities make up a sample of cross-heritages, tell how the social, political, and celebratory aspects of community in the region and in its diaspora give them a sense of nation. Yet, they speak with a consciousness of ethnic divisions, sometimes along the lines of race/politics — alliances, patriarchal leadership, religion — but more often from a lack of knowledge of the construction of any of the ethnic groups.[11] Some of these community activists who have felt exclusion from the solidarity of Black community organizing may take this position.

> **Marise**: Definitely I think that the groups that organized African or Black in Toronto very much want to work from a Black separatist position, focusing on the connections between Africa and the Caribbean. I understand that and support their work. Yet, there needs to be an understanding that the diaspora is as diverse as the region, and that there are people who belong to other communities with a combination heritage, like me. If the focus remains on Africa, then how the colonialists have constructed identities may be dulled in respect of our understanding of how colonial heritage has affected everybody. (Interview 41, 27 September 1995)

∼ Recognizing the issue of sexuality

Similar to the issues of racial identities, issues of heterosexism also became the source of a struggle for Caribbean-Canadian women in their feminist organizing. Lesbianism was misinterpreted as radical feminism, as Maya pointed out earlier. Outreach efforts to retain the participation of a number of politically active, Black, lesbian women were less effective because there was insufficient emphasis placed on issues outside the range of racism and sexism. Audre Lorde, affirming her ways of connecting and reconnecting, says that, "lesophobia and heterosexism" become stumbling blocks to "sisterhood even among Black women who want to claim the site of most multiplied dispossession" (quoted in Boyce Davies 1994: 18). Abena, who was very active in the alternative women's movement, says this about how difference is treated in the female identity among Caribbean-Canadian peoples:

> **Abena**: You know there has been a tremendous amount of homophobia in our community, which we can't deny. As I identified more and more with the gay community, I could feel people turning away and treating me with disdain more and more. I was seen as an oppositional person in this [Black] community, antagonistic to a male leader. (Interview 29, 11 July 1995)

Issues surrounding ethnicities and those connected to heterosexism occupy a political space that remains, unintentionally, in the background of thought for some Caribbean-Canadian women. Priority is usually given to the effects of victimization from White supremacy and male domination. Thus, in Canada, the activism of Caribbean-Canadian women is drawn to develop a movement against the racism and sexism which demoralize them rather than to the broadening of their vision to embrace a collective vision of Caribbean women's identity.

❧ Focusing on racism in community organizing

Caribbean-Canadian women, however, acted out of their consciences to respond to the racism that produced social injustices on a variety of fronts in Canada. They did this independently of White support. From their independent site they focused on the issues of race and gender that plagued immigrant women's lives. Yet, they could participate with Caribbean men in the struggles against racism as perpetuated in immigration policies and against the oppressions of state institutions that significantly criminalized certain groups of men in the community. Several stories will help our understanding of how these women maintained a connection with entire communities affected by the ugliness of discriminatory practices while remaining commited to the eradication of racism. Their tales of community activism display varying levels of intensity, diversity, and complexity, and disrupt the discourse that centres a woman's role in the privacy of home.

Rebeka: I began to feel that the only way I ever talked to anybody was in a meeting. I never had an ordinary conversation with anyone for a long time. It was moving from one meeting to another. (Interview 43, 11 December 1995)

Annzinga: Yes, I know of a social life for many years only through fundraising gatherings either in community halls or somebody's home, where we could take the children other than dragging them with us to do demonstrations. This was my fulfillment socially as it remained connected to the struggle. (Interview 45, 16 September 1996)

Black community organizing

To confront systemic racism in Canadian society, Caribbean-Canadian women, in a leadership role, helped greatly to mobilize Black and Caribbean communities by forming community organizations which engaged in both practical and advocacy work. The activities of many of these organizations need to be fully explored and addressed through other sources. However, one of these broad-based community organizations, The Black Secretariat, exemplifies the independence of many of the Caribbean-Canadian women who undertook enormous responsibility to keep this organization afloat. Founded in 1986, The Black Secretariat was established as an umbrella organization to unify Black politics and enhance Black identity.[12] Annzinga was one of the co-founders; Olive served as a consultant on the Board of Directors; and Zindzi, who took office as President in the 1990s (along with a few others, not included in this book) financed the many anti-racism efforts of this organization when it became difficult to acquire government funding. In my role as its first Executive Director, with a small but diligent staff, we published the first *Black Directory* in Toronto. The objectives of this publication were to acknowledge the diversity of organizations in the struggle; to provide a resource that enabled users to formalize networking in the Caribbean diaspora; and mainly to unify and identify the collective in advocacy efforts against racism in the province of Ontario.[13] As a result of the survey that produced this directory, The Black Secretariat staged its first conference, "Up the Organization". This conference aimed at meeting the leadership needs for community organizing among the increasing numbers of groups which identified with the impact of racism and marginalization as a combined inhuman issue in society. Later in the nineties, The Black Secretariat, continuing its comprehensive approach, instituted The Black Network as a formal strategy that worked to transform public policy. For example, in the city of Toronto it won the struggle against Avon corporate management to remove billboard advertisements, which portrayed negative images of Black women. Next, the Network, through community mobilizing, was instrumental in having the Scarborough Board of Education adjust its zero tolerance policy, which was constituted in the 1990s. The Board was persuaded to remove the considerable bias contained in its policy towards Black children, particularly boys. This community organization, then, is an example of a creation of space for Caribbean women who were able to display leadership and organizational and advocacy skills.[14]

ᘯ Organizing around immigration issues

Some Caribbean-Canadian women showed similar ability when they moved in separate spaces to display activism which ranged from the confrontational to the reformist. As I mentioned before, oppressions of racism and sexism were integral to immigration/refugee issues and attacked people when they were most vulnerable. Thus, it was not surprising that Caribbean-Canadian women in their use of the ethic of independence became fully involved, sometimes on the basis of their own experiences. A few of these women in my study speak of life around the struggle for justice for migrants to Canada.

> **Vanessa**: I started an organization with a group of people, New Vision Canada. We got agreed that newcomers to Canada might benefit from a better understanding of the Canadian political system. Some help that way would enable them to feel better connected and to take a more active part in the society. (Interview 12, 14 May 1995)

Vanessa's activism appears to have a connection with the issues advocated by a middle-class, educated group whose opportunities for integration are mostly positive and whose marginalization could not be measured equally with a working-class group, as is in the next case.

> **Lucinda**: I was a single mother with four kids, doing well I think, in my job, and living in Metro housing. Mr. H. recommended me to the Children's Aid Society (CAS) as a role model to families coming to the Society. I volunteered with the West Indian Moms and Daughters Support Group set up there, and realized that moms had lots of sons, too, so I initiated the program, West Indian Volunteer Youth Program, and linked young men who had been well adjusted to serve as role models. We did linking and special tutoring. I ran the program from the basement of my home, and got donations of furniture and computer equipment from Humber College, Toronto.
>
> In 1985, I converted this program into an organization, and named it The West Indian Volunteer Community Support Services.[15] My goal was to focus on Caribbean women's issues of migration, the reasons they had to come to Canada, and what happened when they came into this society. I was concerned that the immigration process was instrumental for the situation of Black kids in crisis, like it is today. (Interview 24, 24 June 1995)

Lucinda's story demonstrates that there is a link between independence and community for Caribbean-Canadian women as they commit themselves through the use of agency to rectify the experiences of culturally defined bias. Her initiative to lead these groups indicates her consciousness of cultural racism inherent in the services of mainstream organizations, and her understanding of a Caribbean ideology based on a strict connection to community in order to validate life in human ways. Community, as a desired principle in containing the significance of a Caribbean woman's identity, is also exemplified in Cheryl's story.

> **Cheryl**: You remember there were lots of people in the 1980s coming from Trinidad and Guyana as refugees? Well, I don't know where they got our names or how they knew I was involved

in politics, but, before you knew it, people were calling my house for help day and night. It was always, what to do?, they asked. (Interview 10, 22 August 1994)

In Yelena's story there is an understanding that dominant circumstances can produce interlocking oppressions of race, class, gender, and sexuality. Therefore, in the case of refugee women, she saw that they would require alternative approaches to interact with the mainstream.

Yelena: In my refugee work with women, I try an integrated approach because I can't talk about wife assault in a vacuum. These women have been tortured, raped, and have had children taken from them, so I work in terms of violence from a perspective of race. I make them aware of the system of domination, its intricacies to subjugate, that is, how their skin colour, their language will affect the way they will be treated. (Interview 28, 29 June 1995)

In other words, these contributions to the discourse of Caribbean-Canadian women's activism indicate the efforts that some of these women took to subvert White supremacy and, through their own knowledge of racism, tried to reform some of the ways oppressed people are treated.

❧ Anti-racism organizing in service institutions

There were some Caribbean-Canadian women who brought their acts of subversion into their place of employment. They spoke passionately about their attempts to reform institutional practices in social work agencies, using their professional status to intervene against racist practices. Ariel, who worked assiduously at reform, says:

I had to work hard because of police brutality, the arrogance of racism, the over-representation of our kids placed in foster homes. I believed I did my job to the best of my ability. I am dismayed to hear from my people all those tales of ill treatment, of being put down, of the way they are devalued. (Interview 15, 6 June 1994)

Another social worker, Anne, used her status to develop some controls on the systemic racism in services for children, and acted in resistance this way:

> When I was beginning to see how terrible Black children were being cared for and how they were socially deprived, we formed a Committee for the Welfare and Development of Black Children to monitor and support the system. (Interview 12, 7 June 1995)

Yet another challenged the administration of programs for Black young women, believing that education of service providers would help in the elimination of racism.

> **Yaa**: I worked at a group home, where the majority of teenagers were Black and experiencing the backlash of poorly designed immigration policies which resulted in separated families. They complained that White workers would insult their food, telling them it smells. I clearly documented these complaints, thinking that was a way of exposing White workers' practices. But no! They redesigned the forms, leaving two lines for reporting. I then suggested a workshop, hesitating to call it "anti-racism", and asked for a Caribbean woman as facilitator. They brought in a Jewish woman. In retrospect, I still was able to get the education done. (Interview 10, 29 May 1995)

It is difficult to bring about changes, purely on an individual basis, to racist and negative perceptions that White people in general hold about Black people. Racism is ingrained and indestructible, serving to continuously support an imagined idea, a myth, of White superiority. Therefore, the resilience of Caribbean-Canadian women has to be rooted in a history of resistance that needs to fully revered.

> **Yaa**: I was able to resist some of the racism with the articles I composed with an African focus and published in the newsletter. I celebrated differences with contributions of Black women. I had their pictures on the walls of the shelter during Black History Month. And I made sure they, at least, wrote an anti-racism policy. (Interview 10, 29 May 1995)

Organizing cultural production

But Caribbean-Canadian women's activism also disrupted the ideology of women's role through their initiatives in the site of cultural production. This is a site where, in the 1970s and 1980s, they had little choice but to work with mainstream organizations, often in minor roles as actors. At that time, few themes that related to lived experiences of people from Africa, Asia, or from among Amerindians worldwide were evident in theatres in metropolitan societies like Toronto and Montreal. Establishing an alternative theatre that would reflect, in the main, Africa and the Caribbean seemed like a task of considerable magnitude for female Caribbean migrants. Yet, some of these women believed that to produce a theatre that targeted the needs of Caribbean and Black peoples was a means of challenging the stereotypical ideas of dependency of migrants on the mainstream in constituencies of racial construct. Therefore, the birth of Black Theatre Canada (BTC), in 1972, was a strategy of resistance to the persistent racial construction of plays that favour White themes and were correspondingly dominated by White people. The purpose of this Black theatre was to build a cultural identity specific to the ethos of Black and Caribbean peoples and to provide artistic opportunities and employment for the many who had been marginalized in the Canadian scene.

This theatre, which closed for the lack of funding in 1988, produced some of the most successful projects. It will, most of all, be remembered for its staging of *Caribbean Midsummer Night's Dream* in 1983 (Braithwaite and Benn-Ireland 1993). Lena, who initiated and administered this project largely with her own earnings, says:

When Toronto's Theatre Workshop Productions changed for the season, I was not one of them. I jokingly said, "You know what? I am going to start my own theatre" and laughed. Although the starting of any Black organization is a very political thing, Black Theatre Canada started as a joke. The motivation was cultural; the effect on our lives was political. I had tremendous impetus to do it, and I don't know where it came from. I wanted to express myself: I am Black. I had arrived at a point where I realized that there are things Black people stand for, there are things we express which show our culture and could be done in drama, which was my *raison d'être* for this Theatre. (Interview 27, 28 June 1995)

The other major theatre in the Black community, Theatre in the Rough, was an event that overlapped the existence briefly of Black Theatre Canada. Lauretta, who joined the BTC in 1978, worked as Artistic Director and Executive Director while Lena was on sabbatical leave. Lena's courage inspired her and she developed a theatre that would be more directly connected to the struggle.

> **Lauretta**: When Theatre in the Rough got started, we tended to do anti-apartheid work in 1986. I will never forget our first play, as it seemed to have offended the sensitivity of some people as someone wrote Prime Minister Trudeau to complain we were an anti-White movement. We were a theatre organization, not even funded by Canada Council. Our mission was to serve as a social action theatre: 50% of our work focuses on authenticating Caribbean and African identities, while 50% is how people interact with each other. Our definition of "theatre" is not European, not modern either; we are out of my experience: Moi aussi, j'ai Dominique! That is of the Caribbean: a cultural race of people. (Interview 21, 14 June 1995)

Thus, another theatre originated by Caribbean women continued to the end of the twentieth century with political objectives to eliminate racism through education and information.

Using popular culture as a practice in the movement became an integral part of strategic activity for survival of identity and of reducing alienation from the mainstream. It enhanced the role of these Caribbean-Canadian women who linked culture to social issues in Canadian society. Aretha, a high school teacher, was moved to initiate a youth dance group in Waterloo, Ontario, because of a combination of her love for stage dancing and her concern about Black youth, and the effects of racism on their identities.

> **Aretha**: My yearning to keep dancing and my concern for the welfare of youth of a Caribbean background and other Black

youth was the result of my founding a Saturday morning experience of dance for these young people. We eventually entered multicultural events and through these experiences I became co-founder and cultural chair of the Caribbean Canadian Cultural Association (CCCA) of Kitchener-Waterloo. Not only did we dance at these Saturday programs, but we added an academic and athletic component. Unfortunately, by the early eighties, when kids got older and moved on, adult volunteers dwindled as did the spirit of CCCA. (Interview 34, 29 August 1995)

These stories illustrate the social and political consciousness that was inherent in redefining the identities of these Caribbean-Canadian women. They were treated with Canadian racism, yet they could exhibit strengths for doing what was not expected of them as "women" and, particularly, as "immigrant women" in Canada. The diversity they brought into their activism is a mark of how they were able to reconstruct the legacy of resistance, learned from "home", to do whatever was necessary for liberation from racial dominance. This consciousness was also pervasive in their approaches to strategize liberation from sexual dominance.

❧ Feminist organizing: The Caribbean way
Community activism for many Caribbean-Canadian women appeared to be a strategy to reform racist practices in Canada. It may be seen as part of the larger revolutionary Black movement that percolated throughout North America, Europe, and the Caribbean. There was indeed no militancy attached, but there was a consistent and dedicated approach. These women acted as their consciences dictated to reduce levels of degradation and, at the same time, to explore their own self-definition. Gradually, over the period of the eighties, some Caribbean-Canadian women politicized women-centred issues and boosted the process of an alternative women's movement in Canada. The picture embraced the involvement of migrant women of colour and First Nations women in a movement to give recognition to their feminist perspectives, leadership, and organizing skills for the first time in Canada.

Emerging from an initiative taken by the Ontario government in 1983, both the Ontario Coalition of Visible Minority Women (OCVMW) and the National Congress of Black Women of Canada

(NCBWC)were founded. These organizations enabled women of colour to direct their focus on policies of race relations and multiculturalism as these had such an impact on their lives, mainly as migrant women. OCVMW and NCBWC proved to be sites from which very many women could explore the historic factors of colonialism that produced them as migrants to a neo-colonial country. These organizations facilitated, on the one hand, a consolidation of identities of Caribbean and Black women, and, on the other hand, engendered collaborative efforts between this group and the wider circle of female migrants, as well as First Nations women. For example, these organizations developed, collectively, strategies as "watchdogs" of their recommendations to governments and thus were able to monitor the implementation of policies (Agnew 1996; Gabriel 1996).

The National Congress of Black Women of Canada (NCBWC) was preceded by the Canadian Negro Women's Club, founded in 1951.[16] Its continuity, however, is related to the agency that some Caribbean-Canadian women used to radicalize its aims so as to broaden its political scope and to incorporate the diversity of women coping with interlocking oppressions of race, class, and gender. Nikki, who was one of the "movers" in this thrust for Black and Caribbean women's liberation, tells the story:

> You see, there was a history dating back to the National Black Coalition, which was a male-dominated organization. Kay Livingstone,[17] tired of the sexism, organized a conference in 1973. She invited Black women from across Canada and Detroit as well. It caught fire, and meetings continued to be held yearly, for example, in Montreal, Halifax, and so on. In 1976, when I got deeply involved, we passed a resolution to draft an idea for a national organization for Black women, since ad hoc meetings never get anywhere. Hence, it came to Windsor in 1977.
>
> I was a member of the Steering Committee, and we drew up a Constitution, developed communication strategies, and so on. Information was mailed to 200 (Black) women across this country, Canada. By 1979, when a report was due, the appointed coordinator disappeared. I therefore called a meeting which was held in Winnipeg in 1980. My work was applauded, and people suggested I remain in a key role; thus, I became the first President of the National Congress of Black Women in Canada. (Interview 22, 17 June 1995)

This reformation of a Black and Caribbean women's organization at a national level in Canada was a political statement to disrupt the "immigrant woman" identity and to disperse patriarchal images of these women's dependence on men or Whites. NCBWC continued to grow as a political organization at several levels: municipal, provincial, and national. In the nineties, there were 26 chapters. These were actively engaged in various areas that affected specific groups in their communities, such as youth and seniors, as well as maintaining their goals of education for Black women's empowerment. While the National Congress of Black Women of Canada was a major component of the alternative women's movement identified with Black nationalism, some of its members had allegiances with the Ontario Coalition of Visible Minority Women.

> **Aita**: In 1983, evidence was very clear for those Caribbean women engaged with the Human Rights Commission [that] minority women were being pushed around and were in need of a collective voice. I was then an employee of the Ontario Women's Directorate (OWD), and I was made Coordinator of a committee to advance some initiatives around mobilizing visible minority women. My responsibility was for outreach, which I did, across the province, to migrant women and including First Nations women. I held meetings with groups of Chinese, Korean, African, Black Francophone, Philippino, and other diversity of women wherever I located them, Thunder Bay, Kitchener, and so on. Yet, there were few Canadian women of African descent present. (Interview 20, 14 June 1995)

A fully inclusive mobilization of women of colour at a provincial level by a Caribbean-Canadian (Black) woman was a formidable task, given the fear Whites hold that Black political power is confrontational. Thus Aita's function on the Committee, which included White "feminists", was often contested. However, her persistence to challenge the system was commendable.

> **Aita**: These OWD meetings eventually culminated in a conference called "The Visible Minority Women: Racism, Sexism and Work". Well, it was a ground swell — while we expected 100–200 women, 500 women turned up. We had workshops from which

there was a collective agreement to form our own organization as we are from different backgrounds and we are known as "visible minority women". That became the starting point of the Coalition of Visible Minority Women. (Interview 20, 14 June 1995)

This provincially funded conference produced impressive results, such as the creation of a momentum for racially identified women to affirm solidarity through formations of ethnicized community groups, like the First Nations women who had been consolidated previously. For Black (Caribbean) women, the need was the same.[18] Yet, there were other concerns. Annzinger observed that even though disparate groups might have deepened the political movement, enabling these women from diverse backgrounds to rationalize their differences, there was also a need for a site upon which they could heal the marginality that racism produces. She says:

It bothered me that the issues raised at the Conference might have been dealt with by women in their specific community groups before this event. Another of my concerns was the future of this success: a report would be published and then what? We needed to have follow-up by some kind of body to pursue action around recommendations. I then began talking to women about continuity, and their responses made me secure a separate room, and I invited them to attend a caucus meeting. Many of the representatives from the Black and visible minority groups came, and there the Ontario Coalition of Visibility Women was solidified.[19] (Interview 45, 1 October 1996)

Thus, with the formation of this umbrella organization, Canadian migrant women of the 1980s, either racialized or homogenized as Black or visible minority, made some gains towards their own liberation. Black (Caribbean) women in particular recalled the existence of a Black women's national organization in Canada, the NCBW, and agreed to constitute a Toronto chapter among those present. Maya, a participant who was searching for a space to give privilege to her potentials, says:

The formation of the Congress of Black Women, Toronto Chapter, was an amazing result of the 1983 Conference as it moved Black consciousness to a feminist consciousness based on our own experiences with men in organizations and men in our lives. Suddenly that sense of freedom, as opposed to the kind of forces that I felt closing in on me, helped me to see that it was not only racism but sexism as well. (Interview 26, 27 June 1995)

These Caribbean-Canadian women spoke of feeling better prepared to materialize their ideals of leadership in contexts in which existed the possibility that their worth as human beings could be devalued and reduced. They continued to enforce rules of networking as a principal strategy in the struggle to eliminate forces of racism.

> **Bianca**: We met and did a lot of work at Annzinga's kitchen table. We were the group that decided the focus of that Chapter. We emphasized we needed to deal with real issues, as opposed to being a social club, right? We did the groundwork for a Constitution. We also did the same for the Coalition since the objectives were the same: grass roots organizing. These organizations were about raising issues around jobs, employment, and housing. (Interview 2, 18 August 1994)

❧ Caribbean feminism in Canada

Caribbean-Canadian women remained faithful to defining themselves through both the ethic of independence and the Caribbean legacy of resistance. That is, they acted with preparedness to blur the lines between their private and public lives. Their lifestyles became a convergence of community and broad-based politics and non-traditional family living.

> **Bianca**: I had a support system: my mother, my brother, and my uncle. If I wanted to do more, I could have, because I wanted to be there for my children, though they have a different view, that is, I was always going to meetings and dragging them along as well. (Interview 2, 18 August 1994)

This *alternative women's movement* was transforming gender ideologies through family values in order to deviate from hegemonic standards that might influence political norms. These Caribbean-Canadian women community activists, while experiencing the conflict in the system dominated by patriarchal values, maintained a commitment to be agents of resistance strategies against race. In employing agency at the micro level, they made their contribution to revolutionary change which Blacks worldwide sought in general. These women indicated that they had also benefited from intellectual development which would create alternate lifestyles.

> **Aita**: Maya and I had engaged in some profound political work at the intellectual level, resulting in our being honest and straightforward. Therefore, we devised communal living that included her spouse and our two sons. We engaged in sharing our money and so on. But best of all, our home was an open space for many women to come and share issues. Some of the time it was abuse, and they wanted, temporarily, shelter in our home. (Interview 20, 14 June 1995)

This example of a private/public milieu for politicizing serious issues for survival emphasizes a Caribbean female identity which bears marks of agency, independence, and resistance in the Caribbean (Black) ideology.

The voices of Caribbean-Canadian women were heard regularly within their specific communities in the struggle against racism and sexism that encompasses the disparate contestations that men and children experience. An example of fairly frequent encounters with authorities can be found in Aita's words to the then Ontario Minister of Citizenship and Minister Responsible for Women's Issues. She says:

> In the course of advancing the status of culturally and racially diverse populations of Ontario, as well as in the course of advancing the status of women, immigrant and visible minority women should not be left behind, neglected or ignored. We are not asking for special treatment. Within the struggle for equality, equality for one group is not the same as for another, simply because we are not all at the same starting line. (Quoted in Gabriel 1996: 189)

Aita's words demonstrate that these Caribbean-Canadian women were engaged in radicalizing their approaches and initiatives to race and gender discrimination in Ontario. Their style of community organizing had serious implications for public confrontations and demonstrations primarily against the nation's racist practices. Added to that, the alliance between the Congress of Black Women, Toronto Chapter, and the Ontario Coalition of Visible Minority Women served as a powerful space from which Caribbean-Canadian women joined with other racial minority women to vigorously pursue race and gender equality. These groups constituted themselves as strategists to formulate plans and programs that might prove useful to eradicate a system of unequal opportunities for racial minorities in Canada.

> **Aita**: Employment equity, though now talked a lot about, was a leading matter on the agenda of the Coalition and the Congress. We, of these organizations, led this movement, nobody else. We wrote briefs on domestic workers' situation, we wrote on every issue around work you can think about. (Interview 20, 14 June 1995)

Therefore, this alternative women's movement continued to bring representatives from every constituency of the Coalition (Koreans, Sikhs, Chinese, First Nations, and others) to interface with municipal and provincial authorities. One example of the Coalition's advocacy program is its advice to the City of Toronto to institute regulations in regional centres that would respect women's differences (newcomers) based on age, physical ability, as well as cultural and religious practices. For example, the Coalition asked for more appropriate accommodation to ensure women's privacy and for a waiver on fees for use of these facilities to meet the needs of women in adjustment to the Canadian environment. The work of this organization was recognized and applauded by others in the crusade for rights against racism and sexism as being unique in making people aware of difference among a diverse number of visible minority women in the city of Toronto (Das Gupta 1986).

In 1996, the Ontario Coalition of Visible Minority Women was a vibrant organization that was steadfast in continuing the strategies of resistance which the founding members had established. Thus, Naomi, the Executive Director at that time, says:

> Among our programs are the advocacy ventures, the language
> instruction, the occupation instructional for health care workers,
> and the ESL program. We also have many ongoing projects such
> as the wife assault/sexual assault education and the AIDS education
> for frontline health care providers. We maintain our mission to
> keep in touch with grassroots problems. (Interview 43, 26 March
> 1996)

In addition, the alliance between the Coalition and the Congress
(Toronto Chapter) continued to exhibit the strengths of an ethnically
mixed leadership, which was exemplified when both organizations
undertook an initiative to approach the Ontario government for public
funding so as to conduct a rather ambitious project (co-operatives) which
seemed to be appropriated by White organizations.

> **Annzinga**: My experience in organizing tenants to form an
> association in a downtown apartment building helped my interest
> to be sustained in low-cost housing. So I checked and found
> people in the progressive left, that is, the White and predominantly
> middle-class, were becoming the beneficiaries of all the co-op
> housing being built in this city [Toronto]. From my perspective,
> the alternate housing project instituted by the government [Ontario]
> wasn't benefiting the poor tenants and minorities. Therefore, I
> started the process with the Congress, putting through applications
> and the works. But after some negative experiences applying
> singly, we did a joint venture: the Congress of Black Women
> (Toronto Chapter) and the Ontario Coalition of Visible Minority
> Women. This was successful.[20] (Interview 45, 16 September 1996)

Expansion of political activities developed at varying degrees of
magnitude in other provinces in Canada, Quebec, Manitoba, and so on,
indicating that the Caribbean woman-driven role of community activism
carried with it not only an ethic of independence, but an ethic of caring
as well.[21] In Kitchener-Waterloo, Aretha, as she earlier said, cultivated her
dance troupe. She tells us about her transformation into political activism
in her community:

It became evident that having "tea" was not enough. We began to examine issues that surfaced in our area: numerous discriminatory practices and inequities, like harassment, family violence, workplace problems. These and more we saw as affecting people, but more clearly, Black and immigrant women. When some of these women managed the Canadian language, their profiles increased, but with Black women, they remained "invisible". I contacted the Toronto Chapter, attended their meetings, and so on. Then in 1988, the Kitchener-Waterloo Chapter was born, with me as President, and a membership of 12. (Interview 34, 29 August 1995)

The dawning of a Caribbean woman's identity

&

Feminist organizing for Caribbean-Canadian women brought about extensive gains to the Black and Caribbean communities. Caribbean-Canadian women, consistently recognized as "Black" and "immigrant women", broke ground in the institutions of mainstream society in these ways. First, at the institutional level, I refer to advocacy work carried out mainly by the Congress of Black Women (Toronto Chapter) and the Ontario Coalition of Visible Minority Women in the city of Toronto, which enabled the transformation of Ontario government policies that had previously excluded the needs of Black women and women of colour. These policies began to be promulgated within the framework of a Black identity which had been erased in the homogenized identity of "woman" that prioritized White women. Examples of changes could be seen in the provision of services to women, which were changed to recognize "visible minority women" as a category for ethno-specific services. As a result, recognition had to be given to the needs of specific cases in Black and "visible minority" communities with an emphasis on cultural differences. Also, at the level of organizational changes, Black women could be seen spearheading positions of advocacy and, in particular, training. Municipal and provincial authorities recognized executives of the Congress of Black Women Chapters as bodies working towards social change in Canada. Thus, these women were recognized as consultants by mainstream institutions, particularly the police and the education system in Ontario and Quebec.

At the individual level, many of these Caribbean-Canadian women acquired positions as directors, particularly of school boards, and some held positions as senior administrative heads in the education system. Of women in my study, Olive was appointed Director of the Ontario Anti-Racism Secretariat; Annzinger served as co-Chair of the Ontario Criminal Justice Commission; Aita and Maya who both began community activism while holding clerical positions, moved into more significant roles — Aita as a Policy Analyst at the City of Toronto and Maya as a Research Consultant on racial minority issues with the Ontario government; Aretha served on the Board of Directors of Wilfred Laurier University. These are a few examples which present the outcomes of the activism of Caribbean-Canadian women involved in producing the alternative women's movement.

The alternative women's movement in the 1980s and the 1990s of the twentieth century is a significant proof of the collective building of an identity. This movement was comprised of dedicated Caribbean-Canadian women who, as we see in this study, showed a commitment to egalitarian democracy. It provided support for issues which were not relegated to the sphere of women in the gender category, but which directly affected these activists who understood and were committed to community as mothers, sisters, wives, partners, and so on. The *alternative women's movement* in Canada helped define the Caribbean woman's identity; that is, it was a space where Caribbean-Canadian women made a contribution to *home* in Canada through collective resistance to domination.

Notes

1 Standard English translation: *Some day it is obliged to happen.*

2 Refer to Chapter Three of this book.

3 Meaning: Estate tenement house or logies.

4 I borrow meanings from Martin Carter's (1969) recognition of dehumanization in slavery, Walter Rodney's (1981) references to disparate locations of working people of Guyana, and Meiling Jin's (1990) notion of marginality among indentured workers to emphasize the depth of oppression among the diversity of Caribbean peoples.

5 Standard English translation: *I was tired of the assumption that I was a naïve and good girl that would not oppose any ideas.*

6 Black Canadian women, born in North America, had developed, before this period, different sites of organizing. For example, in 1951, the Canadian Negro Women's Club

was founded in Toronto. The purpose was to raise consciousness and to bring public awareness to the merits of Black life in Canada. In order to exert influence at a national level, many of its members were represented in organizations like the Young Women's Christian Association, the Medical Association of Canada, and the National Council of Churches.

7   "Everyday racism", as theorized by Philomena Essed (1991), is a body of prevalent "systematic, recurrent and familiar practices", which distinguishes it from racism at the macro level — the political charting of lack of access to resources (3–4). Experiences of everyday racism are located in the stories that people relate about life in their social contexts.

8   The film production of *Children Are Not the Problem* was among the social action objectives of the Congress of Black Women (Toronto Chapter) in 1988, as well as advocacy work with the Black Action Defense Committee, a male-dominated organization against police racial profiling and targeting of Black men in the Toronto community.

9   Dr Earl Lovelace, author, remains resident in the Caribbean for long periods of time and has published many novels about the struggle for identity to obscure ethnicity. He received an honorary Doctor of Letters from the University of the West Indies in 2002.

10 Kamla has served at times as an executive member of the Caribbean Cultural Committee, a male-dominated cultural organization in the Toronto community since 1967.

11 I acknowledge Professor Sherene Razack's contribution to this argument about mutual exclusion between the majority groups: African and Indian.

12 To the best of my knowledge, the founders of this organization also included Black women and men who were born in Canada, together with Caribbeans.

13 By 1990, *The Black Directory* was in its fourth edition. It listed 162 community organizations; each entry provided vital information about programs, areas served, population, contact person, and telephone number. The *Directory* also included sections on professions and businesses, media, and churches.

14 The Black Secretariat, up to end of the twentieth century, as much as I could ascertain from one of its volunteers, remained an organization identified more with information giving and less with advocacy work.

15 This organization now has townhouse facilities in a metropolitan housing project in Etobicoke, from which location it conducts advocacy programs, an information and referral service, and a wide range of support services to Caribbean youth and other disadvantaged families.

16 This fact is documented briefly in *Embers*, February/March 1991, which discusses the history of the Congress of Black Women in Canada after ten years of survival.

17 Kay Livingstone was among the African-Canadian women activists who initiated community organizing against racism in Canada.

18 The Conference report categorizes the identity of the Conference Advisory Committee as Black. Of the 14-member team, four are from the Caribbean.

19 The National Organization of Immigrant and Visible Minority Women of Canada evolved from a growing awareness that the ills of racism and sexism must be articulated

at a national level. See Hernandez (1987: 17–18).

20   Barsa Kelley Cooperative Housing, a 134-unit cooperative, targeted to accommodate racial minority people, is situated on Lakeshore Boulevard West, Toronto, and was completed in 1999. This housing complex is named after Barsa Kelley, who was a very ardent activist in the formation of the Coalition and who was killed in the Air India crash in 1982.

21   Several chapters of the National Congress of Black Women of Canada were formed in these areas to enter the struggle against racism and sexism. Stories of their activities have not been documented and are lost to this book.

NINE

I Know Who I Am:
A Caribbean Woman in Canada:
Ay, Ay, is know, ah know, we![1]

The interconnected histories and the interrelated experiences of Caribbean women were created through shared and mixed experiences of colonialism. Although adversity was meted out differently in varying contexts of race, colour, and class in these histories, Caribbean-Canadian women have an understanding of survival that produces a culture of resistance. Nevertheless, in creating a collective identity, my arguments do not intend to obscure or minimize the brutality that brought untold damages to the psychical identities of several generations of African people in the Caribbean. Rather, my reasoning purports to show how individual identities, in proximity under colonial domination, bear certain resemblances and similarities. My work acknowledges the centrality of an African identity in the complex diversity of the Caribbean, because it has been, and remains, an empowering and continuing force in the continuum of Caribbean culture. My work brings into focus, however, the totality of experiences of colonialism that has produced collective resistance and, hence, a collective identity. In particular, the voices in this book, representing people of different descent, establish that there is collective resistance in disparate activism in sites of oppression in Canada. Their stories also show how these Caribbean-Canadian women employ an ethic of independence that redefines the representation of an "immigrant woman" identity. Therefore, collectively, they have a notion that *home* taught them resistance, and hence they were able to transport that learning to Canada where they chose to make another home.

We are able to reconceptualize subjectivity in demonstrating how the historical processes of genocide, servitude, slavery, indentureship, and colonialism have influenced the educational responses that subordinated groups make to domination. Mapping histories to learn about interconnections is justifiable in approaching identity through the lens of diversity in the Caribbean. It removes some of the weaknesses found in homogenizing identity and in assessing these women only by external characteristics, which become a means of objectifying them. The historical continuum serves as the foundation for return to and examination of the many components that constitute and reconstitute our subjectivities. It is in this uninterrupted flow of activities to define one's image that subjectivities are formed. Of these, we have discussed those Caribbean-Canadian women who grasp the power to act aggressively within patriarchal and imperialist systems, because they know how to negotiate within limits of the discourses which construct them. Discourses, as postmodern theory has instructed us, constitute individuals, but, as well, the individual may constitute themselves. According to Cornel West (1992b), "agency, capacity and ability" embody significance that "accentuates" the humanity of the oppressed and encourages the idea that we, as individuals, are active in "making and remaking ourselves" (29).

Thus, in this book, subjects demonstrate that the oppressed may or may not use a politicized identity and that the colonizer's identity can be rejected, re-examined, redefined, or reworked. But oppressions of subordination remain a strong reason for changing that identity from being static, using resistance as the dynamic instrument for any changes. (Just imagine, a Caribbean-Canadian [Black] woman [Yaa] in her first job, at the entry level in one of Canada's largest banks, engages in activities to unionize a group of tellers, all of whom are White women, against continued labour exploitation.) Our stories, as Caribbean-Canadian women, demonstrate the struggle each of us experienced in order to displace dominant ideologies which construct migrant women, among oppressed people, as unworthy of citizenship in Canada. Conscious of the iniquities of racism and sexism, we collectively were able to take that course of action to transform different sites of contestation by engaging in centring the self intellectually to disrupt the process of victimization.

A Caribbean woman's identity emerges from the many individual acts in which these women engaged to affirm their strengths and revisit their social histories, thereby forming a collective resistance. Resistance, therefore, is reconceptualized to include multiple and concrete social and cultural actions that systematically address issues of everyday racism and institutional racism. In turn, these actions influence change in public policies and practices in many areas, including housing, education, corporations, and social services, as well as in the cultural sphere. These experiences serve to transform a Black woman's identity. Moreover, these Caribbean-Canadian women's acts of resistance have transformed the images of "visible minority" women in the widest sense. They have played a central role in establishing spaces that change the image of the identity of migrant women from various parts of the world from one of passivity to one of assertiveness. They have been able to demonstrate that they can contest public policies and practices that are discriminatory to racialized women and other oppressed groups alike, at all levels of government — in health and education institutions, social service agencies, and so on.

This study of experiences of Caribbean-Canadian women in Canada, and how they survive enables us to recognize the uniqueness of home as an educative institution. This group of women remembers home and reimagines it, in various ways, as a site where adults resisted in order to survive. In spite of our understanding of home as a site of contestation and contradictions for people in general, it predominates in the imaginations of these Caribbean women as a site of learning. While resistance activities here in Canada have been diverse, they were all inspired through learning at home. It is memory of home that taught these women to meet multiple challenges of life. This learning was re-enacted in different approaches to community activism during a time when revolutionary ideas and actions were prevalent among the Black oppressed groups who sought to eradicate racism and colonialism.

Throughout this book, I emphasize the point that learning to survive is connected to histories of oppressions and to the ways in which communities, subordinated and exploited by hegemonic powers, are sustained. Thus, the study enables us to understand that the identities of these Caribbean-Canadian women have been constructed to take up a legacy of learning which has enabled them to produce acts of anti-subordination towards systems of exploitation and oppression. I repeat, their histories are interconnected. Therefore, we can not only reflect on how and where we have learned to survive, but we can also recognize the many components which centralize the educational setting of home for many Caribbean peoples.

Survival for these women has been due primarily to the use of strategies of resistance, mainly manifested in the areas of education, networking, and community activism. In these areas, an *ethic of independence* was employed. Independence, I argue and the study shows, contains a moral value that enhances strengths of self-esteem, assertiveness, and self-reliance, which are not to be construed as negative forms of liberal behaviour. The courage to use agency that produces independence, in order to engage continuously in forms of resistance, sometimes comes from knowing the social history of one's background. To be an agent working against subordination also requires a critical analysis of one's ongoing experiences. This is the way I interpret Tan Georgie's instruction to me when she admitted to her method of weekly checking the list of things she had done and ticking off those that "got her troo",[2] eliminating those that did not help. In other words, we look to experience for direction; yet, we must be mindful that "experience" is defined as being socially produced. We are required to investigate how history has positioned us to come to know ourselves (Bannerji 1991; Scott 1992).

I argue that an individual, a Caribbean-Canadian woman in particular, having reached that point in self-definition, perseveres with a particular kind of courage to sustain that sense of who she wants to be, what beliefs she holds around social justice, and what reserves she can foster and use to counter vulnerability. It is in this role of self-analyst that a woman can understand her needs and thus gain a sense of control, which is the opposite of *powerlessness or victimhood*. The centring of the self so that she can organize politically, in groups or individually, to resist dominant ideologies contributes to social change,[3] as these Caribbean-Canadian women have done. Their acts of resistance do not exclude the fact that no one can be free from conditioning. As Frantz Fanon (1967) in his *Black Skins, White Masks*, points out to us, it would not be uncommon for the colonized to internalize some of the values of the colonizer. However, a Caribbean woman needs to understand and to know that she, as an individual, is connected to a community, from which she has every right to create a specific site within which she can use an ethic of independence to activate a response to various oppressions. The use of this ethic, while it is not subsumed by other values, such as nurturing, is a means of preserving self-dignity. Also, independence becomes an obvious tactic for a Caribbean woman to use when she becomes sensitive to the predicament that forms of domination are controlling or abusing either her private life or the public life of her community.

A model of defining "identity" to improve critical pedagogy

If we centralize the ethic of independence to examine Caribbean women's relations with the world, then we have to tap into their history, where we find that these women have multiple identities. *They do not comprise a one-dimensional identity.* Our consciousness of both multiple identities and differences enables us to break down the stereotypes configured around race, class, gender, and sexuality. Identity — viewed in the binaries of Black/White; women/men; African/Indian — is problematized, because the subjects of this study, excluded from the centres of cultural and political power, formed their own subjectivities in the margins of that power in order to survive. They construct subjectivities which have "connecting threads" (Brah 1998) in strategies of education, networking, and community activism. That is, their ways of surviving reflect their own creativity, out of diverse realities, to produce what they consider best for removing societal pressures which would victimize them as well as their communities. Many of them exercised self-reliance when they moved beyond boundaries established for women in the patriarchal sense. Thus, identity has to be understood in relation to community, and it is rooted in it. "I see myself not as an individual. I don't see myself as the 'I', 'Me', 'Yaa': I see myself as much connected to a community" (Interview 10, 15 June 1995). In the face of racist attacks and practices, we define this community as beyond biological ties and friends to include many groups of people who represent a trope — Black. Education, in broad terms, was the means, and networking was the base of involvement. These precipitated community activism in major cities of Canada, including Montreal, Toronto, and Kitchener-Waterloo.

Therefore, this study provides ideas about improving critical pedagogy in education. A Caribbean woman's identity in Canada can be described as a *ramajay* (to use a Trinidad word), which means that it embodies an eclectic combination of improvizations, free-spiritedness, and profundity, all of which resist homogeneity. As historical products of genocide, servitude, slavery, indentureship, and colonialism, a Caribbean woman can use her agency to redefine her identity in multiple ways. They are subjects neither to be romanticized nor demonized. It is her political history that has enabled her to develop responses, reactions, and inventions to resist injustices and domination, and, at times, these actions cause them to be misunderstood as "dysfunctional", "aggressive", and so on.

This book is intended to bring a new understanding of a Caribbean woman's identity, particular as she resides in Canada or in the diaspora. It is an understanding that explains how many Caribbean women act as agents, "rebels and spitfires", in community organizing to resist the adversities of domination that emerge in situations of categories: race, class, gender, or sexuality. Caribbean women in Canada are among many other women of colonized and oppressed peoples who help us not only to imagine there can be a better world, but who, in many respects, provide one for us.

Notes

1   Standard English translation: *Of course, I do know who I am.*
2   Standard English translation: *Succeeded.* Yet its meaning implies the difficulties of the struggle.
3   George Dei (1994) forms a similar conclusion in his study of the activities of Ghanaian women in agriculture. He argues that these women's application of "little used subsistence strategies" in agriculture is a response to severe economic recession in Ghana, and is significant to social change.

References

Abu-Laban, Yasmeen, and Daiva Staisulis. (1992). Ethnic pluralism under siege: Popular and partisan opposition to multiculturalism. *Canadian Public Policy* xvii(4): 365–86.

Adamson, Nancy, Linda Briskin, and Margaret McPhail. (1988). *Feminist organizing for change: The contemporary women's movement in Canada.* Toronto: Oxford University Press.

Adeleman, Jeanne, and Gloria Equidanos. (Eds.). (1995). *Racism in the lives of women: Testimony, theory and guides to antiracist practices.* New York, London: Harrington Park Press.

Afroz, Sultana. (1995). The unsung slaves: Islam in the plantation Jamaica. *Caribbean Quarterly* 41(3/4): 30–44.

Agnew, Vijay. (1996). *Resisting discrimination: Women from Asia, Africa and the Caribbean and the women's movement in Canada.* Toronto: University of Toronto Press.

Allahar, Anton. (1993). Unity and diversity in Caribbean ethnicity and culture. *Canadian Ethnic Studies* 35(1): 71–83.

Anderson, Benedict. (1991). *Imagined communities.* London, New York: Verso.

Anderson, Margaret, and Patricia Hill Collins. (Eds.). (1992). *Race, class, and gender ideology.* 2nd ed. Belmont, California: Wadsworth.

Anderson, Patricia. (1986). Conclusion: Women in the Caribbean. *Social and Economic Studies* 35(2): 291–324.

Anderson, Wolseley W. (1993). *Canadian immigrants: A socio-demographic profile.* Toronto: Canadian Scholars' Press.

Aptheker, Bettina. (1989). *Tapestries of life: Women's work, women's consciousness, and the meaning of daily experience.* Amherst, MA: University of Massachusetts Press.

Atteck, Helen, and Philip Atteck. (2000). *Stress of weather: A collection of original source documents relating to a voyage from China to Trinidad, West Indies in 1862* (in conjunction with a family chronicle). St. Catharine's, ON: Wanata Enterprises.

Badillo, Jalil Sned. (1995). The island Caribs: New approaches to the question of ethnicity in the early colonial Caribbean. In Neil L. Whitehead (Ed.), *Wolves from the Sea* (61–89). Leiden: KITLV Press.

Bakan, Abigail, and Daiva. Stasiulis. (1997). *Not one of the family: Foreign domestic workers in Canada.* Toronto: University of Toronto Press.

Balutansky, Kathleen M., and Marie-Agnes Sourieau. (Eds.). (1998). *Caribbean creolization: Reflections on the cultural dynamics of language, literature, and identity.* Barbados, Jamaica, Trinidad and Tobago: The Press of the University of the West Indies.

Bannerji, Himani. (1991). But who speaks for us? In Himani Bannerji et al. (Eds.), *Unsettling relations: The university as a site of feminist struggles* (67–107). Toronto: Women's Press.

Barriteau, Eudine. (1995). Theorizing and development policy and practice in the Anglophone Caribbean: The Barbados case. In Marianne H. Marchand and Jane L. Parpart (Eds.), *Feminism/postmodern development* (142–58). London and New York: Routledge.Barrow, Christine. (1986). Finding the support: A study of strategies of survival. *Social and Economic Studies* 35(2): 131–72.

Barrow, Christine. (1988). Anthropology, the family and women in the Caribbean. In Patricia Mohammed and Catherine Shepherd (Eds.), *Gender in Caribbean development* (156–167). Mona, Jamaica: Women and Development Studies Project, University of the West Indies.

_____. (1996). *Family in the Caribbean: Themes and perspectives*. Kingston, Jamaica: Ian Randle.

_____. (Ed). (1998). *Caribbean portraits: Essays on gender ideologies and identities*. Kingston, Jamaica: Ian Randle and the Centre for Gender and Development Studies.

Baukje, Miedema, and Nancy Nason-Clark. (1989). Second-class status: An analysis of the lived experiences of immigrant women in Fredericton. *Canadian Ethnic Studies* 21(2): 63–73.

Beckles, Hilary McD. (1987). *Black rebellion in Barbados: The struggle against slavery*. Bridgetown, Barbados: Carib Research and Publications Ltd.

_____. (1988). *Afro-Caribbean women in resistance*. London: Karnak House.

_____. (1989a). *Natural rebels: A social history of enslaved Black women in Barbados*. London: Rutgers/Zed Books.

_____. (1989b). *Whites servitude and Black slavery in Barbados, 1627–1715*. Knoxville, TN: University of Tennessee Press.

_____. (1992). Kalinago (Carib) resistance to European colonisation of the Caribbean. *Caribbean Quarterly* 38(2/3): 1–14; 123–24.

_____. (1999). *Centering woman: gender discourses in Caribbean slave society*. Kingston, Jamaica: Ian Randle Publishers.

Belgrave, Valerie. (n.d.). *Ti Marie*. London: Heinemann.

Berg, Bruce L. (1998). *Qualitative research methods for the social sciences*. 3rd ed. Toronto: Allyn and Bacon.

Besson, Jean. (1995). Religion as resistance in Jamaican peasant life: The Baptist Church, Revival Worldview and the Rastafari movement. In Barry Chevannes (Ed.), *Rastafari and other African-Caribbean worldviews* (43–76). Basingstroke, Hampshire: Macmillian; The Hague: Institute of Social Studies.

Best, Lloyd. (1985). West Indian society: 150 years after abolition. In Jack Hayward (Ed.), *Out of slavery: Abolition and after* (132–58). London: Frank Cass.

Birbalsingh, Frank. (Ed.). (2000). *Jahaji: an Anthology of Indo-Caribbean fiction*. Toronto: TSAR.

Bobb, Yvonne, with Jeannine Locke. (1959, September). Are Canadians really tolerant? *Chatelaine* 34.

Bolland, Nigel O. (1992). Creolization and Creole societies: A cultural nationalist view of Caribbean social history. In Alistair Hennessey (Ed.), *Intellectuals in the twentieth-century Caribbean* (50–79). London and Basingstoke: Macmillan Caribbean.

Boyce Davies, Carole. (1994). *Black women, writing and identity: Migrations of the subject*. London and New York: Routledge.

Boyd, Monica. (1975). The status of immigrant women in Canada. *Canadian Review of Sociology and Anthropology* 12(4): 406–16.

———. (1986). Immigrant women in Canada. In R.J. Simon and C.B. Brettell (Eds.), *International migration: The female experience*. Totowa, NJ: Rowman and Allanheld.

———. (1987). *Migrant women in Canada: Profile and politics*. Ottawa, ON: Research Division, Immigration Canada and the Status of Women Canada.

———. (1991). *Migrating discrimination: Feminist issues in Canadian immigration policies and practices*. Working paper series. Centre for Women Studies, Feminist Research. London: University of Western Ontario.

Brah, Avtar. (1992). Difference, diversity and differentiation. In James Donald and Ali Rattansi (Eds.), *Race, culture and difference* (126–46). London: Sage.

———. (1998). *Cartographies of diaspora: Contesting identities*. London and New York: Routledge.

Braithwaite, Edward. (1971). *The development of a creole society in Jamaica, 1770*–1820. Oxford: Clarendon.

Braithwaite, Rella, and Tessa Benn-Ireland. (1993). *Some Black women in Canada*. Toronto: Sister Vision Press.

Brand, Dionne. (1984). A working paper on Black women in Toronto. *Fireweed* 19: 17–43.

———. (1988). Blossom: Priestess of Oya, Goddess of winds, storms and waterfalls. In *Sans Souci; and other Stories* (31–42). Stratford, ON: Williams-Wallace.

Brathwaite, Edward Kamau. (1971). *The development of a Creole society in Jamaica, 1770–1820*. Oxford: Clarendon Press.

———. (1974). *Contemporary omens: Cultural diversity and integration in the Caribbean*. Mona, Jamaica: Savacou Publications.

Brereton, Bridget. (1993a). The development of an identity: The Black middle class of Trinidad in the later nineteenth century. In Hilary Beckles and Verene Shepherd (Eds.), *Caribbean freedom: Economy and society from emancipation to the present* (274–83). Kingston, Jamaica: Ian Randle.

———. (1993b). Social organisation and class, racial and cultural conflict in nineteenth-century Trinidad. In Kelvin Yelvington (Ed.), *Trinidad ethnicity* (33–54). London and Basingstoke: Macmillan Caribbean.

———. (1995). Text, testimony and gender. In Verene Shepherd, Bridget Brereton, and Barbara Bailey (Eds.), *Engendering history: Caribbean women in historical perspective* (63–93). Kingston, Jmaica: Ian Randle.

Brodber, Erna. (1982). *Perceptions of Caribbean women: Towards a documentation of stereotypes*. Cave Hill, Barbados: Institute of Social and Economic Research, University of the West Indies.

———. (1986). Afro-Jamaican women at the turn of the century. *Social and Economic Studies* 35(3): 23–50.

Brodie, Jane. (1996). *Women and Canadian policy*. Toronto: Harcourt Brace.

Burnet, Jean. (Ed.) (1986). *Looking into my sister's eyes: An exploration in women's history*. Toronto: The Multicultural History Society of Ontario.

Burton, Richard D.E. (1997). *Afro-Creole: Power, opposition and play in the Caribbean*. Ithaca, NY: Cornell University Press.

Bush, Barbara. (1981). White "ladies", Coloured "favourites" and Black "wenches": Some considerations on sex, race and class factors in social relations in White Creole society in the British Caribbean. *Slavery and Abolition* 2(3): 245–62.

_____. (1990). *Slave women in Caribbean society, 1650–1838*. Bloomington, IN: Indiana University Press.

Butler, Judith. (1990). *Gender trouble: Feminism and the subversion of identity*. New York: Routledge.

_____. (1992). Contingent foundations: Feminism and the question of "postmodernism". In Judith Butler and Joan W. Scott (Eds.), *Feminists theorize the political* (1–21). London: Routledge.

CAFRA News. (1991). Newsletter of the Caribbean Association for Feminist Research and Action, 1986–. Tunapuna, Trinidad and Tobago: The Association.

Calliste, Agnes. (1989). Canada's immigration policy and the domestics from the Caribbean: The second domestic scheme. In *Race, Class, Gender: Bonds and Barriers. Socialist Studies: A Canadian Annual* 5: 133–65.

_____. (1993). Women of exceptional merit: Immigration of Caribbean nurses to Canada. *Canadian Journal of Women and Law* 6: 85–102.

Campbell, Carl. (1992). *Cedulants and capitulants: The politics of the Coloured opposition in the slave society of Trinidad, 1783–1838*. Newtown, Port of Spain, Trinidad and Tobago: Paria Publishing.

Carew, Jan. (1989). Columbus and the origins of racism in the Americas. *Race and Class* 30(1).

Carr, Ernest A. (1966). Civil strife. In G.R. Coulthard (Ed.), *Caribbean literature and beyond*, London: University of London Press.

Carr Ernest A., and A.M. Clarke. (n.d.) *Ma Mamba and other stories*. Port of Spain, Trinidad and Tobago: Fraser Printerie.

Carter, Martin. (1969). I come from the nigger yard. In *Selected Poems* (61–63). Georgetown, Guyana: Demerara Publishers Ltd.

Cartey, Wilfred. (1991). *Whispers from the Caribbean: I going away, I going home*. Los Angeles, CA: University of California and the Center for Afro-American Studies.

Carty, Linda, and Dionne Brand. (1988). "Visible minority" women: A creation of the Canadian state. *RFR/DFR* 17(3): 31.

Chamberlin, Mary. (1997). *Narratives of exile and return*. London and Basingstoke: The Macmillan Press Ltd.

Chittister, Joan. (1998). *Heart of flesh: a feminist spirituality for men and women*. Grand Rapids, Michigan: William B. Eerdmens Pub; Ottawa: Novalis.

Clarke, Austin. (1990). *Pigtails 'n Breadfruit*. Toronto: Random House Canada.

Cohen, Marjorie Griffin. (1993). The Canadian women's movement. In Ruth Roach Pierson, Marjorie Griffin Cohen, Paula Bourne, and Philinda Masters (Eds.), *Canadian Women's Issues* 1: 1–97.

Cohen, Robin. (1992). The diaspora of a diaspora: The case of the Caribbean. *Social Science Information* 31(1): 159–89.

Collins, Patricia Hill. (1990). *Black feminist thought: Knowledge, consciousness and the politics of empowerment*. New York: Routledge.

Cooper, Afua. (1992). *Memories have tongue*. Toronto: Sister Vision Press.

Coopsammy, Madeline. (1985). Immigrant. In Lorris Elliot (Ed.), *Other voices* (23–25). Toronto: Williams-Wallace.

Cox, Edward. (1984). *Free Coloreds in slave societies in St. Kitts and Grenada, 1763–1833*. Knoxville, TN: University of Tennessee Press.

Craton, Michael. (1982). *Testing the chains: Resistance to slavery in the British West Indies*. Ithaca, NY: Cornell University Press.

_____. (1986). From Caribs to Black Caribs: The Amerindian roots of servile resistance in the Caribbean. In Gary Y. Okihiro (Ed.), *In resistance: Studies in African, Caribbean and Afro-American history* (96–116). Amherst, MA: University of Massachusetts Press.

———. (1993). Continuity not change: The incidence of unrest among ex-slaves in the British West Indies, 1838–1876. In Hilary Beckles and Verene Shepherd (Eds.), *Caribbean freedom: Economy and society from emancipation to the present* (192–244). Kingston, Jamaica: Ian Randle.

Dadzie, Stella. (1990). Searching for the invisible woman: Slavery and resistance in Jamaica. *Race and Class* 32(2): 21–38.

Das, Mahadai. (1988). *Bones.* Leeds: Peepal Tree Press.

Das Gupta, Tania. (1986). *Learning from our history: Community development by immigrant women, 1958–1986.* Toronto: Cross Cultural Communication Centre.

Davidson, Sarah. (2002, September). Does prayer work. *O: The Oprah Magazine.*

Davies, Bronwyn. (1990). Agency as a form of discursive practice: A classroom scene observed. *British Journal of Sociology of Education* 11(3): 341–61.

Dei, George J. Sefa. (1994). The women of a Ghanaian village: A study of social change. *African Studies Review* 37(2): 121–47.

de Lauretis, Teresa. (Ed.). (1986). *Feminist studies/critical studies.* Bloomington, IN: Indiana University Press.

Enloe, Cynthia. (1989). *Bananas, beaches and bases: Making feminist sense of international politics.* London: Pandora Press.

Epstein, Rachel. (1983). Domestic workers: The experience in BC. In Linda Briskin and Linda Yanz (Eds.), *Union Sisters: Women in the Labour Movement.* Toronto: Women's Educational Press.

Espinet, Ramabai. (1991). Barred: Trinidad 1987. In Carmen C. Esteves and Lizabeth Paravisini-Gebert (Eds.), *Green cane and juicy flotsam: Short stories by Caribbean women* (80–85). New Brunswick, NJ: Rutgers University Press.

———. (1993). Representation and the Indo-Caribbean woman in Trinidad and Tobago. In Frank Birbalsingh (Ed.), *Indo-Caribbean resistance* (42–61). Toronto: TSAR.

Essed, Philomena. (1990). *Everyday racism: Reports from women of two cultures.* Alameda, CA.: Hunter House.

———. (1991). *Understanding racism: An interdisciplinary theory.* Newbury Park, NJ: Sage Publications.

Estable, Alma. (1986). *Immigrant women in Canada: Current issues.* A background paper for the Canadian Advisory Council on the Status of Women. Ottawa: Canadian Advisory Council on the Status of Women.

Fanon, Frantz. (1967). *Black skins, white masks.* New York: Grove Press.

Ferguson, Moira. (1993a). *The Hart sisters.* Lincoln, NB: University of Nebraska Press.

———. (Ed.). (1993b). *The history of Mary Prince: A West Indian slave; related by herself.* Ann Arbor, MI: The University of Michigan Press.

———. (Ed.). (1987). *The history of Mary Prince, a West Indian slave, related by herself.* London: Pandora (originally published London and Edinburgh: Westley and David, 1831).

Ferreira, Jo-Anne S. (1994). *The Portuguese of Trinidad and Tobago.* St. Augustine, Trinidad and Tobago: Institute of Social and Economic Research, University of the West Indies.

Finch, Janet. (1984). "It's great to have someone to talk to": The ethics and politics of interviewing women. In Colin Bell and Helen Roberts (Eds.), *Social researching: Politics, problems, practice* (70–87). London: Routledge and Kegan Paul.

Fleras, Augie, and Jean Leonard Elliott. (1992). *Multiculturalism in Canada: The challenge of diversity*. Scarborough, ON: Nelson Canada.

Ford-Smith, Honor. (1989). *Ring ding in a tight corner: A case study of funding and organizational democracy in Sistren, 1977–1988*. Toronto: Women's Program, International Council for Adult Education.

———. (1994). *Peeling back the skin: Whiteness and gender in late colonial Jamaica*. Unpublished M.A. thesis, University of Toronto.

Foucault, Michel. (1979). *Discipline and punish: The birth of the prison*. New York: Random House/Vintage Books.

Freire, Paulo. (1992). *The pedagogy of the oppressed*. Trans. Myra Bergman Ramos. New York: Continuum.

French, Joan. (1995). Women and colonial policy in Jamaica after the 1938 uprising. In Saskia Wieringa (Ed.), *Subversive women: Historical experiences of gender and resistance: Women's movements in Africa, Asia, Latin America, and the Caribbean* (121–46). London: Zed Books.

French, Joan, and Honor Ford-Smith. (1986). *Women, work and organisation in Jamaica*. Kingston, Jamaica: Sistren.

Fung, Richard. (1990). *My mother's place* [videorecording]. Vancouver: Fungus.

Gabriel, Christina. (1996). One or the other? "Race", gender, and the limits of official multiculturalism. In Janine Brodie (Ed.), *Women and Canadian public policy*. Toronto: Harcourt Brace.

Gilroy, Paul. (1993). *The Black Atlantic: Modernity and double consciousness*. Cambridge, MA: Harvard University Press.

———. (1997). Diaspora and the detours of identity. In Kathryn Woodward (Ed.), *Identity and difference*. Thousand Oaks, CA: Sage.

Glaser, Barney G., and Anselm L. Strauss. (1967). *The discovery of grounded theory: Strategies for qualitative research*. New York: Aldine de Gruyte.

Gonzalez, Nancie L. Solien. (1969). *Black Carib household structure: A study of migration and modernization*. Seattle, WA: University of Washington Press.

Gordon, Colin. (Ed.). (1977). *Power/knowledge: Selected interviews and other writings 1972–1977 by Michel Foucault*. New York: Pantheon Books.

Gordon, Derek. (1987). *Class, status and social mobility in Jamaica*. Mona, Jamaica: Institute of Social and Economic Research, University of the West Indies.

Gordon, Monica. (1981). Caribbean migration: A perspective on women. In Delores M. Mortimer and Roy S. Bryce-Laporte (Eds.), *Female immigrants to the United States: Caribbean, Latin American, and African experiences* (14–55). RIES Occasional Papers 2. Washington, DC: Smithsonian Institution.

Gouveia, Elsa. (1965). *Slave society in the British Leeward Islands at the end of the eighteenth century*. New Haven, CT, and London: Yale University Press.

Grewal, Inderpal. (1994). Autobiographic subjects and diasporic locations: Meatless days and borderlands. In Inderpal Grewal and Caren Caplan (Eds.), *Scattered hegemonies: Postmodernity and transnational feminist practices* (231–54). Minneapolis, MN: University of Minnesota Press, 1994.

———. (1996). *Home and harem: Nation, gender, empire, and the cultures of travel*. Durham, NC: Duke University Press.

Hall, Douglas. (1989). *In miserable slavery*. London: Macmillan Caribbean.

Hall, Stuart. (1992). New ethnicities. In James Donald and Ali Rattansi (Eds.), *Race, culture and difference* (252–59). London: Sage.

Handa, Amita. (2002). *Of silk saris and mini-skirts: South Asian girls walk the tightrope of culture.* Toronto: Women's Press.

Harris, Claire (1992). *Drawing down a daughter.* Fredericton, NB: Goose Lane.

Hart, Richard. (2002). *Slaves who abolished slavery: Blacks in rebellion.* Barbados, Jamaica, Trinidad and Tobago: University of the West Indies Press.

Harvey, Franklyn. (1974). *Rise and Fall of Party Politics in Trinidad and Tobago.* Toronto: New Beginning Movement.

Hawkins, Freda. (1991). *Critical years of immigration: Canada and Australia compared.* 2nd ed. Montreal and Kingston: McGill-Queen's University Press.

Head, Wilson A. (1975). *The Black presence in the Canadian mosaic: Perception and the practice of discrimination against Blacks in Metropolitan Toronto.* Toronto: Ontario Human Rights Commission.

Henderson, Thelma. (1988). The Contemporary women's movement in Trinidad and Tobago. In Patricia Mohammed and Catherine Shepherd (Eds.), *Gender in Caribbean development* (63–70). Mona, Jamaica: Women and Development Studies Project, University of the West Indies.

Henry, Frances, Carol Tator, Winston Mattis, Tim Rees (Eds.). (2000). *The colour of democracy: Racism in Canadian society.* 2nd ed. Toronto: Harcourt Brace Canada.

Hernandez, Carmencita R. (1987). The foundation of NOIVMWC. *Canadian Women's Studies* 8(2).

Higman, B.W. *Slave populations of the British Caribbean, 1807–1834.* Baltimore, MD: The Johns Hopkins University Press, 1984.

Hill, Lawrence. (1996). *Women of Vision: The Story of the Canadian Negro Women's Association, 1951–1976.* Toronto: Umbrella Press.

Ho, Christine. (1989). "Hold the Chow Mein, Gimme Soca": Creolization of the Chinese in Guyana, Trinidad, and Jamaica. *Amerasia* 15(2): 3–25.

_____. (1991). *Salt-water trinnies: Afro-Trinidadians immigrant networks and non-assimilation in Los Angeles.* New York: AMS Press.

_____. (1984). *Feminist theory: From margin to center.* Boston, MA: South End Press.

_____. (1990). *Yearning: Race, gender and culture.* Toronto: Between the Lines.

_____. (1993). *Sisters of the yam.* Toronto: Between the Lines.

Kayode, James. (2002). Sat hails "Holi" land as Christians, Hindus, and Baptists celebrate together. *Internet Express.* March 31.

James, C.L.R. (1980). Making of the Caribbean people. In *Spheres of existence: Selected writings* (174–187). London: Allison and Busby.

_____. (1989) The *Black Jacobins: Toussaint L'Ouverture and the Santo Domingo Revolution.* New York: Vintage Books.

James, Selma. (1985). *Strangers and sisters: Women, race and immigration.* Voices from the Conference: "Black and Immigrant Women Speak Out and Claim our Rights". Bristol: Falling Wall Press.

Jin, Meiling. (1990). Strangers on a hostile landscape. In Ramabai Espinet (Ed.), *Creation Fire: a CAFRA anthology of Caribbean women's poetry* (129–132). Toronto: Sister Vision Press.

Johnson, Howard. (1987). The Chinese in Trinidad in the late nineteenth century. *Ethnic and Racial Studies* 10(1): 82–95.

Kerr, Paulette. (1995). Victims or strategists? Female lodging house keepers in Jamaica. In Verene Shepherd *et al* (Eds.), *Engendering history: Caribbean women in historical perspective* (197–212). Kingston, Jamaica: Ian Randle.

Khan, Aisha. 1993. What is a "Spanish"? Ambiguity and mixed ethnicity in Trinidad. In Kelvin Yelvington (Ed.), *Trinidad ethnicity* (180–207). Knoxville, TN: The University of Tennessee Press.

Kincaid, Jamaica. (1988). *A small place*. New York: Penguin Books.

_____. (1991). *Lucy*. New York: Penguins Books.

Klass, Morton. (1961). *East Indians in Trinidad: A study of cultural persistence*. New York: Columbia University Press.

Knight, Franklin W. (1990). *The Caribbean: The genesis of a fragmented nationalism*. 2nd ed. New York: Oxford University Press.

Krathowohl, David R. (1993). *Methods of educational and social science research: An integrated approach*. New York and London: Longman.

Krauter, J.K., and Morris Davis. (1978). *Minority Canadians: Ethnic groups*. Toronto: Methuen.

Kuhn, Thomas. (2000). *Internet Encyclopedia of Philosophy*.

Lamming, George. (1953). *In the castle of my skin*. London: Longman.

_____. (1996). Concepts of the Caribbean. In Frank Birbalsingh (Ed.), *Frontiers of Caribbean literature in English* (1–14). London: Macmillan Caribbean.

Lemke-Santangelo, Gretchen. (1996). *Abiding courage: African American migrant women and the East Bay Community*. Chapel Hill, NC: The University of North Carolina Press.

Li, Peter S. (Ed.). (1990). *Race and ethnic relations in Canada*. Toronto: Oxford University Press.

Liverpool, Hollis "Chalkdust". (2000). *Rituals of power and rebellion: The Carnival tradition in Trinidad and Tobago, 1763–1962*. Chicago, IL: Research Associates School Times Publications/Frontline Distribution Int'l Inc.

Loker, Zvi. (1991). *Jews in the Caribbean: Evidence on the history of the Jews in the Caribbean zone in colonial times*. Jerusalem: Institute for Research on the Sephardim and Oriental Jewish Heritage.

Look Lai, Walton. (1993). *Indentured labor, Caribbean sugar: Chinese and Indian migrants to the British West Indies, 1838–1918*. Baltimore, MD: The Johns Hopkins University Press.

Lorde, Audre. (1984). *Sister outsider*. Trumansburg, NY: The Crossing Press.

Lovelace, Earl. (2002). Requiring of the world. In Funso Aiyejina (Ed.), *Earl Lovelace: Growing up in the dark (Selected Essays.* (229–232). San Juan, Trinidad and Tobago: Lexicon Trinidad Ltd.

Lowenthal, David. (1972). *West Indian societies*. New York, London, Toronto: Oxford University Press.

Macklin, Audrey. (1992). Foreign domestic worker: Surrogate housewife or mail order servant? *McGill Law Journal* 37(3): 681–761.

Mahonney, Maureen H., and Barbara Yngvesson. (1992). The construction of subjectivity and the paradox of resistance: Reintegrating feminist anthropology and psychology. *Signs* 18(1): 44–73.

Mama, Amina. (1995). *Beyond the masks: Race, gender and subjectivity*. London: Routledge.

Mangru, Basdeo. (1993). *Indenture and abolition: Sacrifice and survival on the Guyanese sugar plantation*. Toronto: TSAR.

_____. (1996). *A history of East Indian resistance on the Guyana sugar estates, 1869–1948*. Lewiston, Queenston, Lampeter: The Edwin Mellen Press.

Manning, William. (1995). *My name is Eva: A biography of Eva Smith*. Toronto: Natural Heritage/Natural History Inc.

Mansingh, Laxmi, and Ajai Mansingh. (1999). *Home away from home: 150 years of Indian presence in Jamaica, 1845–1995*. Kingston, Jamaica: Ian Randle Publishers.

Martin, Biddy, and Chandra Talpade Mohanty. (1986). Feminist politics: What's home got to do with it? In Teresa de Lauretis (Ed.), *Feminist studies/critical studies* (191–212). Bloomington, IN: Indiana University Press.

Massiah, Joycelin. (1983). Women in the Caribbean Project: An overview. *Social and Economic Studies* 35 (2): 1–29.

_____. (1986). Women in the Caribbean project: An overview. *Social and Economic Studies* 35(3): 1–20.

Mathurin, Lucille. (1975). *The rebel woman in the West Indies during slavery*. Kingston, Jamaica: African Caribbean Publications.

McCree, Roy Dereck. 1999. The Chinese game of "whe whe" in Trinidad: From criminalization to criminalization. *Caribbean Quarterly*, 1–5.

Meeks, Brian. (2000). *Narratives of resistance: Jamaica, Trinidad, the Caribbean*. Barbados, Jamaica, Trinidad and Tobago: The University of the West Indies Press.

Melville, Pauline. (1997). *The ventriloquist's tale*. London: Bloomsbury.

Mohammed, Patricia. (1985). The women's movement in Trinidad and Tobago since the 1960s. *Concerning Women & Development* 11, 12. Barbados: University of the West Indies.

_____. (1988). The "Creolization" of Indian women in Trinidad. In Selwyn Ryan (Ed.), *The independence experience, 1962–1987* (381–97). Toronto: University of Toronto Press.

_____. (1989). Women's responses to the 70s and 80s in Trinidad: A country report. *Caribbean Quarterly* 35(1–4): 36–45.

_____. (1995). Writing gender into history: The negotiation of gender relations among Indian men and women in post-indenture Trinidad society, 1917–1947. In Verene Shepherd *et al.* (Eds.), *Engendering history: Caribbean women in historical perspective* (20–47). Kingston, Jamaica: Ian Randle.

Mohammed, Patricia, and Catherine Shepherd. (1988). *Gender in the Caribbean*. Cave Hill, Barbados: Women and Development Project.

Mohanty, Chandra Talpade. (1991). Cartographies of struggle: Third world women and the politics of feminism. In Chandra Talpade Mohanty, Ann Russo, and Lourdes Torres (Eds.), *Third world women and the politics of feminism* (1–50). Bloomington, IN: Indiana University Press.

Montejo, Esteban. (1968). *The autobiography of a runaway slave*. Miguel Barnet (Ed.), Jocasta Innes (Trans.) Toronto: The Bodley Head.

Moodie Kublalsingh, Sylvia. (1994). *The Coco Panyols of Trinidad*. London: British Academic Press.

_____. (1997). Professions of faith: A teacher reflects on women, race, church and spirit. In Kim Marie Vaz, (Ed.), *Oral narrative research with Black women* (24–37). Thousand Oaks, CA: Sage.

Moody, Joycelin. (1997). Profession of faith: a teacher reflects on women, race, church and spirit. In Kim Marie Vaz (Ed.), *Oral narrative research with Black women*. (24–37). Thousand Oaks, CA: Sage.

Moore, Brian L. (1993). The social impact of Portuguese immigration into British Guiana after emancipation. In Hilary Beckles and Verene Shepherd (Eds.), *Caribbean freedom: Economy and society from emancipation to the present* (52–160) Kingston, Jamaica: Ian Randle; London: James Curry.

Morrissey, Marietta. (1989). *Slave women in the new world: Gender stratification in the Caribbean*. Lawrence, KA: University Press of Kansas.

Morton, Patricia. 1991. *Disfigured images: The historical assault on Afro-American women*. New York: Praeger.

Naidoo, Josephine C. (1977). *The East Indian in Canadian context: A study in social psychology*. Waterloo, ON: Wilfred Laurier University.

———. (1978). Canadian perspectives on East Indian immigrants. Paper presented at the 10th Anniversary Conference of the Canadian Society for Asian Studies. Guelph, ON: University of Guelph.

Nettleford, Rex M. (1970). *Mirror mirror: Race and protests in Jamaica*. Kingston, Jamaica: W. Collins and Sangster.

———. (1979). *Caribbean cultural identity: The case of Jamaica*. Los Angeles, CA: Center for Afro-American Studies and UCLA Latin American Center.

———. (1993). *Inward stretch, outward reach: A voice from the Caribbean*. London: Macmillan.

Ng, Roxanna. (1982). Constituting ethnic phenomenon: An account from the perspective of immigrant women. *Canadian Journal of Ethnic Studies* 7(1): 97–108.

———. (1988). *The politics of community services: Immigrant women, class and state*. Toronto: Garamond Press.

Ng, Roxanna, and Tania Das Gupta. (1981). Nation builders? The captive labour force of non-English speaking immigrant women. *Canadian Journal of Women's Studies* 3(1).

Ng, Roxanna, and Alma Estable. (1987). Immigrant women in the labour force: An overview of present knowledge and research gaps. *RFR/DFR* 16(1): 29–33.

Ng, Roxanna, and Judith Ramirez. (1981). *Immigrant housewives in Canada: A report*. Toronto: Immigrant Women's Centre.

Ng, Winnie. (1982). Immigrant women: The silent partners of the women's movement. In Maureen Fitzgerald, Connie Guberman, and Margie Wolfe (Eds.) *Still ain't satisfied!* (249–56). Toronto: Women's Press.

Nichols, Grace. (1989). Home truths. In E.A. Markham (Ed.), *Hinterland: Caribbean poetry for the West Indies and Britain* (98–101). London: Bloodaxe Books.

Ochs, Carol. (1993). *Women and spirituality*. Totowa, NJ: Rowman and Allanheld.

Odie-Ali, Stella. (1986). Women in agriculture: The case of Guyana. *Social and Economic Studies* 35(2): 241–85.

Patterson, Orlando. (1993). Slavery, alienation and the female discovery of personal freedom. In Arien Mack (Ed.), *Home: A place in the world* (160–87). New York: New York University Press.

Patton, Michael Quinn. (1980). *Qualitative evaluation methods*. Beverly Hills, CA: Sage.

Payne, Anthony, and Paul Sutton. (Eds.). (1993). *Modern Caribbean politics*. Baltimore, MD: The Johns Hopkins University Press.

Personal Narratives Group. (Eds.). (1989). *Interpreting women's lives: Feminist theory and personal narratives*. Bloomington and Indianapolis, IN: Indiana University Press.

Peterson, Elizabeth A. (1992). *African American women: A study of will and success*. Jefferson, NC: McFarland and Co.

Pierson, Ruth Roach. (1993). *Canadian women's issues: Twenty-five years of women's activism in English Canada*. Toronto: J. Lorimer.

Powell, Dorian. (1986). Caribbean women and their response to familial experiences. *Social and Economic Studies* 35(2): 83–130.

Powell, Patricia. (1993). *Me dying trial*. London: Heinemann.

REFERENCES

Praetorius, Ina. (1998). *Essays in feminist ethics*. Leuven, Belgium: Peeters.

Prince, Althea. (1993). Body and Soul. In *Ladies of the night and other stories*. Toronto: Sister Vision Press.

Puar, Jasbir K. Writing my way "home": Travelling south, Asian bodies and diasporic journeys. *Socialist Review* 24(4): 75–108.

Ralston, Helen. (1991). Race, class and gender and work experiences of South Asia immigrant women in Atlantic Canada. *Canadian Ethnic Studies* 23(2): 129–139.

Ramesar, Marianne Soares. (1994). *Survivors of another crossing*. St. Augustine, Trinidad and Tobago: University of the West Indies, School of Continuing Studies.

Razack, Sherene. (1991). *Canadian feminism and the law: The Women's Legal Education and Action Fund and the pursuit of equality*. Toronto: Second Story Press.

_____. (1998). *Looking white people in the eye*. Toronto: University of Toronto Press.

Reddock, Rhoda E. (1988). *Elmer Francois*. London: New Beacon Books.

_____. (1990). The Caribbean feminist tradition. *Womanspeak* 26/27: 12–14.

_____. (1993). Indian women and indentureship in Trinidad and Tobago: Freedom denied. In Verene Shepherd and Hilary Beckles (Eds.), *Caribbean freedom: Economy and society from emancipation to the present* (225–37). Kingston, Jamaica: Ian Randle; London: James Curry.

_____. (1994). *Women, labour and politics in Trinidad and Tobago: A history*. London: Zed Books.

_____. (1999). Jahaji Bhai: The Emergence of a Dougla Poetics in Trinidad and Tobago. *Identities* 5(4): 569–601.

_____. (Ed.).(1996). *Ethnic minorities in Caribbean society*. St. Augustine, Trinidad and Tobago: Institute of Social and Economic Research, University of the West Indies.

Rennie, Bukka. (1969). *The Genius of our own*. Unp. Mimeo.

_____. (1998). *Fighting or fighting up*. Internet Express. *Opinion*. 10 August.

Resources for Feminist Research (RFR/DRF). (1987). Immigrant women 16(1).

Rhys, Jean. (1992). *Wide Sargasso Sea*. New York: Norton.

Riley, Joan. (1987). *Waiting in the twilight*. London: Women's Press.

Roberts, Helen. (1981). *Doing feminist research*. London: Routledge and Kegan Paul.

Rodney, Walter. (1981). *A history of the Guyanese working people, 1881–1905*. Baltimore: The Johns Hopkins University Press.

Rohlehr, Gordon. (1990). *Calypso & society in pre-independence Trinidad*. Port-of-Spain, Trinidad: Gordon Rohlehr.

Ryan, Selwyn, (Ed.). (1991). *Social and occupational stratification in contemporary Trinidad and Tobago*. St. Augustine, Trinidad and Tobago: Institute of Social and Economic Research, University of the West Indies.

Said, Edward W. (1993). *Culture and imperialism*. London: Chatto and Windus.

Sanders, Andrews. (1987). *The powerless people: An analysis of the Amerindians of the Corentyne River*. London: Macmillan Caribbean.

Sangari, Kumkum, and Sudesh Vaid (Eds.). (1990). *Recasting women: Essays in Indian colonial history*. New Brunswick, NJ: Rutgers University Press.

Schuler, Monica. (1980). *"Alas, Alas, Kongo": A social history of indenture African immigration in Jamaica*. Baltimore, MD: The Johns Hopkins Press.

Scott, Joan W. (1992). Experience. In Judith Butler and Joan W. Scott (Eds.), *Feminists theorize the political* (22–40). London: Routledge.

Scott, Yvonne Kesho. (1991). *The habit of surviving: Black women's strategies*. New Brunswick,

NJ: Rutgers University Press.

Segal, Daniel. (1993). Race and colour in pre-independence Trinidad and Tobago. In Kelvin Yelvington (Ed.), *Trinidad Ethnicity*. Knoxville: The University of Tennessee Press. (81–115).

Senior, Olive. (1991). *Working miracles: Women's lives in the English-speaking Caribbean*. London: James Curry; Bloomington, IN: Indiana University Press.

Seydegart, K., and G. Spears. (1985). *Beyond dialogue: Immigrant women in Canada, 1985–1990: A plan of action arising from a national consultation commissioned by Multiculturalism Canada*. Ottawa, ON: Erin Research Inc.

Shepherd, Verene. (1993). Emancipation through servitude: Aspects of the conditions of Indian women. In Hilary Beckles and Verene Shepherd (Eds.), *Caribbean freedom: Economy and society from emancipation to the present* (245–50). Kingston, Jamaica: Ian Randle.

———. (1995). Gender, migration and settlement: The indentureship and post-indentureship experience of Indian females in Jamaica, 1845–1943. In Verene Shepherd et al. (Eds.), *Engendering history: Caribbean women in historical perspective* (233–57). Kingston, Jamaica: Ian Randle.

———. (1996). Control, resistance, accommodation and race relations: Aspects of the indentureship experience. In David Dabydeen and Brinsley Samaroo (Eds.), *Across the dark waters: Ethnicity and Indian identity in the Caribbean* (65–87). London and Basingstoke: Macmillan Caribbean.

Shepherd, Verene A., and Glen L. Richards (Eds.). (2002). *Questioning Creole: Creolisation discourse in Caribbean culture*. Kingston, Jamaica: Ian Randle.

Sherwin, Susan. (1992). *Feminism and bioethics*. Toronto: Faculty of Law, University of Toronto.

Silvera, Makeda. (1989). *Silenced*. Toronto: Sister Vision Press.

———. (1991). Remembering G and other stories. Toronto: Sister Vision Press.

Silvestrini, Blanca G. (1989). *Women and resistance: Herstory in contemporary Caribbean history*. The 1989 Elsa Goveia Memorial Lecture. Mona, Jamaica: Department of History, University of the West Indies.

Singh, Kelvin. (1988). *Bloodstained tombs: The Muhurram massacre 1884*. London and Basingstoke: Macmillan Caribbean.

Singh, Simboonath. (2001). Cultures of exile: Diaspora identities. *International Journal of Theory and Research* 1(3): 289–304.

Sio, Arnold A. (1987). Marginality and free Coloured identity in Caribbean slave society. *Slavery and Abolition* 8: 166–82.

Slinger, Dr Francis ["The Mighty Sparrow"]. (1967). *Education is essential*. Quintessential Millenium Series.

Smart, Ian Isidore, and Kimani S.K. Nehusi. (2000). *Ah come back hom: Perspectives on the Trinidad and Tobago carnival*. Washington, DC, and Port-of-Spain: Original World Press.

Spivak, Gayatri. (1990). *Postcolonial critic: Interviews, strategies, dialogues*. New York: Routledge.

Springfield, Consuelo López (Ed.). (1997). Introduction: Revisiting Caliban: Implications for Caribbean feminisms. *Daughters of Caliban: Caribbean women in the twentieth century* (xi–xxi). Bloomington and Indianapolis, IN: Indiana University Press.

Stasiulis, Daiva K. (1987). Rainbow feminism: Perspectives on minority women in Canada. *RFR/DFR* 16(1): 5–9.

REFERENCES

Stivers, Camilla. (1993). Reflections on the role of personal narrative in social science. *Signs: Journal of Women in Culture and Society* 18(2): 408–25.

Stolzoff, Norma. (2000). *Wake the town and tell the people: Dancehall culture in Jamaica.* Durham and London: Duke University Press.

Strauss, Anselm. (1987). *Qualitative analysis for social scientists.* New York: Cambridge University Press.

Strauss, Anselm, and Juliet Corbin. (1990). *Basics of qualitative research: Grounded theory, procedures, and techniques.* Newbury Park, CA: Sage.

Sullivan, Edmund. (1990). *A critical psychology and pedagogy: Interpretation of the personal world.* New York: Bergin and Garvey Publishers.

Terborg-Penn, Rosalyn. (1986). Black women in resistance. In Gary Y. Okihoro (Ed.), *In resistance* (188–209). Amherst, MA: The University of Massachusetts Press.

Thorpe, Marjorie. (1975). *Beyond the Sargasso Sea.* Ph.D. thesis. Montreal: McGill University.

Turritin, Jane Sawyer. (1976). Networks and mobility: The case of West Indian domestics from Montserrat. *Canadian Review of Sociology and Anthropology* 13(3): 305–20.

Upadhyay, H.C. (1991). *Status of women in India.* Vol. 1. Daryaganj, New Delhi: Anmol Publications.

Vassell, Lynette. (1995). Women of the masses: Daphne Campbell and "left" politics in Jamaica in the 1950s. In Verene Shepherd et al. (Eds.), *Engendering history: Caribbean women in historical perspective* (318–33). Kingston, Jamaica: Ian Randle.

Vaz, Kim Marie. (Ed.). (1997). *Oral narrative research with Black women.* Thousand Oaks, CA: Sage.

Vertovec, Steven. (1992). *Hindu Trinidad: Religion, ethnicity and socio-economic change.* London and Basingstoke: Macmillan Caribbean.

Wade-Gayles, Gloria. (Ed.). (1995). *My soul is a witness: African American women's spirituality.* Boston, MA: Beacon Press.

Wallis, Maria, Wenona Giles, and Carmencita Hernandez. (1988). Defining the issues in our own terms: Gender, race and state — Interviews with racial minority women. *RFR/DFR* 17(3): 43–48.

Wariboko, Waibinte. (1995). The status, role and influence of women in eastern delta states of Nigeria, 1850–1900: Examples from New Calabar. In Verene Shepherd et al. (Eds.), *Engendering history: Caribbean women in historical perspective* (369–83). Kingston, Jamaica: Ian Randle.

Warner, Marina. (1998). Siren/Hyphen; the Maid beguiled. In Christine Barrow (Ed.), *Caribbean portraits: Essays on gender ideologies and identities,* (361–376). Kingston, Jamaica: Ian Randle and the University of the West Indies Centre for Gender and Development Studies.

Weedon, Chris. (1987). *Feminist practice and poststructuralist theory.* Oxford: Basil Blackwell.

West, Cornel. (1992, Summer). A matter of life and death. *October* 61: 20–23.

————. (1993). *Keeping faith: Philosophy and race in America.* New York: Routledge.

Williams, Brackette F. (1996). Women out of place: The gender of agency and the race of nationality. New York: Routledge.

Williams, Eric E. (1970). *From Columbus to Castro: The history of the Caribbean, 1492–1969.* London: Andre Deutsch.

Wiltshire, Faith. (1990). *Woman/Speak!* 26/27.

Wiltshire-Brodber, Rosina. (1988). Gender, race and class in the Caribbean. In Patricia Mohammed and Catherine Shepherd (Eds.), *Gender in Caribbean development* (58–75). Mona, Jamaica: University of the West Indies.

Winks, Robin. (1971). *Blacks in Canada.* New Haven, CT: Yale University Press.

Woodward, Kathryn. (Ed.). (1997). *Identity and difference.* Thousand Oaks, CA: Sage.

Yelvington, Kevin. (Ed.). (1993). *Trinidad ethnicity.* London and Basingstoke: Macmillan Caribbean.

Yon, Daniel. (1995). Identity and differences in the Caribbean diaspora: Case study from Metro-Toronto. In Alvina Ruprecht and Cecelia Taiana (Eds.), *In the hood: The reordering of culture: Latin America, the Caribbean and Canada* (479–97). Ottawa, ON: Carleton University Press.

Young, Iris Marion. (1990). *Justice and the politics of difference.* Princeton, NJ: Princeton University Press.

Index

INDEX

DR. YVONNE BOBB-SMITH teaches Caribbean Studies both at Ryerson University and at New College, University of Toronto. She has facilitated workshops on issues of identity, gender, Caribbean popular culture, and community organizing. She was the first Executive Director of the Black Secretariat of Canada, where she coordinated the production of its first directory of Black organizations in Toronto.